BLACK BOSTONIANS

BLACK BOSTONIANS

Family Life and Community Struggle in the Antebellum North

JAMES OLIVER HORTON
AND
LOIS E. HORTON

HM
HOLMES & MEIER PUBLISHERS, INC.
NEW YORK • LONDON

First published in the United States of America 1979 by
Holmes & Meier Publishers, Inc.
30 Irving Place
New York, N.Y. 10003

Great Britain:
Holmes & Meier Publishers, Ltd.
131 Trafalgar Road
Greenwich, London SE10 9TX

LIBRARY OF CONGRESS CATALOGING IN PUBLICATION DATA

Horton, James Oliver.
Black Bostonians.

Bibliography: p.
Includes index.
1. Afro-Americans—Massachusetts—Boston—Economic conditions. 2. Afro-Americans—Massachusetts—Boston—Social conditions. 3. Afro-American families—Massachusetts—Boston. 4. Boston—Economic conditions. 5. Boston—Social conditions. I. Horton, Lois E., joint author. II. Title.
F73.9.N4H67 1979 974.4'61'00496073 78-24453

ISBN 0-8419-0445-6

MANUFACTURED IN THE UNITED STATES OF AMERICA

Cover photo courtesy of the Society for the Preservation of New England Antiquities

Contents

Preface

This is a book about working people who lived in Boston during the decades before the Civil War. Like most nineteenth-century workers, these Bostonians struggled constantly to maintain homes and families. Most of them worked long, hard hours and hoped that by doing so they could secure a brighter future for their children. Theirs were typically American dreams of mobility and opportunity. Yet their dreams were often denied them by the force of racial discrimination.

The first black Bostonians, like the first white Bostonians, were immigrants. They came to this growing commercial seaport city in 1638 as "perpetual servants" from the West Indies. It was not automatic that New England, Massachusetts, or Boston would become a slaveholding area. Considering the inability of that region's soil or climate to support large-scale agriculture, it might be surprising that slavery should become implanted in this stronghold of Puritanism. As early as 1641 there were efforts to limit the conditions under which people could be enslaved. In 1700 a Boston committee took steps to discourage the importation of black slaves. Despite these efforts, by 1715 slavery was a fact of life for old New Englanders.

Slavery in the Puritan commonwealth was distinct from its southern counterpart in many important ways. Although New England slaves were held at a level below that of indentured servants, they generally possessed more rights and legal protections than southern plantation slaves. They were more than "inventory," having the right to own property, to receive trials, and to sue in the courts. Yet they were less than free persons since their families were often separated, they had little control over their labor, and their tenure as servants was for life.[1]

The black population of New England remained small throughout the colonial period, never more than sixteen thousand, and colonial Massachusetts' black population never rose much above 2 percent of the colony's population. By the mid-eighteenth century, however, Boston had one of the North's major concentrations of blacks. In 1752, 10 percent of the city's population was black, numbering just over fifteen hundred persons.[2]

As colonial Boston huddled close to the seafront wharves, so did the residences of most of the blacks. Boston blacks were generally the slave servants of wealthy white merchant families or were laborers in the commercial establishments that crowded the docks. A few slaves were employed in skilled trades, but often laws enacted at the insistence of white artisans limited the use of slaves in areas that might put them in direct competition with skilled white workers. Even after such laws disappeared, tradition prevented most blacks, slave or free, from entering skilled trades. Blacks were engaged in virtually every industry in New England; many worked in shipbuilding and seafaring, both of which were important to the Boston economy. Well into the nineteenth century, large proportions (often as much as half) of the crews of whaling vessels were black.[3]

The Revolutionary period saw a decline in Boston's black population. When wealthy Tories fled the city, many took their slaves with them to settle in Nova Scotia and other areas of eastern Canada.[4] On the eve of the Revolution, there were fewer than seven hundred blacks in all of Suffolk County. During the war, many slaves escaped to the British forces and were transported to Europe; other blacks were freed as a result of their service with the colonial forces. By 1790, the black population of Suffolk County had risen from its pre-Revolutionary level to just under eight hundred, but never again during the century did it reach the levels of the 1750s.[5]

Since most Boston slaves worked and often lived in close contact with their masters, master-slave relationships were most often strongly paternalistic. Sometimes this paternalism worked to the advantage of the slave. It meant, for example, that although the integrity of the slave family was subordinate to the economic concerns of the master, slave marriages were encouraged. New England slaves were required to abide by the laws and regional traditions concerning marriage.

Boston slaves were far from free, but their lot was better than that of slaves in the South. Indeed, it was their recognized right to bring suit, an action that allowed them to break the bonds of slavery in the commonwealth. By the last decade of the eighteenth century, slavery had been abolished in Massachusetts. Blacks emerged into the light of a freedom, which, if not complete, was at least an important stimulus to continued struggle toward equality and full citizenship.

Being a Bostonian carried a proud heritage steeped in a love of freedom. Being a black American carried a heritage of slavery. Both heritages included a willingness to struggle for liberty. Black Bostonians were immersed in both traditions. They had stood with other patriots on the battlefields of the American Revolution. In the nineteenth century, they formed the vanguard for the eradication of human bondage in the South.

Acknowledgments

In the course of researching this book, we have been fortunate in receiving the advice and guidance of more friends and colleagues than we can adequately acknowledge here. Yet a number of them deserve special thanks. John P. Roche and Pauli Murray were among those who guided the project in its formative stage. Stanley Engerman, Lawrence J. Friedman, Elizabeth Pleck, and Kenneth Lockridge each gave the manuscript a thorough reading and provided valuable criticism. Charles Tilly contributed helpful suggestions, support, and encouragement at a crucial juncture. The manuscript also profited from the close and perceptive reading of Herbert G. Gutman.

Others who have contributed important suggestions are Lawrence Glasco, Phyllis Palmer, Noralee Frankel, and Leo Ribuffo. Valuable assistance and advice on gathering and analyzing statistical data were provided by Raymond Shortridge, Maris A. Vinovskis, and Eric Austin. Dwight Herbert, Susan Green Henderson, and Mark Henderson lent important and capable research assistance.

Gratitude is expressed to Arthur LaBrew, who made his copies of nineteenth-century Boston playbills and concert programs available to this project. Special thanks is also extended to Kate Kaminski, Pauline Klumpp and Nancy L. Smith for their assistance in the preparation of this manuscript.

We would also like to thank the staffs of the Andover Newton Theological Seminary Library, the Boston Public Library, the Moorland Spingarn Collection of the Howard University Library, the Library of Congress, and the National Archives. Byron Rushing, director of the Museum of Afro-American History in Boston, made the resources of the museum available to us.

At important points in the research, the project received much-appreciated funding from the Irving and Rose Crown Fellowship Program at Brandeis University, the Rackham Faculty Research Grant Program at the University of Michigan, and the Center for Afroamerican and African Studies at the University of Michigan.

There are those who should receive extraordinary thanks, for without their support and scholarly advice this project could not have been completed. Idus A. Newby and Marvin Meyers have both given much to this study. To the extent that it makes a scholarly contribution, they are largely responsible.

Finally, we would like to thank Michael James Horton for his patience, understanding, mathematical computations, and enthusiasm.

Introduction

Throughout the antebellum period, the black population of Boston organized itself to deal with local and national problems. The social characteristics of this small community determined, in part, the nature of its organization. Because those who constituted the community were largely poor and were excluded from many of the social services of the city, informal, cooperative solutions were found to their common problems. This cooperation, which was in some ways a reaction to discrimination by the wider society, became an important factor in the development of black social activism.

The task of serving this poor, diverse, and transient community was difficult, but the necessities of individual survival spurred communal action. Black Boston was not a monolithic society. Class and social differences existed, and occupation, geographic origin, and skin color often defined differences in residence, job skills, and association. There were disagreements over questions of integration and separation, cooperation with whites, or independent black action. Yet all blacks were unified in the belief that the basic rights of citizenship ought to be extended to Americans of African descent. Class distinctions became more important after the Civil War. The relatively small size of the community and its involvement in actions against slavery tended to diminish the impact of class during the antebellum period.

The black family was particularly important since it became the cooperative model extended to other institutions built on the same principles of sharing. These institutions, particularly the church, were the foundation upon which a community was built, one that developed the strength to deal with shared problems. From these institutions and organizations came community leaders who spurred the denunciation of local racism and national slavery, verbalizing their interconnection. Despite the transience of many blacks—especially unskilled workers and fugitives from slavery—important institutions provided a continuity in black community life. They eased adjustment to the new city and provided the mechanisms for migrants to become involved in ongoing community action.

The organizations established to meet survival needs also provided the framework for social protest. Except for the existence of these community institutions, the explosion of protest activity might not have taken place in

Boston in the pre-Civil War decades. Slavery loomed as the most blatant symbol of racial injustice and was thus a chief object of black protest. For many in the community who had suffered personally under the dread institution, or for the many more whose friends and relatives had labored or remained under its yoke, slavery was more than a symbol: it was an intimate and personal enemy. It was natural, then, that abolition would become the major protest activity and the protection of fugitives who had escaped from slavery a major concern.

Other protest activities that concerned black Bostonians resulted from the discrimination faced daily in the city. Efforts directed toward the improvement of black education, the integration of public transportation, accommodations, and entertainment facilities represented an attempt to provide an equal status for blacks in Boston. The existence of such extensive social protest organizations in a city recognized by its black population as one of the most liberal in the country may appear contradictory. Yet Boston's reputation for relative racial tolerance fostered optimism, which in turn encouraged protest organization. Furthermore, each success provided an incentive for greater protest and more extensive organization.

It may be argued that cooperation forms a major theme for all American society. Few Americans have been able to exemplify the myth of rugged individualism. In the small farming communities of the Midwest, in the mining camps of the far West, on the plains of the frontier, and in the working-class slums of eastern cities the historical experience of the masses of Americans reflects the extent to which cooperation often overshadowed individualism. To the extent that this is true, the experience of blacks illustrates in the extreme the need for cooperation, a need that is a part of the historical experience of most Americans.

Unlike most histories, this book studies those individuals who were neither rich nor politically powerful. In this sense, it is a social history of working people. It is unique among studies of black history in that it examines the lives of pre–Civil War blacks, most of whom were not slaves themselves and did not live in the region of slavery. This is not a book of "first blacks." Individual achievement is seen as most important within the context of family, group, or community membership. This study moves beyond previous works to place discrimination and social protest in the context of family and community life.

It is especially difficult to study poor, working-class people in the nineteenth century, and even more difficult when they are black. A few letters and diaries have survived, but these do not begin to flesh out the picture of community life. There was no sustained black press in Boston before the Civil War, and although city newspapers provide some information about local blacks, they tend to focus upon exceptional individuals. The activities of black leaders, special achievers, and lawbreakers were almost certain to appear in print, but those of the average wage earner and family member were just as certain not to. Even the *Liberator*, with its special interest in the black community, was not likely to provide much information concerning the daily lives of common black working people.

Black newspapers published in other cities, such as New York City's *Colored American*, give valuable information about the political life of Boston blacks, reporting on organizations and gatherings. Accounts of such activities are often sketchy, but sometimes there are estimates of audience size and a listing of officers. Some of the most helpful information can be found in the classified ads placed by Boston's black businessmen. A boardinghouse advertisement might include a description of services provided and the character of the clientele. Some boardinghouses catered to sailors. Others explained that there were whites as well as blacks among the residents. Geographical location and proximity to the church or to the local black residential area were often included, indicating the importance of such information to potential residents. A close analysis of this data reveals much about the structure and character of the black community.

Obituaries and editorials were used profitably, although allowances had to be made for the particular biases inherent in such data. Beyond this, newspaper circulation figures provided clues to the degree of literacy in the community. The geographical reporting area gave information on the extent of communication with other cities and the concern for, and awareness of, common problems. Other documents, like wills and organizational and institutional records, helped to illuminate social networks. Yet all these sources proved inadequate for illustrating the world of black Boston.

Such works as Theodore Hershburg's important examination of antebellum Philadelphia blacks, the studies of Stephen Thernstrom and Peter Knights on antebellum white workers, and Elizabeth Pleck's analysis of post-Civil War black Boston suggested techniques applicable to this study.[1] Each of these studies makes extensive use of government documents, particularly the United States census. Starting in 1850, the census provides extensive individual-level information such as name, age, race, occupation, and place of birth. Individuals are located in family and household groups, which allows some analysis of living arrangements. For the purpose of this study, the entire black population listed in the census of Boston in 1850 and 1860 was coded and computerized. This information was supplemented by data gathered from selected Boston city directories issued between 1800 and 1830, all directories issued between 1830 and 1860, and by Boston tax records and vital statistics.

There are, of course, important problems in using these documents. Although they do bring to light much data on otherwise obscure individuals, even these documents are biased toward the most stable and secure segment of the population. Although information is provided for both laborers and business owners, the laborer is more likely to be missing from public records even if he did not actually leave the community. Because poor people were likely to drift from one residence to another within the community, or to live in the homes of others, they were more likely than stable property owners to be missed by the census taker or official record keeper.[2]

In order to minimize problems of underenumeration and error, the data from these public sources were combined. This method proved extremely worthwhile, for example, in establishing occupational patterns among Boston's blacks. The census is the most important source of occupational data after 1850. Prior to that year, occupational information was developed by combining city directories and tax records. This was necessary because city directory data alone was not sufficient to establish occupational patterns.[3]

In 1830, for example, with only 14 percent of black household heads listed in the city directory, about one-half of them were listed as employed in semi-skilled or unskilled jobs. More complete information, not quite as biased toward the more stable middle class, can be obtained by combining sources. City directories and tax records combined for 1840, for example, give the occupations of over 50 percent of the black household heads in Boston. These sources indicated that over 68 percent of the workers held unskilled and semi-skilled occupations, a figure comparable to census figures for 1850 and 1860.

Another interesting benefit resulting from combining sources is the possibility of finding occupations for those individuals listed in the city directory as having no occupation. In almost every case, those so listed whose occupations could be obtained through other sources were doing semi-skilled or unskilled work. Research conducted by Leonard Curry into the usefulness of city directories suggests that although city directories may not be as complete as the census, they are useful in estimating the proportional representation of various occupational levels.[4]

One of the most useful tools for historians seeking to understand black society is also one of the most underused data sources—the pension records of the Veterans Administration.[5] For the nineteenth century, the pension records of the Civil War are most useful. These records contain far more information than that related directly to the war or to military life. Those applying for government pensions were required to provide written statements by witnesses as verification of claims. Sometimes these written statements were very concise and simple, but frequently they amounted to a biography of the claimant, a detailed description of the relationship between the claimant and the witness and, on occasion, an autobiography of the witness. For those interested in the daily life of the masses of black people, the pension records can be the most valuable source available.

Pension records most closely approximate the private diaries and letters of those who left no such personal records. The people who applied for pensions included the wounded or the widows of those who had died as a result of the war. There is every reason to believe that while almost all of the other records discussed might be slanted toward the more affluent members of society, pension records may well be one of the most valuable sources for the less affluent and the poor. Blacks had a disproportionately high casualty rate in the Civil War, as well as in most other wars, making the pension records especially valuable for the student of black nineteenth-century history.

The statements included in these records provide information about the lives of claimants before and after the war. Since many applicants did not request pensions until late in their lives, it is not unusual to find Civil War pension applications dated after 1900. Frequently the claimant's life can be traced before, during, and after the war, making it possible to speculate as to the effect of the war experience on the lives of many of those who participated in it. The possibilities for the uses of this data source seem to be limited only by the imagination and creativity of the historian.

An exciting aspect of researching this study was the constant demand for inventiveness. If the history of working people is ever to be understood, it will depend on the development of new historical sources and novel uses of more traditional data. Recently there has been a trend toward categorizing and separating historical methodologies into the quantitative and the non-quantitative. This trend can be counterproductive unless historians understand the complementary nature of these methods. Traditional and statistical history can and must be combined to achieve a more complete and sophisticated historical analysis of the lives of working people, black or white. It is hoped that this study, by blending these techniques, will contribute to further advances in social history research.

1/Profile of Black Boston

It was a cold, snowy evening in early January 1832. On Boston's Beacon Hill, a young black boy, William C. Nell, stood huddled against the snow that swirled up Smith Court from Belknap Street. The flickering gas lights illuminated the street in front of the African Meeting House where the boy stood straining to catch a glimpse of the gathering inside.

This was an important meeting, he knew, the climax of an exciting year for Boston's black community. Peering through the frosted windowpane, he could see Mr. Garrison, who for the past year had been editing the newspaper called the *Liberator*. This small sheet with its ringing denunciation of slavery had created excitement among blacks in Boston. Most agreed that Garrison's newspaper and its promise of white support would bring new power to their long struggle against slavery in America.[1]

In the basement of the meetinghouse, which regularly served as classrooms for the African School, a number of men discussed the establishment of a regional society dedicated to the abolition of slavery. Plans were made for the organization's constitution and a preamble was signed. The small group left the hall exhausted and excited, braving the snow and the cold wind of the New England winter.

At the corner, most turned up Belknap Street, heading toward the fashionable residences at the top of Beacon Hill. Here, overlooking the nation's fourth largest city, was the State Capitol building, a brick and marble structure with an impressive golden dome. In the shadow of the Statehouse, spreading westward to Charles Street, lived many of the city's most prominent industrialists, who blended by residence, interest, and marriage with the old aristocratic mercantile families. In the thirty years since the turn of the century, New England's manufacturers had converted small localized businesses to a multimillion-dollar textile industry. This process was facilitated by the advent of water power, machine technology, corporate organization, and capital accumulation. Most of this industrial capital was invested in the large factories in towns outside of Boston, where the wealthy cotton manufacturers—the Lowells, Cabots, Appletons, and Lawrences—found superior water power and a cheap, exploitable labor supply. Banking and other financial institutions flourished in Boston, providing lucrative fields of investment for the city's rich but only limited employment opportunity for the city's poor.[2]

The growing wealth and status of this new industrial class resulted in their control of one-fifth of the nation's spindles, one-third of Massachusetts' railroad mileage, and two-fifths of Boston's banking capital by 1850. Since their wealth was closely tied to cotton, their economic and political interests were closely tied to the South. Exercising their influence and power, these gentlemen of property and standing played a significant role in the anti-abolitionist movement in Boston and were generally not supportive of drives for racial equality.[3]

North of the Statehouse, occupying the lower slopes of the hill, were the residences of another group of Bostonians, black Bostonians. In contrast to their affluent white neighbors at the top of the hill, those of this largest black

Table 1

BLACK POPULATION OF BOSTON, 1830–1860

Year	*Total Population of Boston (thousands)*	*Black Population*	*% of Total Population*
1830	61.4	1,875	3.1
1840	84.4	1,988	2.4
1850	136.9	1,999	1.5
1860	177.8	2,261	1.3

SOURCE: Peter R. Knights, *Plain People of Boston, 1830–1860* (New York, 1971), p. 29.

Table 2

LARGEST NORTHERN URBAN BLACK POPULATIONS, 1860 [a]

City	*Black Population*	*% of Total Population*
Philadelphia	22,185	3.9
New York City	12,472	1.5
Brooklyn, New York	4,313	1.6
Cincinnati, Ohio	3,737	2.3

SOURCE: Hollis, Lynch, *The Black Urban Condition* (New York, 1973), p. 4.

[a]Even though these cities have black populations much larger than Boston, the percentages of blacks in their total populations are comparable to the percentage in Boston.

enclave in the city, one-third of the city's almost 1,900 blacks in 1830, lived in a world far removed from the wealth and power just a few blocks away.[4]

The work of those few who initiated the New England Anti-Slavery Society on that snowy evening in 1832 provided avenues for some whites to break free from the political and financial concerns of Beacon Hill's aristocracy and to join blacks in their struggle against slavery. Yet few broke through the barriers of Boston's black world to understand the plight of their darker Boston neighbors.

Black Beacon Hill met white Beacon Hill on Belknap Street (later Joy Street), a narrow cobblestone way that climbed from Cambridge Street to the summit near the Statehouse. Two-level attached brick dwellings formed boundaries broken occasionally by the network of alleyways honeycombing the area.

The snows of winter muted the sounds of horses' hoofs. The smell of smoke from green wood sold to the poor at discount prices greeted vendors, whose songs announced their wares. Winter meant that social activity was indoors. Only the sounds of children, who seemed to consider the slopes their private slide, greeted passersby as they hurried from workplaces to the warmth of their homes.

The passing of winter brought the black community to the steps and streets. Although some adults complained of too much noise from the children who played outdoors in warmer weather, Boston did not have large numbers of black children. There were proportionately fewer blacks than whites under ten years of age throughout the antebellum period.[5] Life in this poor community was hard, sometimes too hard for the very young. Although studies conducted in 1848 and again in 1854 reported that the birthrate among the blacks was the highest in the city, many black babies did not survive their first year.[6]

Partially because of its higher infant mortality rate, black Boston tended to be statistically older than the city's white population. It was mainly a young adult society, with the vast majority no older than thirty-five years. Although many more women than men passed through the daytime streets, to and from market or transporting the laundry which provided a living for many, in reality, there were only slightly more women than men in the black community. Since women tended to live a bit longer than men, the imbalance was greater among those fifty years of age and older.

The residential concentration of the relatively small black population distorted the perception of those who passed through the community, making it seem larger than it actually was. As this concentration increased, so that by 1860 almost two-thirds of the city's blacks lived on Beacon Hill, the lower slopes were thought of by most as "Nigger Hill," solidly black. This was not true. Even in the most segregated areas blacks and whites lived adjacent to one another or shared the same dwellings.[7]

Ironically, during the two decades before the Civil War, when economic and social pressure created even greater separation from most whites, an increasing number of white faces and Irish brogues blended with the other sights and sounds of black neighborhoods. This condition reflected the growing number of Irish immigrants who arrived in Boston during the 1850s, limited by prejudice and poverty to less attractive areas of the city.[8] Often, a dramatic rise in the number of Irish in a neighborhood resulted in a decline in the area's black population. This was the case in ward two between 1850 and 1860. Competition for jobs and housing engendered animosity between blacks and Irish, and much of the black flight from ward two was undoubtedly an effort by blacks to shield themselves from hostility and harrassment. Since they were still barred from many neighborhoods, these families moved into predominently black sections.

Cambridge Street, at the bottom of the hill, did not mark the limits of the black community. Blacks were also concentrated on the streets immediately to the north in the area, in ward five, now occupied by the Massachusetts

Table 3

BLACK RESIDENCE BY WARD, 1830–1860

Ward	*1830*	*1840*[a]	*1850*	*1860*
1	107	148	120	160
2	193	693	115	73
3	42	8	31	101
4	46	138	112	32
5	185	202	221	277
6	605	1088	1219	1395
7	450	26	16	5
8	38	6	1	4
9	11	17	19	40
10	64	3	8	47
11	28	32	73	79
12	106	66	64	48
TOTAL	1875	2427	1999	2261

SOURCE: Lemuel Shattuck, *Report to the Committee of the City Council/Report of the Joint Special Committee on the Census of Boston for 1845* (Boston, 1846); *Seventh United States Census* (1850); *Eighth United States Census* (1860).

[a]Ward boundaries were redrawn in 1838. This may account for what seem to be striking changes in the populations of wards between 1830 and 1840.

Table 4

RESIDENTIAL CONCENTRATION OF BLACKS IN BOSTON, 1830–1860

Year	*Four Wards of Largest Black Concentration*	*% of Black Population Residing in Those Wards*
1830	2, 5, 6, 7	76.4
1840	1, 2, 5, 6	85.1
1850	1, 2, 5, 6	83.8
1860	1, 3, 5, 6	85.5

SOURCE: Knights, *Plain People of Boston,* p. 31.

General Hospital. A third important black neighborhood was located near the wharves of the North End. This had once been the largest black neighborhood in the city, but by 1830 it was losing ground to the other areas. It had become notorious as a district of crime and vice which worried police authorities and satisfied the needs of sailors and gentlemen alike.[9]

Boston, then, was a racially separated but not totally segregated city. In this respect, it paralleled many other nineteenth-century cities. Detroit and Cleveland, for example, showed "no evidence of the existence of well-defined ghettoes before 1890."[10] In both cities, blacks and poor immigrants shared

Table 5

INDEX OF DISSIMILARITY SHOWING RESIDENTIAL SEGREGATION OF BLACKS AND WHITES IN 1860 [a]

Boston	61.3
Chicago	50.0
Cincinnati	47.9
Indianapolis	47.2
Philadelphia	47.1
New York	40.6

SOURCE: Ira Berlin, *Slaves without Masters* (New York, 1974), p. 257.

[a]Boston's ward six (Beacon Hill area) accounted for more than one-third of the Index of Dissimilarity for that city. A higher index value denotes greater segregation.

neighborhoods. Boston, however, was the most segregated city in the country by 1860.

Boston's black neighborhoods reflected the diversity of their people. On the streets and in the shops, many different dialects and accents could be heard. Although by the mid-nineteenth century, less than half of black Bostonians had been born in Massachusetts, almost two-thirds had been born in the North. Most were from states along the east coast. William Cortland, for example, was from New York. He and his wife, Rachael, had come to Boston in the 1840s and he had secured a job on a cargo vessel. Abraham Church was a native Pennsylvanian who came to Boston in search of work in the mid-1840s. Since he was over forty years old and unskilled, there was little chance that he could find more than menial labor to support his family. His wife and a child, probably hers from a previous marriage, were both native New Yorkers, but by mid-century this family of non–New Englanders made their home and a simple living in Boston.[11]

Mingled with the tones of these northerners were the softer drawls of southern-born blacks whose proportion of the population grew from 17 percent in 1850 to almost one-quarter by 1860. Most, like William Paine, a thirty-year-old seaman, had come north from Virginia in search of work and a better way of life. Paine's wife, Maria, also a native Virginian, did menial work to help support the family and to fill the days that William spent at sea. Of those blacks born in the South, 48 percent in 1850 and 53 percent in 1860 were born in Virginia.[12]

Generally, both northern- and southern-born blacks were from the east coast. Few had been born in the then new western areas such as Wisconsin or Michigan or in the western South. Although there is no way to determine an individual's order and number of residences from his birthplace, the overwhelming concentration of Atlantic Seaboard birthplaces among Boston blacks seems to indicate that eastern black migration, like general American migration, followed the major Atlantic trade route. The route from the eastern South seemed to be through Philadelphia and New York. Each of these cities had sizable black populations and organized black communities.

Increasingly evident during this period was a sprinkling of foreign accents. The clipped tones of British and Canadian English and the musical strains of West Indian speech were peppered with the brogue of Irish-born blacks and the accents of Spanish, French, and African dialects to lend a cosmopolitan flavor to Boston's black community. Many foreign-born blacks were descendants of American blacks who had fled to the English during the American Revolution to escape slavery in the United States. Others had been freed in 1834 by the abolition of slavery in the British Empire or during the 1820s as Latin American nations gained their independence.

A few had come to the United States and finally to Boston to escape political persecution. Emilius Mundrucu had been an officer in the Brazilian army. His involvement in political dissension had forced him to leave Brazil. After a short stay in Haiti and Venezuela, where he met the Latin American liberator Simón Bolívar, Mundrucu settled first in New Bedford and then in Boston. By 1830 he had entered into the business partnership of Mundrucu and Bautista Clothing on Ann Street in Boston's North End. Mundrucu married a native of Massachusetts and by mid-century had five children, one of whom worked with him in the clothing shop.[13]

Table 6

NATIVITY OF BOSTON BLACKS

Region	*% of City's Black Population*	
	1850	*1860*
Massachusetts	44.8	39.4
New England (including Massachusetts)	54.5	48.0
North (including Massachusetts and New England)	63.2	59.1
South	16.6	24.1
Foreign	9.0	15.8

SOURCE: *Seventh United States Census* (1850) and *Eighth United States Census* (1860).

As diversity was striking to the ear, variety was conspicuous to the eye. Black Boston was a colorful place. The long bright dresses and multicolored bandannas worn by many of the women highlighted the many shades of complexion which characterized the people. Skin tones from yellowish tints to deep rich ebonies created a kaleidoscopic scene, contrasting sharply with the rest of Boston, which became even less variegated by midwinter. Blind to the nuances of color, official records reported only two categories—black and mulatto. According to these sources, there were proportionately more mulattoes in Boston's black society than in other northern black communities.[14] There was no correlation between place of birth and skin color. This is especially interesting since there were proportionately more mulattoes among free blacks living in the South than among northern blacks by 1860.

Boston's mulattoes were generally more skilled, held more property, and were a bit less residentially separated from the white society than the darker members of their race. Although mulattoes were only 18 percent of the black work force in 1850, they accounted for one-quarter of the most skilled. By 1860 this overrepresentation was even greater. While mulattoes were 34 percent of the black work force, they were 53 percent of the skilled workers.

Apparently, lighter skin operated to the blacks' advantage in antebellum Boston as it did for blacks generally in late nineteenth- and twentieth-century American society. Between 1850 and 1860 mulattoes were less likely to live in predominantly white areas of the city. The animosities that led to a greater concentration of Afro-Americans of all shades after 1850 were undoubtedly also responsible for the migration of larger numbers of mulattoes to "Nigger Hill."

Differences in birthplace and skin tone contrasted with a relative sameness in economic condition. This was evident as evening brought black working people back into the neighborhoods. Black women returning from domestic jobs in the homes of the wealthy provided crucial sources of income for many households. By mid-century, domestic work was the most frequent occupation for the city's blacks. Black men made their way from North End docks or midtown commercial areas. These were laboring men who worked with their hands and their backs. Their skills were few, the work sporadic, and the pay pitifully low. Three-quarters of them were semi-skilled or unskilled workers, mostly day laborers and seamen. Fewer than one-third were skilled workers or small shopkeepers. To be a hairdresser, a barber, a blacksmith, or a used-clothing dealer, the most common skilled or entrepreneurial occupations among blacks, was to be a person of relatively high standing in the community.[15]

There were regional concentrations within specific occupations. Although southern-born blacks accounted for only a little more than one-quarter of those listed with occupations in the census of 1850, they accounted for 40 percent of the black barbers and hairdressers listed. They accounted for 60 percent of the black carpenters, and ran three of the five black boardinghouses in the city. Boston's only black printer in 1850 was born in Virginia. The situation was much the same in 1860, when 40 percent of all black skilled craftsmen were southern born.

The higher percentages of southern-born blacks working as skilled craftsmen in Boston reflected, in large part, the significant number of free blacks and slaves employed in skilled labor in the antebellum South. Although the majority came north to take unskilled work, a substantial number brought skills which they put to good use in their new home.[16]

Michael Milliken and his family exemplify the most common pattern for southern-born black migrants to antebellum Boston. Michael was born in Virginia, and his wife, Katherine, was born in Washington, D.C. Michael was a carpenter by trade, and by the late 1840s he, his wife, and their three children were living in East Boston. Like most southern migrants, the Millikens had not come directly to Boston. The birthplaces of their children indicate that Boston was one of a number of cities along the Atlantic coast in which they had lived. The family moved relatively short distances during the 1830s and 1840s. This pattern paralleled that of white families moving from the East to the Midwest during the same period.[17]

Foreign-born black workers were the least skilled workers in the city. They were concentrated to a greater extent than either northern or southern born in the occupations of laborer, seaman, and domestic. By the last decades of the antebellum period, these foreign-born blacks bore the brunt of increasing job competition with white unskilled immigrant labor.[18]

Since steady employment was difficult for unskilled blacks to secure, most were familiar with a variety of jobs. Caesar Gardner, for example, held jobs as a day laborer, a bootblack, a seaman, and a waiter between 1830 and 1844. James Johnson was similarly versatile, holding jobs as a waiter, a laborer, a tender, and a teamster between 1844 and 1860.[19]

For a few blacks, a change of jobs meant a rise in occupational level. John Henry was born in New Jersey and came to Boston in the 1830s. He took odd jobs as a day laborer and finally sought relief from the Overseers of the Poor in 1839. During the early 1840s, he was fortunate enough to secure a position as a seaman. This proved to be temporary, however, for by 1848 he was again taking jobs as a laborer. The next two years were a period of great prosperity for Henry, and he accumulated $1,500. He opened a small grocery shop in his residence on Belknap Street in the early 1850s. In twenty years, Henry had risen from the bottom of the economic ladder to a relatively prosperous position in black society. John Henry was one of a small number of blacks who were upwardly mobile during this period.[20]

Thomas Smith from New York worked as a laborer during most of the 1840s to support his wife and son. He worked as a porter during the early 1850s and by 1860 had acquired his own clothing shop. For many unskilled or semi-skilled blacks, opening small, independent, community-based businesses was an important means of advancement, but most were not nearly so fortunate. Most at the bottom of the economic scale remained there throughout the antebellum period. Insofar as there was occupational mobility within black society, it occured within the low-level occupational group—as the unskilled sometimes became semi-skilled. The rise of a worker into the skilled or entrepreneurial group was extremely rare.[21]

Occasional exceptions to this rule were young black men and those new to the city who accepted temporary work while preparing for more permanent careers. Edward M. Bannister, arriving from St. Andrew, New Brunswick, took odd jobs before opening his own hairdressing salon. Finally, after a fortuitous marriage to a wealthy businesswoman, Bannister gained prominence as an artist and converted his salon to a studio. Like Bannister, another member of Boston's black professional class began his working life at a menial level. Robert Morris worked as a servant and clerk to Ellis Gray Loring, a well-known Boston attorney. Later, he was admitted to the bar as one of Boston's first black lawyers.[22]

There were also those in skilled and entrepreneurial occupations who were downwardly mobile, indicating the precarious existence of Boston's more prosperous blacks. For at least two years, William R. Woodroff operated a clothing store. Yet in 1839 he died as an inmate of the poorhouse.[23] George C. Clary also operated his own clothing shop in the 1830s which he converted to a hairdressing salon in 1841, but by 1848 he was no longer able to maintain his own business and was forced on the market as a common laborer.[24] Likewise, William Wallace who was an independent hairdresser in 1837 died in the poorhouse two years later. Fortunately, this downward mobility was not a major trend and may be accounted for at least in part by the effects of national depressions.[25]

At the top of the black occupational scale stood a very few professionals—doctors, ministers, teachers, and lawyers. Their numbers were miniscule and, although there was a steady growth in this class, their percentage of the city's total black work force ranged from less than 1 percent in 1830 to about 2 percent in 1860.[26]

The occupational structure of black Boston was comparable to that of other northern cities. In Buffalo (1855 and 1875), Troy, New York (1860 and 1880), and New York City and Brooklyn (1860) 68 percent to 81 percent of black workers were in the lowest occupational categories.[27] Although the vast majority of Boston's black workers were unskilled, there were important distinctions between those who worked on a temporary daily basis and those employed more regularly. Traditional class divisions are inadequate for understanding the occupational structure of black society. The occupations of porter and laborer, for example, were generally considered of equal worth in white society—both lower-class jobs. Yet, for blacks, the job of porter was more desirable because most black laborers were employed on the docks where the work was more sporadic and seasonal than that available in the downtown commercial areas for black porters.

Table 7

BLACK OCCUPATIONAL LEVELS, 1850 AND 1860

	1850		*1860*	
		%		%
Professional	7	1.3	20	2.1
Skilled and Entrepreneurial	146	26.7	258	26.4
Unskilled Semi-skilled	394	72.0	698	71.5

SOURCE: *Seventh United States Census (1850) and Eighth United States Census* (1860).

Boston's black workers and their families generally lived in homes that they did not own. At mid-century, only 1.5 percent of black single adults and family heads owned real property. A rise in the percentage of black real property holders to 4.5 percent by 1860 was probably due as much to improved official reporting as to any actual property holding increase. Yet,

Table 8

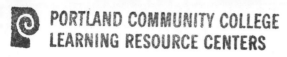

NATIVITY OF BLACK WORKERS, 1850 AND 1860

	Northern Born (%)		*Southern Born (%)*		*Foreign Born (%)*		*Unknown (%)*	
	1850	*1860*	*1850*	*1860*	*1850*	*1860*	*1850*	*1860*
	N=*261*	N=*469*	N=*142*	N=*306*	N=*63*	N=*187*	N=*81*	N=*14*
Professional	1.5	1.9	1.4	2.0	0	2.1	0	7.1
Skilled and Entrepreneurial	30.3	27.1	31.7	29.7	27.0	19.3	6.2	28.6
Unskilled and Semi-skilled	68.2	71.0	66.2	68.3	73.0	78.6	93.8	64.3
Total	47.7	48.1	26.0	31.4	11.5	19.2	14.8	1.4

SOURCE: *Seventh United States Census* (1850) and *Eighth United States Census* (1860).

Table 9

BLACK AND MULATTO WORKERS, 1850 AND 1860

	1850		*1860*	
	Black %	*Mulatto %*	*Black %*	*Mulatto %*
	N = *407*	N = *91*	N = *583*	N = *306*
Professional	1.5	1.1	2.4	1.9
Skilled and Entrepreneurial	24.0	35.2	17.5	37.3
Unskilled and Semi-skilled	74.5	63.7	80.1	60.8
Total	81.7	18.3	65.6	34.4

SOURCE: *Seventh United States Census* (1850) and *Eighth United States Census* (1860).

even the higher percentage described a virtually propertyless community. As was true for other northern black communities, property was not apportioned along traditional economic class lines. Although skilled and entrepreneurial workers were more likely to hold property, one's occupation did not necessarily predict property holdings.[28]

In 1840 George Price and George Thompson were both laborers. Price had no property noted by tax assessors, whereas Thompson was reported to have at least $20,000 in personal property. John Rock, a black doctor, was reported to have no taxable real property and only $500 in personal property. Of the small businessmen in the community, clothing dealers were most likely to own property, probably their own shops. The wealthiest black person in antebellum Boston was a servant, Arran Morris, with $40,000 in personal property. There are no clues to explain how a laborer or a servant accumulated such wealth while professional blacks had so little. Probably such great sums came from white benefactors, perhaps left in a will to a loyal employee.[29]

Obviously wealth like this was unheard of for most blacks. On the eve of the Civil War, per capita property holding was $91. In comparison, the per capita wealth of the entire population of Boston was $872. Even the Boston Irish, poor recent immigrants, had outdistanced blacks by 1860 with a per capita wealth of $131.

Although the black community was economically poor, it was rich in tradition. The oral tradition in particular was strong during the nineteenth century. Young children often became acquainted with the world and their place in it through the stories told by the senior members of the society. Deacon Cyrus Foster was well known and appreciated for his tales of New England blacks during the Revolution and early period of American nationhood. Foster had fought in the Revolution and lived on a small pension he received from the federal government. Much of his time was spent walking and talking about his experiences. Foster and others became community oral historians, respected for their knowledge and their ability to entertain.[30]

During the 1850s William C. Nell transcribed this oral history and included it in the first black-authored regional history. Nell presented his *The Colored Patriots of the American Revolution* to a surprisingly literate black community.[31] In 1850 the census reported that only 14 percent of the city's black adults were unable to read and write. By 1860 the number of blacks who were illiterate had dropped to 8 percent. Massachusetts-born blacks were least likely to be illiterate, reflecting the concern for public education within the state. Northern-born blacks were far more likely to have basic reading and writing skills than southern-born blacks. As might be expected, illiteracy was highest among the lowest skilled workers.[32]

Illiteracy was also higher among older adults. In 1850 the percentage of adults fifty years of age and older who were reported as illiterate was more than twice their proportion of the total black population. Older women were less likely to be literate than older men.

During the 1850s there was a decline in the percentage of illiterates among older adults but a rise in the illiteracy of black women. This change may be partially due to a rise in the number of illiterate southern-born females who came to Boston to work as domestics.

Table 10

ILLITERACY AMONG BLACK BOSTONIANS OVER TWENTY YEARS OF AGE, 1850 AND 1860

	1850		*1860*	
	Number Illiterate	*% Illiterate*	*Number Illiterate*	*% Illiterate*
Massachusetts Born	41	8.7	13	2.5
All New England Born	64	9.5	28	3.7
All Northern Born	77	10.2	38	4.4
Southern Born	72	25.5	61	12.5
Foreign Born	18	11.7	27	8.6
Total	184	13.6	128	7.6

SOURCE: *Seventh United States Census* (1850) and *Eighth United States Census* (1860).

It would be misleading to assume that literacy in the mid-nineteenth century meant anything more than a rudimentary knowledge of reading and writing. Many of those judged literate were, in fact, functional illiterates, able to write little more than their names and, in some cases, unable to read and comprehend a newspaper. Still, the large percentage of those who could read and write even at an elementary level meant that broadsides posted in the community could communicate valuable information to many. This communication was a significant factor in the organization and operation of black protest and mutual aid groups that blossomed in the decades before the Civil War.

The characteristics of black Bostonians and the conditions of their lives suggest both the limits and the potentialities of the black community. The picture of black society presented by an external view of black neighborhoods, however, is incomplete. For insight into what it meant to be black in antebellum Boston, it is necessary to become acquainted with the interior life of the community. Behind the brick facades of "Nigger Hill" and the wooden fronts of the North End, black families and households struggled for survival. In their homes, they found a limited shelter from the often cruel and intolerant world outside.

2/Families and Households in Black Boston

The dipping of the sun across the Charles River signaled the end of the working day for those who labored on the docks in North Boston. For Joseph J. Fatal, it meant the beginning of the long walk toward Beacon Hill. The spring of 1850, like those of most years, was a welcome season for the city's blacks. It meant not only the end of the New England winter, notoriously hard and long, but also a time of decreasing expenses for living. The wood, so vital for warmth in the bitter cold, lasted longer, being used only for cooking and occasionally to ward off the chill of evening. There were fewer expenses for the children's clothing. Most important, spring brought the thawing of the harbor, the return of business to the wharves and needed jobs for laborers like Fatal.

Across Cambridge Street and uphill at South Russell, Fatal paralleled Belknap Street as far as Southac Street. At Southac he turned right, putting Belknap to his back. It was only a short distance from the corner to number two Southac where thirty-four-year-old Joseph Fatal lived with his wife, Mary, and their twelve-year-old son. The Fatal household, like most black households in Boston, was a small one. The average black household in 1850 and 1860 contained four people, usually a married couple with two children.[1]

Prior to 1850, families and households are difficult to reconstruct, since the manuscript census provides only minimal information—listing heads of households by name but giving only the number, sex, and age range for other family or household members. Beginning in 1850, more detailed information is available. In 1850 and 1860, census takers recorded specific data for all members of a household. Although familial relationships were not recorded until 1880, deductions can frequently be made based on name, age, and birthplace of household members. The order of listing in the census also provides important clues to status.[2]

Such deduction was determined to have an extremely high reliability, especially for immediate family members. This deductive method was less reliable, although still over 80 percent reliable, in determining extended family relationships—in-laws, aunts, and uncles. Determination of married sisters or daughters was also highly reliable, but since the determination of cousins was less than 60 percent reliable, this latter relationship will not be examined here. Stepchildren were distinguishable from children taken into the household mainly through comparisons between age and place of birth of child and adult members of the household. This determination had a 75 percent reliability.[3]

Black families were not isolated from other families in the urban Boston environment. Most lived in multiple-family dwellings. In 1850, the Fatals shared their house with the Freeman family and with William Delancy, a hairdresser with a shop in East Boston.[4] The close proximity of the families meant that when forty-year-old Richard Freeman was away at sea, his young wife could visit with Mary Fatal and that the only child of each family had a playmate close at hand. Joseph Fatal had been born in Massachusetts, and Mary had been born in Canada. The young Fatal boy's knowledge of the world was widened beyond the boundaries of his family background, however, not only by his father's tales of the days when he, too, had been a seaman, but by Richard Freeman's stories of his native West Indies and by Mrs. Freeman's narrations of life in the slave state of Maryland.

Many households in black Boston included more than family members. Across the street from the Fatals, for example, was the family of Henry L. Thacker, a waiter. The Thacker family included Henry, his wife, a twenty-one-year-old daughter, and a twenty-five-year-old son who worked as a printer. The Thacker household also included twenty-eight-year-old Lemuel Burr, a southern-born barber with a shop on Court Street in downtown Boston. About one-third of the households in 1850 and about 40 percent in 1860 included boarders.[5]

Taking in boarders probably stemmed from both custom and economic and social necessity. Since blacks were excluded from residence in the city's hotels and from most white boardinghouses, black boarders found lodging in the few black-operated boardinghouses and, most often, in rented rooms in black households.

Frequently boarders were friends and relatives drawn to Boston by reports of possible employment and relative racial tolerance. Boarding provided an important means for new arrivals to be acclimated to city life in Boston. Through their hosts, boarders could be introduced to employment opportunities, social groups, the church, and friends. In over half of the households that had boarders with occupations listed, at least one boarder was employed in the same occupation as a member of the host family. Boarding also served an important function for the host family. In the poor black community of Boston, boarders often provided a necessary additional income. Many married black women who held no outside employment provided household services, like washing and ironing, for boarders in their homes. This arrangement was often economically advantageous for the boarder, too, easing periods of unemployment. After the depression of 1857, the number of boarders increased, perhaps reflecting the function of boarding as one means of dealing with economic adversity. Since women were less likely to be employed than men, taking in boarders also served as a means of support for widows and single adult women.[6]

Boarding was especially common for young single adults who were not yet financially independent. About half of the female single adults and over two-thirds of the male single adults were boarders.[7] After marriage and after young adulthood, when families were being established and becoming more financially secure, black Bostonians were far less likely to live in households

Table 11

PERCENTAGE OF EACH POPULATION GROUP WHO WERE BOARDERS

Boarders	*Married Couples*	*Single Males*	*Single Females*
1850	N = 350	N = 234	N = 407
	11.4	73.1	53.1
1860	N = 396	N = 318	N = 541
	14.4	68.2	47.9

SOURCE: *Seventh United States Census* (1850) and *Eighth United States Census* (1860).

Table 12

SINGLE ADULTS

	1850		*1860*	
		%		%
Boarded with household head of different name	453	70.7	367	42.7
Boarded with household head of same name	62[a]	9.7	289[b]	33.6
Live-in servants	64	10.0	152	17.7
Lived alone	62	9.7	51	5.9
Total	641		859	

SOURCE: *Seventh United States Census* (1850) and *Eighth United States Census* (1860).

[a]12 percent of all single adult boarders.

[b]44 percent of all single adult boarders.

headed by others. As financial opportunities dwindled, the period of boarding extended beyond the twenties so that by 1860 there was a rise in the number of those in their thirties and forties who were still boarding.[8]

Financial hard times increased the likelihood that blacks would turn to relatives for shelter. Perhaps this was an indication that rents charged by relatives were reduced or paid in services rather than in cash. It may also reveal something of the support provided by kin. After the economic depression of the late 1850s, the percentage of those boarding with relatives more than tripled.[9]

Boarders did more than pay rent. Sometimes a boarder's income was pooled with that of other members of the household. Boarders also contributed in other ways to the household economy. A high proportion of boarders were young women and teenagers with no occupations listed in the census. They undoubtedly provided household and child-care services, freeing mothers to take informal jobs important to the family's support.

Taking in boarders was also a manifestation of the responsibility many blacks felt for one another. Herbert Gutman, in his study of the relationships between slaves, noted this feeling of responsibility as the slave community attempted to cope with the lack of individual freedom. Often, Gutman said, communities provided services to individual blacks that were unavailable to them elsewhere.[10] For free blacks in Boston, boarding was one such service. Providing shelter for the homeless was not limited to the boarding of adults. Gutman described the practice of taking in homeless children as a manifestation of community responsibility.[11] This was also true for free blacks in Boston.

Black children without homes of their own were often taken in by black families. Sometimes these families were relatives but, in many instances, ages, surnames, birthplaces, and color suggest that they were not related. In the mid-nineteenth century, between 9 and 12 percent of Boston's black children lived with people probably not their natural parents.

Families taking in homeless children were likely to have children of their own. In 1850 about one-half already had children. As the number of homeless children increased, more families without children took them in.[12] Although most of these children were taken in by two-parent families, a smaller percentage lived in two-parent families than was the case with children living with their natural parents. These children were also likely to be a bit older than the general child population. Well over half of them were over eleven years of age, compared to less than 40 percent for black children generally. The older age of these juveniles suggests their usefulness to host families.

Despite the fact that there were often no apparent familial connections between the children taken into households and the host adults, these children were often treated as members of the family. Familial names (aunt or uncle) were often applied by these children to their hosts, even when no actual kinship existed.[13] Carol B. Stack, who studied relationships in a modern-day black ghetto, noted: "Friends are classified as kinsmen when they assume recognized responsibilities of kinsmen."[14] This was also true for blacks in antebellum Boston. In the 1850s, Susan Hall, a teenager, boarded with the Porter family on Beacon Hill. She was provided with food and shelter in exchange for work in the household. Susan became close friends with the Porter's teenage daughter, Sarah, who introduced her to the world of Boston's black youth. Although it is doubtful that they were actually related, Susan referred to Mrs. Porter as Aunt Lydia.[15]

In some cases, it was apparent that children living with one family were actually members of another family that lived in the immediate neighborhood. Often the child's actual family lived next door to or in the same dwelling as the family with which the child was living. In these instances, the host family was functioning as an extended-kinship system, often providing a service for the child's natural family. This was especially true when both natural parents worked but could not afford to pay for child-care services.

Taking in homeless children was a civic duty not limited to the financially stable. Blacks of all occupational levels, including the unemployed, were likely to take in children. This practice was important among blacks, since Boston's institutions for homeless children admitted only whites. In 1860 the city had at least four institutions serving homeless children. In their total population of 328 there were no blacks. Thus the black household was the heart of the community's system of mutual aid.

The many functions of black households defined the roles of women in the community. Generally, black women exercised a good deal of influence as wives and mothers within the household. Women were responsible for the management of the home. In a time before the general use of preservatives, food shopping was a daily task.[16]

For Mary Fatal, William Johnson's grocery shop at 13 Southac was an easy walk. Often in the company of neighbors, she selected staples there before visiting Junior's oyster shop just across the street. Cartmen brought fresh vegetables in the afternoon, drawing women out of doors to inspect their wares and to share family news and information of community interest.

Much of a woman's day was spent cleaning the house, washing the family's clothes, and preparing the evening meal. Any spare time was used for visiting, a favorite pastime.[17] Sometimes visits were purely social occasions, but often there were other purposes. At one point during the 1840s when a number of mothers decided that something must be done about the loud noise the children made going to and from school, they formed a patrol to curb the disturbances.[18] Loosely structured groups were formed to address such concerns as temperance, unemployment, and needed community services.

Often black married women held two jobs. They ran the household and engaged in other work that brought in additional income.[19] The extent of black female employment cannot be determined from existing records. The census reported few of the working black women. Those most likely to be so reported were generally those who found employment outside of their own homes and those who worked with some regularity for one or a few employers. For those who took in washing, for example, on an irregular and informal basis, the records are very unreliable.[20] There were no black washerwomen listed in the 1850 census. Yet, the city directory listed twenty-five women who took in laundry. Newspapers, letters, tax lists, and other records are also clear that taking in washing was a chief form of employment for black women. The 1860 census was more accurate, listing thirty black washerwomen, but this figure is certainly an underenumeration. Women probably provided laundry service for their boarders, for example. A reading of the various primary sources suggests that well over half of the married women and perhaps as many as three-quarters of the unmarried women and teenage girls were gainfully employed, drawing wages either in cash, produce, or room and board.

This pattern of employment made women an extremely important part of the financial life of the black community. Often, when men could find no jobs or only seasonal or erratic employment, their wives' more continuous income was critical to the maintenance of the household. For most blacks of antebellum Boston, as for most blacks in other cities, the romanticization of womanhood which left females free from the necessities of employment was as inapplicable as it was for poor women generally.

The importance of women to the family economy facilitated an expansion of their social and political influence in community affairs. The expanded role of working women also freed middle-class nonworking black women to be socially and politically active. Most nineteenth-century middle-class women were severely restricted in the roles they could play outside the home by the popular conception of femininity. In contrast, black women found support from their community for their roles as speakers, leaders, and political advocates for abolition, civil rights, and aid to escaped slaves.

Charlotte Forten was from a wealthy Philadelphia family. Her grandfather was James Forten, a sail manufacturer and one of the earliest and most successful black businessmen of the antebellum period. James was also one of the nation's earliest and most active abolitionists. Robert Bridges Forten, James' son, was Charlotte's father. Like James, Robert hated the racial prejudice which he saw around him and spoke out strongly against it and against the human bondage under which his people suffered. At one point, he would not allow Charlotte to attend school rather than allow her to get a segregated education. From her grandfather and her father and from her uncle, abolitionist Robert Purvis, Charlotte learned of the need for constant struggle for racial equality. She developed a strong racial pride and an activist nature which led to her continual involvement in protest activity.[21]

The reforms in which Charlotte was involved raised the eyebrows and brought opposition from the husbands and fathers of her white counterparts who saw such involvement as improper for ladies. Charlotte's activities, however, drew only approval from her family and from her community.

The activism of Charlotte Forten paralleled that of many other middle-class black women. Sarah Parker, Caroline E. Putnam, Joanna Turpin Howard, and Georgianna O. Smith were but a few individuals who were politically active on behalf of their people and were honored by their community for their efforts. To say that the political involvement of black women received greater acceptance by black men than did women's activism among whites does not imply an assumption of sexual equality. Although some local groups contained female officers, no Boston woman represented her city at national black conventions; major community organizations were almost always headed by men.

Women were valued for their importance to the social, political, and economic life of the community, but they were also valued for more traditionally feminine attributes. Marriage patterns illustrate those traits which were desirable for women. First marriages tended to occur when men were in their late twenties and women were in their early twenties. For couples under thirty, a man was generally two years older than his wife. This age gap was greater when men married at a later age. The average man marrying for the second time was in his late thirties or early forties. His wife tended to be in her late twenties. The greatest age differential existed for men marrying after age fifty who were likely to have wives ten or fifteen years their junior.[22]

The age differentials between spouses are not unusual for the mid-nineteenth century. They seem to indicate that youth was valued in a wife while maturity and the relative financial stability that often accompanied it, even in black society, were qualities valued in a husband. For women approaching middle age, the prospects for marriage were not good. Thus aging had a far greater impact on women than on men, who seemed to be able to find young women to marry. In this context, blacks reflected the values of the wider society in which women were valued, to a great extent, for their appearance. Since feminine beauty in America is almost synonymous with a youthful appearance, young women were most desirable. Youth may also have been important for the health, childbearing ability, and longevity that is afforded.

Apparently black women were also judged on the basis of the shade of their complexion. The census listed color in four categories—black, mulatto, Indian, and white. Tables 13 and 14 demonstrate that a strong relationship existed between an individual's skin color and that of his/her spouse. Blacks were much more likely to marry blacks and mulattos were more likely to marry mulattos than would have occurred had color not been an important factor. In 1850, for example, 91 percent of all black men were married to black women. Only 6 percent had mulatto wives, and 3 percent had white wives. The pattern was much the same for mulatto men.

Where marriages occurred between partners of different colors, men were likely to be the darker partner. For example, one-quarter of mulatto women had black husbands while only 1 percent of black women had mulatto

Table 13

MARRIAGES BY COLOR, 1850 [a]

Female	*Male*		
	Black N = 286	*Mulatto* N = *61*	*White* N = *2*
Black N = *263*	260 d = 125	3 d = −77	2
Mulatto N = *75*	18 3 = −70	55 d = 22	
White N = *11*	8	3	0

SOURCE: *Seventh United States Census* (1850) and *Eighth United States Census* (1860).

[a]d = A−E, where A = the observed or actual total and E = that total expected if black males were equally as likely to marry mulatto women as black women and vice versa. For blacks and mulattoes only, $\chi^2 = 259.20$ and $\phi = .88$.

Table 14

MARRIAGES BY COLOR, 1860 [a]

Female	*Male*			
	Black N = *253*	*Mulatto* N = *137*	*White* N = *4*	*Indian* N = *2*
Black N = *222*	213 d = 99	7 d = −77	1	1
Mulatto N = *132*	21 d = −69	107 d = 47	3	1
White N = *40*	18	22	0	0
Indian N = *2*	1	1	0	0

SOURCE: *Seventh United States Census* (1850) and *Eighth United States Census* (1860).

[a]For blacks and mulattoes only, $\chi^2 = 246.43$ and $\phi = .84$.

husbands.[23] This pattern continued in 1860. There was also a rise in the number of interracial marriages from 13 to 44. The majority of the white women involved in these interracial marriages were from Ireland or England, and the men were most likely to be seamen.

Social contact between blacks and whites on a basis which could lead to marriage, then, was more likely to occur for black men whose occupations took them to foreign countries. Most of these couples were married in America. In Boston not only were more Irish-born whites living in black neighborhoods, but there were more than twice as many whites living in the same dwelling as blacks in 1860 as there were in 1850. The data on interracial marriages suggests the paradoxical relationship between the two groups at the lowest end of Boston's economic scale. The residential patterns of Boston facilitated personal contact between the poorest, most oppressed groups, increasing the likelihood of both friction and more amiable relationships among individuals.

Nineteenth-century American culture equated beauty with light, even pale, skin. For some black Boston men, women who most closely approximated the white American image of beauty seemed particularly attractive. The tendency of darker men to seek lighter women, like the tendency of older men to seek younger women, may reflect the extent to which women were valued and judged in physical terms.

Although the woman's role was central to most households, there were some households composed mainly of men. Single men often lived in large North End boardinghouses. This was especially true for seamen and others whose work made them transient members of the community. By mid-century, almost 60 percent of the city's black seamen resided in the North End. The two largest black boardinghouses were located there, in the second ward. They housed twenty-three and twenty-six people, all seamen. Such boardinghouses were more than residences. They performed the function of fraternal organizations and social clubs. For seamen without families, boardinghouses provided companionship and mutual support. They were sometimes small communities offering recreation, social contact, and even protection for their residents.[24]

James Weed, who had come to Boston in the late 1850s in search of work, was well known for the card games he sponsored at one boardinghouse. These games were held regularly on weekends, and the participants varied depending on who was in port at the time. Although there was some drinking, the stakes were usually small, and this was considered a "friendly game."[25] On occasion a boardinghouse regular might become impatient with the congenial but less exciting format of Weed's game and seek outside games. This could lead to serious trouble, as one seaman learned when he became involved with the notorious "alley boys," a local group which also sponsored gambling. Evidently these outside games were less congenial and sometimes disputes led to violence.[26]

Under the threat of violence, one seaman who was unable to pay a gambling debt owed to the "alley boys" asked for and received the protection of his boardinghouse fellows. The sailor, however, refused to learn his lesson about gambling with outsiders. When his boardinghouse could not offer constant protection, he escaped by enlisting in the army.[27]

Many boardinghouse residents developed close comradeships. A seaman in trouble in a distant port often appealed to his boardinghouse community for aid.[28] These single men living in the boardinghouses of the North End considered themselves, in many ways, separate from the more stable married community of black Boston. Although there were many married people and families living in the North End, the term "the hill" was used to refer to the area where most black families lived. When a boardinghouse member got married he was often "lost to the hill."

A man named Fletcher lived in the North End boardinghouse community for many years. He was known as a flashy dresser and a drinker until he "got married, got religion and moved to the hill." By the time of the Civil War he was said to have had only sporadic contact with his old friends, drank only tea, and entertained at home. Although many of his old friends found this change amusing, there was also some resentment at having "lost" a comrade to the "hill."[29]

There was some feeling of separation and disdain on the part of hill residents toward the boardinghouse crowd. These sailors and dock workers were generally younger men whose tastes for excitement and unpolished manners made them undesirable in the eyes of many residents on the hill. This was especially true for the parents of teenage girls. Many would not allow their daughters to associate with North End single men.[30]

The boardinghouse and the hill were thus separate neighborhoods, but it would be an oversimplification to characterize them as completely separate societies. The gulf between these two groups was much narrower than might be expected because of the pressure from whites in Boston, who generally overlooked distinctions among blacks.

Although the vast majority of blacks lived in black households, either as part of families or as boarders, a few blacks lived outside black households. From 8 to 10 percent of Boston's blacks in 1850 and 1860 lived in public institutions or in white households.[31] Of this group, over one-third in 1850 and nearly two-thirds in 1860 were domestic workers living either in white households, white boardinghouses, hospitals, hotels, or at the garrison at Fort Independence.

Live-in domestics tended to be females in their late twenties or early thirties.[32] Male domestics tended to be slightly younger than females.[33] These domestics were most likely to live in the homes of Boston's wealthiest white families. The wealthy of Beacon Hill and the city's central wards employed the majority of these live-in servants. Although this was not high status work, a few domestics, by virtue of their personal contact with the wealthy and the influence that sometimes accompanied it, held positions of some importance within the black community. Robert Roberts was a domestic servant for a wealthy family. This "station of life," he observed, "comprised comforts, privileges and pleasures, which [were] to be found in but a few other stations in which [blacks might] enter."[34] Roberts was the author of a guide for house servants in which he blended a philosophy of the Puritan ethic variety and instruction on becoming the successful house servant. Roberts was also a community leader, serving as delegate to the Second National Convention of Free People of Color in the 1830s. He was an example of the unusual house servants whose parallel could be found in the South where standing in the slave community was enhanced by one's status in the master's household.

A small number of Boston's blacks boarded in primarily white Irish households. Their white associates were, however, likely to have a lower social and economic standing than those of the domestic servants. Often these whites and blacks were co-workers. In a few instances, black men who were interracially married boarded with their wives and children in the home of their in-laws. The practice of boarding with the wife's parents was not unusual within the black community; it was most unusual among interracial couples.

For most black Bostonians, families and households were central to social relations and community life. Poverty and discrimination did not force disorganization, but often actually encouraged organization. Carol Stack found that twentieth-century blacks worked through extensive survival networks, cooperating to provide for one another's needs as the wider society did not.[35] Blacks in the nineteenth century also found it necessary to rely on cooperation and mutual aid. A variety of strategies was occasioned by the necessity to cope with a hostile social and economic environment. Family and household arrangements provided many of these strategies. Where possible, blacks established institutions to serve their needs, supplementing the family's role and binding black people into a community of shared disadvantage.

3/Formal and Informal Organizations and Associations

Alexis de Tocqueville, the French observer of antebellum American society, wrote as follows in his work entitled *Democracy in America*: "Americans of all ages, all conditions, and all dispositions, constantly form associations. They have not only commercial and manufacturing companies, in which all take part, but associations of a thousand other kinds,—religious, moral, serious, futile, general or restricted, enormous or diminute."[1]

Tocqueville's observations were certainly accurate. Nineteenth-century Americans formed organizations at a formidable rate. Like their compatriots, black Bostonians established formal groups and associated informally to provide for community services, to protest discriminatory restrictions, and to lobby for social and political change.

One of the first and most pressing concerns of Boston blacks was the abolition of slavery in Massachusetts. Black actions against slavery in the commonwealth during the seventeenth and eighteenth centuries were largely individual efforts. In 1694, Adam, servant of John Saffin, brought legal action against his master for failure to grant a promised freedom after seven years of service. Adam's plea was granted after considerable litigation. The eighteenth century brought other suits. James of Boston brought action against his former master's son who had refused to follow his father's will and grant James his freedom. James won his claim only after a long and bitter court fight. By the 1770s slaves were suing in the courts of Massachusetts, claiming and being granted freedom as their right. The Revolutionary era brought group action of a kind which set the tone for nineteenth-century community organization and action.[2]

In one of the earliest group actions, several slaves addressed a petition to the Massachusetts legislature on March 18, 1777. In the following years, blacks repeatedly used the petition as their primary means of communication with state and federal governmental authorities. In the petition of 1777, blacks pointed out the inconsistencies between the condition of slavery and the principles of the American Revolution. This became a recurrent theme in nineteenth-century black protest. Boston blacks were acutely aware of the contributions and sacrifices made by members of their race in the fight for American independence and were quick to remind Massachusetts authorities of the pride black Bostonians felt as patriotic Americans. Finally, as a result of a court decision in the case of *Commonwealth of Massachusetts* v. *Jennison* in 1781, slavery was declared unconstitutional within the state. Following this decision, Boston's blacks turned to concerted efforts to improve their condition within their city and the condition of fellow blacks nationwide. In this effort community organizations played an increasingly important role.[3]

One such organization, founded in 1796, was the African Society. A mutual aid and charity organization, the society had an original membership of forty-four. The society's activities drew far wider support than its membership rolls indicated. At the end of services at the African Church, on July 14, 1808, two hundred blacks acknowledged the important work of the society. Many contributed to its collection for the community's needy. The African Society provided social-welfare services in the form of financial relief and job placement to its members and their families. Support was also provided to widows, orphans, and the infirm. In addition to these welfare and insurance functions, the society administered wills, provided for burials, and, in conjunction with the church, attended to members' spiritual needs. As was true of many community organizations, the African Society held its meetings at the African Meeting House, the home of the African Baptist Church, on Beacon Hill.[4]

The African Society, like other community organizations, was both an instrument of socialization and a reflection of community values. As Bostonians, the black community expressed many values that were typical of nineteenth-century American society. Moral living, temperance, self-improvement, and education were themes found in black speeches and writing throughout this period. These virtues were stressed in the laws of the African Society. Morality was encouraged if we are to judge by the society's promise to care for the widow of a member "so long as she behaves herself decently."[5] A widow was expected to live by a strict code of sexual propriety in keeping with the precepts of old Puritan New England.

The African Society made an effort to compel its members to abstain from drink. The organization expressed its strong opposition to drunkenness, ruling that "any member bringing on himself a sickness or disorder by intemperance, shall not be considered as entitled to any benefits of assistance from the society."[6] Intemperance, it was believed, revealed an irresponsible character. A man could not be depended upon by his family when his resources were squandered on drink. His commitment to provide for himself and his family was fundamental to the collective survival. Intemperance was seen as a threat to the community. It was an important obstruction to industry and self-help. In a society where poverty was a central fact of life, those dedicated to finding viable solutions were less than tolerant of those who appeared to be adding to the problem.[7]

In many ways the values expressed by the African Society paralleled those extolled by such twentieth-century black leaders as Booker T. Washington. Members were urged to be clean, thrifty, and law-abiding. "We take no one into the society," the organization warned, "who shall commit any injustice or outrage against the laws of our country."[8] This admonition was indicative of national loyalty felt by Boston blacks in the generation immediately after the Revolution. Later this spirit of legal obedience to national law waned under what appeared to many to be federal favoritism toward the forces of slavery. More important for understanding the loyalties of black Bostonians during the antebellum period was their respect for the laws of Massachusetts, which were often more sympathetic to blacks than those of the federal government. Thus, the society laid heavy stress on "behaving ourselves . . . as true and faithful citizens of the Commonwealth."[9]

The African Society was concerned with the control of crime in the community. Blacks did not accept the presence of crime in their neighborhoods as natural or inevitable. The idea of a culture of poverty in which deviation from the law was expected did not describe the value system of black Boston, except in the very particular circumstances surrounding slave rescues or civil-rights activities.

One of the chief concerns of the African Society was the abolition of slavery. The Society was forthright in its denunciation of slavery and the African slave trade. In 1808 it published a formal antislavery statement. Drawing parallels between the American Revolution and the black man's desire for freedom from slavery, this publication stated: "Freedom is desirable, if not, would men sacrifice their time, their property and finally lose their lives in pursuit of it?"[10] In this, as in other organizational statements, one underlying value was expressed. It was a value central to the developing black community of nineteenth-century Boston, the value of concerted social protest.

Black fraternal organizations, like the mutual aid societies, were important vehicles for community-service work. These fraternal societies, which were organized and grew to maturity in the late eighteenth and early nineteenth centuries, collectively represented another major institution in Boston's black community. The earliest of these was the African Lodge #459, organized in 1787. The founder of this lodge was Prince Hall, a Methodist minister who had served with the colonial army in the American Revolution.[11]

Hall was born in Bridgetown, Barbados, British West Indies in 1748, the son of a white English leather worker and a free woman of African and French descent. Measuring only five feet four inches and of slight build, he was a fiery crusader, urging his followers forward in their tasks, whether it was in the drive for quality education for black children, or to admit blacks to the ranks of George Washington's revolutionary forces, or in his protest against the injustice of slavery or the discrimination experienced by black Bostonians.[12]

In 1775 Hall had become a member of a British Masonic lodge. After the war, he had applied to the American Masons for permission to establish a black lodge in Boston. When his request was denied, Hall applied to the Grand Lodge of England. The African Lodge in Boston was, therefore, established under the auspices of the English order. During the first quarter of the nineteenth century, the African Lodge, later renamed the Prince Hall Lodge, grew in size and influence to become an important part of black social and economic life, drawing members from various economic levels. Its programs of education and community service complemented those of the African Society and the black church.[13]

The African Masonic Lodge was another early forum for the condemnation of slavery and racial discrimination. One of the earliest recorded black antislavery orations was delivered by Prince Hall before the African Lodge on June 24, 1797. In a subtle yet powerful denunciation of the "iron yoke of slavery" and the oppression of blacks, Hall employed Biblical illustrations to instruct and encourage his audience. He implored blacks to overcome their lack of formal education with good judgment and inquiring observation. Portraying God as the protector and defender of the righteous, he cautioned blacks against allowing their fear of the powerful to divide the community. Praising the successful revolution which gained freedom for blacks in Haiti and giving a historical portrait of freedom as the natural estate of black people, Hall emphasized the necessity for mutual aid and solidarity among righteous men.[14]

Hall understood that slavery was only the most blatant example of the injustice suffered by blacks at the hands of white society. He was also vocal in his protest against "the daily insults [met] in the streets of Boston—[especially] on public days of recreation." He denounced the cowards who attacked blacks in mobs, lacking the courage to "face [them] man for man. . . . We may truly be said to carry our lives in our hands, and the arrows of death are flying about our heads. Helpless women have their clothes torn from their backs . . . by a mob or horde of shameless, low-lived, envious, spiteful persons. . . . O, the patience of the blacks."[15] Yet Hall and other black leaders did not generally counsel patience. Hall assured his listeners that both slavery and discrimination were temporary conditions that could be overcome through courage, social action, and faith in an avenging God.

The Masons also provided their share of service to black Bostonians, both members and nonmembers. During the long winter season, the group handed out free firewood and sponsored periodic food drives with supplies collected for distribution to those in need. Weekly "sick dues" were provided for members unable to work, and loans were made to members and their families. In these and other ways, fraternal organizations filled the role now played by governmental social programs.

Although other black fraternal organizations were founded before the Civil War, like the Odd Fellows in 1846, the Masons remained the most influential of these throughout the period.[16] The Prince Hall Masons, despite diligent attempts, were not officially recognized by the Grand Masonic Lodge of

Massachusetts before the Civil War. Yet it was an important group for members and nonmember blacks.

These fraternal organizations were, of course, restricted to men, as was the African Society. In this, Boston black society paralleled the wider society where women and men were generally members of separate organizations. Yet men and women in black society were likely to work together in many other social and political groups.

Membership in some groups was also limited by economics. Often, organizational fees discouraged participation by some unskilled poor workers or the unemployed. The African Society, for example, assessed its members twenty-five cents in the form of an entrance fee and another twenty-five cents for monthly dues. These dues had to be paid for one full year before any benefits were provided to the member. Thus, these financial requirements probably made membership in these groups difficult for all but the more economically stable.[17] Unlike groups like the Brown Fellows of Charleston, South Carolina, these organizations were not an economic or social elite. There were surely a disproportionate number of skilled workers and small businessmen among the membership, but unskilled workers were not totally excluded.[18]

Some organizations had more specific purposes than the promotion of general community service and fellowship. Although the material needs of the community were great, blacks were also concerned about educational and cultural needs. Several groups were organized to provide an outlet for dramatic and intellectual creativity. One of these groups was the Adelphic Union Library Association formed in 1838. This organization encouraged intellectual debates in the community and offered lectures for the considerable sum of fifty cents for each ticket or seventy-five cents for the seasonal series.[19] Significantly, at a time when women were generally excluded from public lectures, the predominantly black Adelphic Union opened its meetings to all, regardless of color or sex.

The community also sponsored a drama group. During the late 1840s the Histrionic Club was formed. Like the Adelphic Union, this group included men and women, drawing the cast for its productions from the local community. Many of the pieces performed by the Histrionic Club were written by William C. Nell, the local community leader and historian. Nell also took part in the various community-sponsored debating societies like the Boston Philomanthean Society or the Young Men's Literary Debating Society.[20]

There were also organized black women's groups, which, like other community organizations, provided a number of different services. The Afric-American Female Intelligence Society formed in 1832 was both a literary and a mutual-aid organization. Like the Adelphic Union, it attempted to provide an intellectual forum by sponsoring lectures and conducting studies, and by using these educational services for moral uplift. It also provided special services to its members in the form of health insurance and other types of relief. Like the early fraternal and mutual aid groups, the Afric-American Female Intelligence Society held to a strong code demanding "good moral character" from its members and sought to become a positive moral force in the community at large.[21] Like its fraternal counterpart, the Afric-American Female Intelligence Society charged substantial fees for membership. Entrance fees were twenty-five cents and monthly dues were twelve and one-half cents, somewhat less than the African Society but still a sizable sum for poor people. In addition, there were fines levied against members who failed to attend meetings without a "satisfactory apology." Again, these fees probably limited the membership of this organization.[22]

There were other educational and community service groups like the Daughters of Zion (1845) and the Female Benevolent Firm (1850). Black women also formed social action groups directed at specific social evils.[23] During the early 1830s, Jane Putnam and Susan Paul joined with other black women to form a temperance society. In April 1833 this group was largely responsible for 114 blacks taking the "cold water pledge" denouncing liquor. Two years later, as a result of its efforts, the New England Temperance Society of People of Color was formed. This latter organization maintained its headquarters in Boston.[24]

As the fees charged by some groups were likely to restrict their membership, the focus of particular groups was likely to do the same. Thus, temperance groups were most likely to attract those most committed to the middle-class values that temperance represented. Conspicuously underrepresented in these groups were the laborers, sailors, and other unskilled workers. Arrest statistics and newspaper accounts make it clear that the cause of temperance was no more universally adhered to in black society than it was in white society.

Blacks also provided for the education and intellectual stimulation of their children. In the early 1830s the Juvenile Garrison Independent Society was organized. This group of youths, mostly teenagers, sought to provide education for themselves and services for their community. They sponsored lectures, community fix-up self-help projects, and antislavery rallies.[25]

It would be hard to imagine a black community in which music did not play a trenchant role. Black Bostonians enjoyed a wide variety of musical forms, including the gospel singing traditionally associated with the black church, classical European forms, and the more earthy sounds associated with black working classes. The black church often served as concert hall and practice center for musical performances. During the antebellum period, blacks were especially active in sponsoring musical concerts. Almost every month there was some special event in which community members took part, performing with a number of community orchestras and bands. In April 1833, for example, a concert was held at the African Baptist Church by the Baptist Singing Society. A small seven-piece orchestra, which included Peter Howard, a barber, playing clarinet, opened the program with "The Overture to the Marriage of Figaro." Mrs. John T. Hilton, wife of a hairdresser, performed a vocal solo, followed by a vocal trio selection. Later that year, the adult mixed chorus, which included Susan Paul and James G. Barbadoes, a hairdresser, performed with a four-piece band.[26]

Children were an important part of the musical life of the community. There were several youth choirs, like the Garrison Juvenile Choir, which performed its first concert in 1833 at the African Baptist Church, and the Primary School Number Six Choir, directed by Susan Paul. In these groups, black children learned to read music and were introduced to the works of classical and semiclassical composers. A number of opportunities for private or group instruction were also available. Usually the church served as the classroom, and almost daily it provided a place for vocal training, band or orchestra rehersal, or musical tutoring. For some time, Sunday evenings were reserved for the "Singing School for Sacred Music," a twenty-six lesson series, with a tuition cost of one dollar for ladies and two dollars for gentlemen.[27]

The classrooms of the black schools also served as a place for musical presentations. In 1843, a musical concert featuring the volunteer choir was presented at the "infant school rooms" on Beacon Hill. In April 1844, the Holmes Waltz and Vaudeville Band performed in the small auditorium of the black Smith School.[28]

The selections performed by various musical groups in the black community often exhibited the cultural influence of white Boston society, including selections from European operas, major classical works, and semiclassical sacred music. This music probably had as little meaning for most working-class blacks as it did for most working-class whites. It may be charged that only those blacks or whites concerned with social status consciously cultivated a taste for the European music commonly associated with "high culture." Indeed, most of the performers themselves were from the skilled, entrepreneurial, or professional occupational groups. Yet unskilled and semiskilled workers were also represented. In 1844, the director of one of the juvenile choirs was Miss Frances Allen, daughter of Jesse Allen, a laborer. George Washington, who worked alternately as a bootblack, waiter, and laborer, was a member of the Attucks Glee Club in the late 1850s, while his wife Rachel sang with the volunteer choir. It is impossible to determine the occupational representation in concert audiences, but considering the occupations of the performers, it is reasonable to assume that there were at least some workers from all occupational groups in the audiences. It may be true that some people attending these concerts were imitating proper Boston society (which in turn, it could be claimed, was imitating proper European Society). Yet many black Bostonians, like many white Bostonians, were genuinely interested in widening both their own and their community's cultural experience.[29]

Several times during the year, fraternal groups presented large music festivals and dances. These gatherings, open to nonmembers, generally had greater appeal for those less interested in classical concerts. One such affair was the "Soiree Musicale" sponsored by the Odd Fellows during the 1840s. Organization members marched in full regalia to the hall already crowded with party goers. Entertainment for the evening included vocal and instrumental presentations followed by dancing. Although the mood was gay and the music more suited to general tastes, these gatherings tended to attract a predominantly middle-class or upwardly mobile group. The young single unskilled laborers were likely to pass up such gala parties for the less formal and perhaps for them more comfortable setting of the "North End."[30]

The centers for gambling and vice that catered to the less lauditory needs of the community were generally, although not exclusively, located in the North End. The black seamen and dock laborers who lived there during the pre–Civil War era shared this area with working-class immigrants. They also shared the area's entertainment facilities like the "Bella Union" dance hall on Hanover Street.[31]

In these underworld taverns and barrooms, which were decorated with pictures of nude women, black laborers and seamen gambled and socialized. Such places featured refreshments and entertainment that allowed patrons to escape the troubles of an unjust and oppressive world. "New York gin" flowed freely while black and white men joined in one of the city's few integrated environments to smoke cabbage-leaf cigars and enjoy the favors of "vermillion cheeked women in low-necked dresses."[32] There they were served raw clams and participated in various games of chance. One favorite "sporting event" was the notorious rat pits, where dogs and rats fought to the death for the amusement and profit of spectators. Supplying rats for these games provided a living for a few blacks like Jum, who collected as much as five dollars a night for his work.[33]

Blacks could also find music for dancing in the boardinghouses of the North End. One popular dance band was a black trio composed of unskilled laborers who played music part time for their own enjoyment and for additional income.[34] Frequently, those who lived on Beacon Hill visited these boardinghouses to enjoy the musicians and singers who performed there.[35]

The North End was an area of particular concern to the Boston police, a constant source of irritation to black temperance reformers, and a challenge to church missionaries. Excessive drinking was a problem for many in the North End. In April 1855, a black sailor was found dead in his boardinghouse bed. He had died of "lung fever" aggravated by alcoholic drink.[36] Often, intoxication was a major contributing factor to crimes of violence, as when James Marshall, "crazy drunk," assaulted James Brown, a fellow laborer, with a hatchet. Drunken quarrels resulting in arrests were not unusual, especially on weekends.[37]

North Enders, black and white alike, were often prominent in the crime statistics of the city. During the summer of 1854, the Boston police averaged two thousand arrests a month. The majority of those arrested were immigrants; although specific figures are not available, blacks, no doubt, accounted for a fair share.[38] Most of those arrested were charged with minor crimes, and most were never convicted. On the day of the census in 1850 and 1860, there were thirty-four blacks incarcerated as criminals or juvenile delinquents. The institutionalization of black juveniles was questionable, since the two boys, aged twelve and thirteen years, held in the House of Reformation in 1850 were charged only with idleness. Interestingly, both boys were listed with occupations. One was a shoemaker, possibly the youngest in the city, and the other was listed as a domestic. Apparently they had been unemployed at the time of commitment. Luckily, laws on idleness were not strictly enforced against the unemployed, for if they had been, local and county jails would have supported much of the black community.[39]

Blacks charged with criminal acts in 1850 represented almost 10% of those held in the House of Corrections. Although the single most common crime among blacks was drunkenness, over one-third of those had been charged with violations of public morality. Five blacks, all women, were held for "nightwalking," six (five men and one woman) were held for fornication, and one young mulatto Frenchman was held for the operation of a house of prostitution. Others held included seven for robbery and housebreaking, four for assault, and one for disorderly conduct. Blacks were disproportionately represented among those incarcerated for prostitution, which was doubtless an effect of the poverty in black society, the tendency for black prostitutes to be arrested with greater frequency than white, and the coincidence of those who happened to be in jail on the day of the census.

The census of 1860 listed over one-third of those blacks incarcerated as thieves. Only two inmates were listed as arrested for violations of public morality, one black man for operating a house of prostitution, another for indecent exposure. Six were arrested for drunkenness and six for assault. There were also two arrested for idleness and two children held for truancy. The shift from crimes of morality in 1850 to crimes of theft by 1860 may be a reflection of worsening economic conditions in the black community. The peculiarities of census-taking, which was at best a spot check of inmates held at a specific time, and the eccentricities of police arrests, which seldom provide a representative sample of criminals, may combine to render any conclusions based on this data suspect. It is sufficient to say that in the city's correctional facilities, unlike most public facilities in Boston, blacks were overrepresented.

More reliable sources of crime statistics are the various reports of correctional institutions. Figures drawn from these sources indicate that throughout the antebellum period blacks accounted for between 5 percent and 15 percent of inmates of jails and houses of correction. The usefulness of these statistics is limited by their failure to indicate specific crimes. There is no way of determining the seriousness of an inmate's crime.[40]

Of course, not all black vice was confined to the red-light district of the North End. The more respectable areas of Beacon Hill, too, had their share. For twenty-five cents per person, entertainment was provided by several black women whose performance began at "the witching hour of night."

Gentlemen patrons, many of whom were white, enjoyed the erotic dancing while liquor was served. Men of various ages and political persuasions, "Know-Nothings and Know-Somethings," apparently enjoyed the performance, as shows were often crowded to capacity.[41]

Among poor people, visiting was often a chief form of entertainment. Black Bostonians frequently exchanged visits. Usually some food was served—Lydia Porter was apparently known for her coffee and pie. It was also customary to play cards, and much visiting went on around a table. Generally, this was a very quiet affair, but occasionally visits got out of hand even on Beacon Hill. In October 1855, for example, the police had to be called to a house on Southac Street because of "turbulent visitors." Nine people were arrested for disorderly conduct. It is not clear whether alcohol was involved.[42]

If blacks were not likely to be teetotalers, they were at least under some social pressure to maintain sobriety. The church and the various black temperance groups maintained a steady stream of circulars, lectures, and newspaper articles against drink, which "will destroy us and all we hold dear."[43] One boardinghouse run by Joel Lewis on Southac Street advertised itself as a "Temperance boarding house" in a "very pleasant and healthy part of the city." The ad was clear that it catered to "genteel persons" and that references were required.[44]

Upwardly mobile blacks were most susceptible to this temperance pressure. Yet it would be an oversimplification to dismiss those trapped at the very bottom of black society as simply vice-ridden drunkards. Often for them the gambling table offered their only hope for the future and the bottle their only escape from the present. In this underworld, the black hustler lived and profited by his wits. He often swindled whites who found the illicit entertainment attractive. Black hustlers preyed on blacks as well, forcing black women into prostitution, tricking unwary fugitives out of their money, and sometimes delivering them into the hands of slave catchers for a price.[45] Yet many fugitives were sheltered among the hustlers, gamblers, and common laborers. Although underworld blacks were not likely to join formally organized groups, they were well represented among those who used direct action for social protest.[46] Many of those arrested during attempts to rescue fugitive slaves from the authorities were North End laborers and seamen who were not members of an antislavery society.

There were diversions in black society that were peculiarly middle class and those that catered to the lower classes. There were also many informal community institutions and centers that served all elements. Like boarding arrangements and social activism, these informal gathering places provided contact across lines of community division to involve blacks of various interests and conditions.

In the nineteenth-century black community, as in the contemporary black community, the local barber shop was an important forum for the discussion and exchange of political ideas and community information. Peter Howard's barber shop, for example, was a gathering place for all segments of black society—for those who were likely to be members of formal protest groups and for those who were not. For many, the underemployed and the barely literate, the conversation at Howard's shop was often the only form of political education available. Job openings were posted in the shop, and community information was available there along with tickets for community events. For over twenty years Howard's, located at the foot of Beacon Hill on Cambridge Street, was one of the most popular gathering places in the community.

Although Howard's was well known for its provocative discussions, few outside the community understood the extent of its function—for the shop was an important station on the underground railroad.[47] Through the rear door and the connecting alleys beyond, many fugitives who chose to remain in the city for a time joined other blacks who came to the shop for the services of its proprietor and to share in the fellowship of conversation.

Other barber shops assumed central importance as well. John J. Smith's shop on Howard Street, like Howard's shop, was a meeting place for antislavery forces. In Smith's shop, Charles Sumner could often be found engaged in earnest debate with blacks on the important issues of the day. In this informal setting the United States senator could gauge public opinion and become familiar with the concerns of local blacks.[48]

Black barber shops sometimes became informal clubs with a regular membership. In the early 1860s, a group of regulars from Smith's shop decided to enlist in the Massachusetts black regiment. After signing up as a group, they returned to Smith's for a celebration. "Some got a trim," one witness recalled, "but most got drunk."[49]

Since the services of Boston's financial community were not generally available to blacks, the community provided its own service. There were several grocery stores that became the finance agencies of the community. Services were generally provided in the form of credit, which was particularly important among people susceptible to irregular cash flow. Sometimes such credit made the difference between a family eating an evening meal or not. A few outright loans of cash were made. Before going off to war, several members of the Massachusetts 54th and 55th black army regiments visited local grocery stores to pay off debts.[50] It is not clear whether interest was charged on these loans but, at the least, they promoted good will, fulfilled one's responsibility to the community, and encouraged loyal customers.

Other black-operated shops also functioned as informal community centers. Clothing shops and dry-goods stores were gathering places, and their owners were often active community members. More than one-third of those who could be identified as activists in the census of 1850 and 1860 were proprietors of small businesses.

Despite the great need among blacks, few received formal aid from the city. Records of the Overseers of the Poor and census records show a small and declining number of blacks aided by city facilities in the antebellum period.[51] The small number of black almshouse inmates in the later years may have been partially due to blacks being provided with outdoor relief or to a growing black militancy and accompanying community spirit which might have increased the desire of blacks to care for their own. It may also have been due to the growing numbers of white reformers willing to provide aid through private organizations. The dramatic increase in immigrants seeking assistance severely taxed state and local relief capabilities, making it more difficult for blacks to be judged "deserving poor," eligible for public relief.

Blacks almost always supplied their own social, welfare, cultural, educational, and financial services. The extent of these services was severely limited by the scarcity of community resources. They were provided out of pride and a perception of responsibility but also out of necessity.

4/The Community and the Church

The history of black Americans is closely bound up with the history of the black church. For an oppressed and harassed people, religion provided a solace and a hope for better days to come in this life and in the eternal. For a people shut out of much of American society, with little hope of attaining position and prestige in traditional ways, the church performed many other functions as well. It was a training ground for leaders, a place where common laborers could gain positions of status as deacons and officers of church groups, a place for the education and training of the young, a place for entertainment and social life, and a meetinghouse for the exchange of thought, both political and social, free from the pressures of the white society.[1]

The black church arose in Boston partly as a response to the discrimination faced by blacks in white churches and partly in response to the needs for self-expression which originated in the culture and experience of the black community. A small number of blacks had worshipped in white churches in Massachusetts from early slave days. In the late 1700s, slaves were admitted as members to the First and Second Baptist Churches. There is no record, however, of their having voted, held office, or participated in the various organizations of these churches. In 1790, Phillis Wheatley, poet and former slave, was baptized into the membership of the Old South Meeting House, the church of her former mistress.[2] Yet blacks were not generally accepted by white churches or were segregated into special "Negro Pews . . . where they could hear [but] not see the preacher or be observed by him or the white congregation."[3]

Many of those blacks who attended white churches faced discrimination and humiliation. A few decided on defiant persistence, hoping to outlast those who would bar them from worship in the church of their choice. In the early 1800s, James Easton, a manufacturing blacksmith, and his family were forcibly ejected from the Orthodox Church after refusing to sit in the black section. They subsequently purchased a pew in the Baptist Church at Stoughton Corner. This "excited a great deal of indignation" among some members who attempted to cancel the purchase. Failing in this, members tarred the pew; whereupon the Eastons brought carriage seats to church. The pew was then removed, but the family sat in the aisle. James Easton was a proud and determined man, but repeated insults finally drove the Eastons from the church.[4]

It was this kind of discrimination, in part, that provided the impetus for the formation of black churches and caused the withdrawal of many blacks from white churches. During the late eighteenth century, a handful of blacks met for worship in private homes—their private protest against racial discrimination. These nondenominational, informal gatherings were the beginning of the black church in Boston. By 1789, blacks had been granted the use of Faneuil Hall for religious meetings on Tuesday or Friday afternoon. This group was joined in that year by Thomas Paul, a sixteen-year-old boy who had recently been baptized into a church in Exeter, New Hampshire. Soon Paul assumed the role of an "exhorter," explaining scripture passages to the informal congregation. In 1798, seeking a place for Sunday worship, blacks requested the use of a schoolhouse in Boston's North End where, at that time, the black population was concentrated. They were instead granted the use of a schoolhouse in the West End, a peripheral white neighborhood.[5]

By 1804, Thomas Paul, then thirty-one years old, was the preacher for an increasing group of worshipers. He returned to New Hampshire on May 1, 1805, to be ordained a Baptist minister.[6] Returning to Boston, he set about organizing a formal church. In July, Thomas Paul and Scipio Dalton, then a member of the First Baptist Church, sent the customary letter to the First and Second Baptist Churches asking their aid in constituting a new church. On August 8, 1805, with their white brethren represented, the African Baptist Church was officially organized.[7] The following year a meetinghouse was built on Smith Court, near Belknap (later Joy) Street, to accommodate the large congregation coming to hear the black minister. It was a demonstration of the growing sense of black identity and pride that this meetinghouse was built using only black labor. On December 4, 1806, the Reverend Thomas Paul was installed as pastor of the African Baptist Church.

Although the African Baptist Church was organized as a black church, it did have contact with the white community. In 1812, it became a charter member of the Boston Baptist Association and frequently sent John Hay, John T. Hilton, and Coffin Pitts as delegates to association meetings.[8] The black church also supported the American Baptist Home Mission Society and Foreign Missions. The members originally intended to discourage white membership, maintaining the church's African character. Some whites, however, attracted by the preaching of Thomas Paul, did join and participate. Nor did its sister churches become totally white. A few blacks continued to be added to the rolls of both the First and Second Baptist Churches of Boston until after the Civil War.[9]

By 1819, the African Baptist Church was an established institution with 103 members. It had extended its aid and influence to black communities in other cities, sending its pastor in the summer of 1808 to New York City to establish what later became the Abyssinian Baptist Church, twentieth-century church home of Adam Clayton Powell. Reverend Paul also conducted several revival tours for the Baptist Missionary Society, including at least one successful trip to Haiti. Filling the pulpit during his absences were ministers from the Home Mission Society and two young men from the church who had been called to preach, Eli Ball and Nathaniel Paul, Thomas Paul's son.[10] Throughout the 1820s the church continued to grow. By 1828 the membership had grown to 139.

The divergent views of a growing congregation and dissension over Paul's continual absences created disunity within the church. This condition, combined with Paul's ill health, led to his resignation in 1829. There followed a succession of interim and short-term ministers, fluctuations in membership, and continued internal dissension.[12] Finally, in 1840 forty-six members, led by the Reverend George Black, left to form a new church, which became the Twelfth Baptist Church. The death of Reverend Black a year later left the new congregation without stable leadership until 1848, when Leonard A. Grimes, then a resident of New Bedford, was called to the struggling young church.[13]

The nature of the dissension within the church is unclear. Some have speculated that the split developed because of differences in protest strategy, with some in the congregation favoring integration as a means to racial justice and others favoring separation and black control of black institutions. These differences in strategy clashed in the controversy over the integration of Boston schools. William J. Watkins favored integration to the extent of calling for the abolition of the black church altogether.[14] It is unlikely that these differences caused the split in the Baptist church since the membership of the African Baptist and the Twelfth Baptist contained prominent leaders on both sides of the question. Thomas Paul Smith, a separationist, remained an active member of the African Baptist church together with Coffin Pitts and John T. Hilton, both staunch integrationists, after the Twelfth Baptist church split off.[15]

At least one historian has suggested that the dissension within the African Baptist church centered around differences over the church's involvement in abolition and social reform. According to this argument, adherence to "Baptist orthodoxy" led many blacks to oppose efforts by their fellow members who sought to use the church as a base for antislavery agitation. There is no convincing evidence that this was true.[16] It misinterprets the historical character of the black church. Although the black church has not generally been an agent of political or economic radicalism, it has almost always been an important center for community service and social action. There can be little doubt about the commitment of Thomas Paul to church involvement in social activism. His dedication to the goals of antislavery and the social welfare and civil rights of his people were acknowledged by black and white reformers. Between 1829, when Paul resigned, and 1842–43, when the split became formal, almost every report of church activities filed with the

Boston Baptist Association lists a minister or church representative who can be identified as a social activist.[17]

It might be argued that personal activism need not necessarily suggest a willingness to commit the church as an institution to that activism. However, protest meetings were often held at the church. Frequently the church was the only platform in Boston available to abolitionists; it was an important station on the underground railroad. It is particularly striking that John T. Raymond, who was pastor of the African church from 1841 to 1845, opened that church to "lecturers on the various reforms" who were received by him and "cordially solicited to address his church, in which exercises he participated with credit to himself and satisfaction to others."[18]

A further indication of the African Baptist Church's continued commitment to antislavery and social protest was the activity of its most prominent members and church officers. Between 1840 and 1860, almost every delegate to the Boston Baptist Association was an activist. Many, like Peter Howard, were members of the underground railroad and some, like James Scott, were fugitive slaves. The Twelfth Baptist Church, its minister, and its congregation were even more active.[19]

Disagreement could very well have involved personal differences among the members. In at least one instance there was considerable disagreement and a number of "tumultuous church meetings" when one church member charged another with adultery. This charge rested on the fact that one church member, Thomas Teamoh, a former slave, had brought his former wife out of slavery to Boston after the woman to whom he had been married in Boston died. In receiving this former wife from slavery Teamoh separated the woman from her current husband. Many in the church took a dim view of Teamoh's intention to marry the woman who many considered as already married.[20] This is an example of the kind of moral dilemmas faced by a church whose membership included those whose lives had been disrupted by slavery. This conflict lead to resignations from the church, and it is not unlikely that similar issues stimulated dissension. This might be particularly true during periods when the church lacked strong leadership. The 1830s was clearly one such period in the life of the African Baptist Church.

Paul had offered such leadership, but near the end of his tenure he frequently absented himself and undertook missionary trips. This helps to explain the pressure for his resignation in favor of a minister present to tend to the needs of the congregation. Unable to secure the services of a man with the appeal and magnetism of Paul, the church floundered during the 1830s. The split in the early 1840s might have been the result of personal animosities and differences which arose at a time when no dynamic leader was present to unify the congregation. The Reverend Black was apparently magnetic enough to have attracted a minority of the congregation away from the church when he left. Meanwhile, the African Baptist continued to experience fluctuations in membership and a changing ministry. Significantly, those ministers who remained in the church longest were those who built reputations as social activists and leaders. Both churches continued their activism even though one remained under stable leadership and the other changed ministers frequently throughout the 1850s and 1860s.

The reaction to discrimination and the movement for the creation of black social and religious institutions also led to the formation of the African Methodist Episcopal Church in 1818 and the African Methodist Episcopal Zion Church in 1838. By 1860, there were at least six churches serving the needs of blacks. Among them was the Free Church, later Tremont Temple, established in 1836 as an integrated church in protest of segregated seating in many of Boston's white churches.[21]

In some ways the churches serving Boston's black people were like those serving Boston's whites. The basic Christian philosophy served as the foundation for sermons. Passages were read from the same Bible and generally, services were held at approximately the same hour (although black services were typically longer) on the same day of the week. Beyond these basics, however, the Sunday services in black and white Baptist or Methodist churches diverged sharply.

Scholars who attempt to analyze the importance, the role, or the nature of the black church in terms of standard theological or denominational doctrine generally find the process frustrating. Black churches, whatever their denominations, simply did not conform to the orthodoxy of their white sister churches. They tended to revise not only the tone and texture of church services but also that of the Christian message itself. When, in 1829, David Walker of Boston criticized white ministers and their churches for their inconsistencies on the subject of race and slavery, he was voicing the objections of most blacks who believed that white theologians did not interpret Christianity in a way relevant to the black life experience.[22]

The religious activities in black churches were essentially different from those in white churches. Doctrinal orthodoxy, which sometimes acted as a conservative force among white Christians and argued against church involvement in nineteenth-century social activism, did nothing of the sort in black churches. The conservative stance of the orthodox white church cannot be used to interpret the central thrust of black religion. As black theologian C. Eric Lincoln has said, "Those who attempt to reduce black religion to nothing more than a cryptonym for the prevailing white expression of the faith run the inevitable risk of exposing how little they know about religion, or black people or both."[23]

Black ministers spoke before a congregation of people oppressed by a hostile or, at best, paternalistic society. The Christian philosophy may have been the same, but the emphasis was different. Acutely aware of the immediate concerns of their congregations, most black ministers were more likely to emphasize passages from the Old Testament history of the early Hebrews. The stories of oppression and slavery in Egypt were not lost on congregants, many of whom had themselves been slaves, or who had friends and relatives in slavery. Black ministers inspired and sustained their people with sermons which issued calls for a Moses who would lead black people out of bondage and into the promised land.

The message of the black church had wide appeal for black people of every station. Laborers and domestics gathered with independent businessmen and doctors on Sunday morning or at Thursday night prayer meetings, when the entire congregation was enlivened with musical inspiration from a black choir, or on those evenings when political and social protest leaders held sway in the sanctuary. Not only were blacks of various occupational and social levels members of the same churches, they were also likely to serve on the same committees, to hold church offices together, and to represent the church at religious conventions. Records suggest that, particularly in the Baptist churches, unskilled and semi-skilled workers were active church members.

In the late 1830s, both Cyrus Foster, a black clothier, and George Washington, a bootblack and part-time waiter and laborer, were deacons of the African Baptist Church. During the 1830s, at least half of the representatives sent by this church to the annual convention of the Boston Baptist Association were unskilled or semi-skilled workers. Similar representation was sent by the Twelfth Baptist Church to the North Boston Baptist Association meeting between 1849 and 1857. A few of these delegates were fugitive slaves. Robert Johnson, a waiter, was a fugitive who fled from Boston to St. Johns, New Brunswick, in 1858. While in Boston, he took part in a number of community projects, was a member of the African Baptist Church, and was the church's delegate to the Boston Baptist Association in 1845.[24]

Although many church records have not survived, the evidence which does remain testifies to the importance of the black church in the lives of blacks in antebellum Boston, even among the unskilled, irregularly employed workers. The rough-honed dock worker who gambled in the saloons of the North End and frequented Rosanna York's house for relaxation on Saturday nights was, no doubt, less interested in church school or the Sunday afternoon teas and picnics than in the antislavery message included in the Sunday morning sermons or delivered at abolitionist protest meetings. The antislavery activity of black churches or of black ministers like Peter Randolph, John T. Raymond, Samuel Snowden and his family, Jehial C. Beman, John Sella Martin, and Leonard Grimes offered more than the comfort of traditional theology. These black ministers brought the message of Christianity to the people, emphasizing its social and political concerns and its affirmation of human freedom and justice. The church stood as a spiritual, social, and physical haven for the black community. It also offered continuity and familiarity to blacks migrating to Boston. By 1860, over 60 percent of Boston's blacks had been born outside of Massachusetts; almost one third of these were boarders.[25] Many found hosts and sponsors among relatives and friends already in the city. For those less fortunate, the church provided not only consolation but social contacts and economic aid as well. Blacks were not generally served by labor unions or occupational benevolent associations.

The church, then, was the chief institution for socializing and aiding the adjustment of new residents. For unskilled workers who were most likely to relocate in search of jobs, the church played an especially important role. It was not a coincidence that the only formal employment aid center established for blacks in antebellum Boston was founded by a black minister.[26]

The black church performed indispensable services for the most transient, poorest segment of the black community. It dealt with issues which directly affected them. For blacks of various economic and professional levels, the church was a place in which they might feel comfortable and express their feelings freely. Communication between the minister and the congregation was, then as now, an important part of black religious services. To a far greater extent than in white churches, black services demanded congregational participation. The minister, much like the West African tribal priest, began the sermon or prayer, building the emotional tenor until the congregation responded both verbally and physically—encouraging him with an "Amen" or "Yes, Lord," a rhythmic clapping of hands and patting of feet. The entire congregation could, for a time, find release from the strain of daily cares. The message and the style of the minister was familiar and relevant to blacks of diverse regional, economic, and occupational backgrounds.[27]

In addition to ministers with formal denominational ties, there were a few folk ministers. Although there is little information concerning black folk religion in Boston, there is one account of a voodoo ceremony among southern-born blacks held after the Civil War. The ceremony itself seemed to resemble those practiced more widely in New Orleans. It is very unlikely that such ceremonies were frequent or that the number of practitioners was great before the war, when the southern black population was relatively small. Even during the postwar period, when the number of southern-born blacks increased dramatically, the dearth of information even acknowledging the existence of voodoo practices would seem to indicate its rarity among the city's blacks.[28]

During the antebellum period, Boston's blacks were attracted in greatest numbers to Baptist and Methodist denominations, in part, because of certain similarities to West African religious practices. Melville J. Herskovitz suggested, some decades ago, that the practice of baptism, for example, might have been related to the ritual of West African river cults, transplanted to America by the large number of river-cult priests who had come to the New World as slaves. Scholars have tended to agree with Herskovitz that the African heritage was not destroyed in slavery, but was integrated into the American culture adopted by blacks.[29] The Baptist and Methodist denominations offered considerable independence in the selection and ordination of church leadership. This allowed blacks to become ministers more easily. Then too, most blacks, attracted by the informal style of worship, attended white Baptist or Methodist churches prior to the establishment of independent black churches. It was not surprising that blacks adopted those denominations.

Black ministers have traditionally held special positions of influence and respect within the black community. As the slave preacher held authority over the plantation slaves, the northern urban black community held a special reverence for their religious leaders. The message was the same North and South, slave or free—unity, mutual respect, and resistance. Sometimes the message was shrouded in necessary subtleties, but almost always it was there in the sermons, in the scriptural passages, in the prayers and, of course, in the music of the black church. As one historian aptly described the dilemma of the black minister, "The black preachers faced a problem analogous to that of the early Christian preachers. They had to speak a language defiant enough to hold the high spirited among their flock, but neither so inflammatory as to arouse them to battles they could not win, nor so ominous as to rouse the ire of ruling powers."[30] Boston's black ministers were less restricted by white public opinion than those in many other northern cities, but there remained cause for caution. Even the black minister was not completely immune to the power of the wider society.

Black ministers were not merely important religious leaders. They filled a variety of roles, from offering the opening prayer at protest meetings to leading the campaign to free an individual captured fugitive slave. There were tactical differences in ministerial leadership, just as there were personality differences in the ministers themselves, but there was wide agreement upon desired goals. Thomas Paul was not only a dynamic minister but also a competent organizer. He traveled extensively as a spiritual and social reformer, ministering to blacks in New England and in New York and speaking out for racial justice and freedom. He was based in and acted almost entirely through the organized church, mainly because during the period of his ministry, before 1830, the black church was the strongest, most widespread organization among blacks in the North. He exemplified the union of social and spiritual leadership that characterized the most effective black ministers.

Many succeeding black ministers, having greater choice of organizational backing, operated through antislavery groups as well as through the church. Nathaniel Paul headed his own church in Albany, New York. He was deeply influenced by the antislavery movement, which by the early 1830s was merging black abolitionists with the Garrisonian militants. Nathaniel Paul acted as an agent for the *Liberator,* antislavery speaker, and as agent for the Wilberforce Colony for fugitive slaves in Canada. He opposed efforts to colonize American blacks in Africa, speaking out against the American Colonization Society at the Anticolonization Convention held in London in 1833. Calling for a universal emancipation, he also lobbied for the abolition of slavery in the British Empire.[31]

The growth of Garrisonianism and the international antislavery movement widened the opportunities for black ministers to campaign against slavery and racial injustice. In the early 1840s, John T. Raymond spoke out from the pulpit in the cause of temperance and abolition.[32] He associated with white abolitionists, many of whom were also temperance reformers and shared his views that alcohol was an evil which destroyed human progress. Raymond's theology emphasized freedom, and he used the Bible as an important source of his antislavery zeal. In most cases, black ministers could speak to the concerns of their congregation out of their own experience. Since poverty and discrimination touched the lives of all blacks, ministers were personally familiar with these obstacles. It was not difficult for them to relate to the needs and concerns of laboring people. A minister like Thomas Freeman had been an unskilled laborer himself and knew well the conditions black laborers faced. Bondage was not only within the personal experience of church members but also within the experience of many of their ministers.

Antebellum Boston's best known activist minister was Leonard A. Grimes. Grimes was born of free parents in Leesburg, Virginia. As a boy, he had worked in Washington, D.C., in a butcher shop and in an apothecary shop. He had seen slavery at close range in Virginia and in Washington. His experience working for a slaveholder traveling throughout the South convinced him of the great evil and inhumanity of the institution. Grimes' antislavery feelings were translated into action as he aided a number of slaves to escape bondage. This was an extremely dangerous activity. Many blacks arrested for aiding fugitive slaves were themselves sold into slavery. Grimes was fortunate indeed, for when he was convicted of helping a free black man and his slave wife and seven children escape to Canada, the court sentenced him to only two years in the state prison in Richmond.[33]

After prison, Grimes returned to Washington, D.C., where he worked as a hackman and married Octavis, a native of that city. In the late 1840s, the Grimes family, by then including a daughter and a younger son, moved to New Bedford, Massachusetts. Finally, after the death of Reverend George Black, the Twelfth Baptist Church called Grimes to be its new minister. In November 1848, Grimes found a poor and dwindling congregation of only 23 members, able to pay its minister only one hundred dollars a year. Under the new minister's guidance, the church increased its membership to 250 during the next decade and constructed a church building to house its spiritual and political activities.[34] By the 1850s, Grimes was one of the city's best known abolitionists. Under his leadership the Twelfth Baptist Church became a center for social protest and an important station on the underground railroad.

Grimes was by far the most aggressive of the black activist ministers in antebellum Boston. He spoke out not only against slavery but also worked directly with underground groups to secure freedom for individual fugitives. On a number of occasions, he was involved in planning the escape of fugitives from federal authorities in Boston, much as he had done in Virginia. When all else failed, Grimes and his congregation resorted to purchasing the freedom of individual slaves. For all his antislavery work, however, Grimes was not as involved with formal antislavery organizations as were less active black ministers. His work was almost exclusively through his church. It is not hard to understand the appeal of this man who operated directly, often in unorthodox ways, to aid fugitives. So many members of Grimes' congregation were fugitives themselves that his church was commonly called the "fugitive slave church."

Some black ministers, less likely to operate in Grimes' direct and unorthodox style, were more likely to work through antislavery societies. Often these ministers were better known for their organizational work than for their work in their churches. Jehial C. Beman, first pastor of the African Methodist Episcopal Zion Church in Boston, became increasingly important in reform groups based outside his church. Beman was born in Connecticut. Although he had not personally experienced slavery, his father, who had escaped from bondage, had made him aware of the evils of the institution. A strong advocate of antislavery and civil rights, Beman was active not only as an abolitionist but also in efforts to improve public education for blacks. Some of his congregation expressed the hope that his preaching and his letters written to parents would maintain a "lively interest in the education of [black] children."[35] Beman also reached out to those in need, ministering to black seamen and dock laborers of Boston's North End. Finally, he established an employment agency to aid blacks with low-skill levels in finding work.

The work for which Beman was best known was antislavery. When, in 1839, Beman broke with Garrison, he helped establish the New England Abolition Society. This new group rejected Garrison's policy of nonresistance, favoring a political approach to antislavery. After 1840 Beman served as assistant secretary to the American and Foreign Anti-Slavery Society, an anti-Garrisonian group that split with the American Anti-Slavery Society.[36] He came under considerable criticism for his attack on Garrisonianism from Boston blacks, most of whom were Garrison supporters in the early 1840s. The dispute was not one of goals, but rather one of tactics. Beman and a number of other blacks from several cities in New England and New York supported the Liberty party and later the Free Soil party and encouraged blacks to use political action for antislavery goals. In his fights against slavery and racism, Beman was far more orthodox and more politically oriented than Grimes. Beman was less likely to be involved in the rescue of individual fugitives than in campaigning among blacks for Liberty party candidates. Grimes and Beman were two different personalities, one aggressive and independent, the other an organizer. Each had his own very definite ideas on strategy, but both agreed on the basic necessity for racial equality, opportunity, and liberty.

Another black minister with a distinctive brand of activist style was John Sella Martin. Born into slavery in 1832 in Charlotte, North Carolina, Martin was sold away from his parents while still a child. He spent much of his childhood in Georgia and Louisiana. In 1856, Martin escaped from slavery and resided for a time in Chicago and Detroit, where he studied for the ministry. In the late 1850s, he became minister to a church in Buffalo, New York, before serving as interim pastor of Boston's Tremont Temple and finally as minister of the African Baptist Church.[37] Martin became an outspoken advocate of political abolition, campaigning from the pulpit for the Republican party. He supported Lincoln in the presidential election of 1860 because of the candidate's free-soil commitment and because other candidates offered nothing to blacks.[38]

Although Martin was a Bostonian for fewer than four years, he was extremely influential among Boston's blacks. His political abolitionism, which was in opposition to Garrisonianism, attracted far less criticism than the earlier political stance of Jehial Beman. By the late 1850s and early 1860s, Boston blacks were far more willing to depart from Garrison's non-political approach as political parties took positions more hostile to slavery.

John Sella Martin was one of the most intellectual of Boston's black activist ministers. Although born a slave, he was one of the few antebellum blacks to formally study theology. His brand of reform reflected his more intellectual style. His antislavery messages were likely to draw upon liberal philosophy or political and social history. In the late 1850s, his sermons on Nat Turner drew large crowds. Martin was likely to work with integrated groups like the Massachusetts Anti-Slavery Society. He was, for example, one of the featured speakers at memorial services for John Brown. When services were simultaneously held for Brown, one which only blacks attended, the other an integrated group, Martin spoke before the integrated group. Public speaking was a talent which Martin put to good use, but he was not likely to take direct action like Grimes or work as an active member of a national organization like Beman. Martin was a persuasive speaker and an independent reformer. During the Civil War he moved to Washington, D.C., where he continued his struggle.

Obviously, John Sella Martin, having been a slave himself, had strong feelings on the subject of abolition. Although white churches and their ministers could afford the luxury of ignoring slavery, as many in the North who were not outright proslavery did, the concerns and life experiences of congregations and ministers made it impossible for black churches to remain indifferent on the subject. Another former slave who became an active Boston minister was Peter Randolph. Born in Virginia, Randolph secured his freedom and came to Boston in the late 1840s. He was one of sixty-six former slaves who came as a group seeking a better life in the city. Randolph was the informal leader of the group, mainly because he was the only one who could read and write. About half of the group remained in the city, finding jobs and education for their children. After working at a number of jobs, including one as janitor at Harvard University, Randolph became a traveling lecturer, speaking to audiences about his experiences in slavery.[39]

Randolph and most of the others in his group joined the African Baptist Church. He was later ordained by Leonard A. Grimes in the Twelfth Baptist Church and became a traveling minister. In the 1850s he was minister to the home for elderly black women on Phillips Street. After a short pastorship in New Haven, Connecticut, Randolph returned to Boston to establish the Ebenezer Baptist Church.[40] Like Grimes, Raymond, and Martin, Randolph combined his spiritual message with one of particular relevance for black Bostonians. His personal life experience lent authority and urgency to his attack on human bondage and racial discrimination.

Some ministers spent much of their lives in the fight for freedom. For more than a quarter of a century, Samuel Snowden ministered to a growing and enthusiastic congregation in the African Methodist Episcopal Church on May Street on Beacon Hill. His forthright attacks on slavery and his efforts to improve the lives of local blacks, most notably black seamen, attracted many black activists to his church. David Walker was not only a member of Snowden's congregation but also a personal friend of the outspoken minister.[41]

Snowden's church attracted not only activists but the unskilled and fugitive slaves as well. Like both Baptist churches in Boston during the 1840s and 1850s, the A.M.E. Church was a stop on the underground railroad.[42] Not only was Snowden active through his church; the activities of his children indicate the extent to which he was personally committed to social reform. At least four of his eight children became abolitionists and social reformers. Like the children of Thomas Paul, Snowden's children carried on his work after his death.

In the 1850s and 1860s, two of Snowden's daughters worked with an organization established to aid and protect fugitive slaves who came to Boston. They took several fugitives into their homes, providing them with food and clothing in addition to shelter.[43] Two of Snowden's sons became followers of a more militant strategy, arming themselves against slave hunters.[44] One of his sons, Isaac, participated in an effort to break through Harvard University's policy of not admitting black students. In 1850, he and another black student, Daniel Laing, enrolled in Harvard's medical school. Although they were admitted, student and faculty protest was such that both students were forced to withdraw after one semester.[45]

Snowden's activism was carried out through non-church-related groups as well as through his church. He was a member of a committee of Boston blacks who represented their city in 1831 at the National Convention of Free People of Color. He joined with that body in its strong denunciation of the efforts of the American Colonization Society. During the 1830s, Snowden was a counselor to the New England Anti-Slavery Society and, like most Boston blacks, was a strong supporter of William Lloyd Garrison.[46]

The activism and political influence of black ministers was common not only in antebellum Boston, but throughout the history of black people in America. Generally these ministers were supported by and responsible to the black community. They were more independent of white society than other blacks who were dependent almost entirely upon white employers for the support of their families. Because black ministers found their constituencies within the black community, they were less socially and politically responsible to whites. They could speak out on controversial subjects like antislavery and civil rights with some immunity from white backlash. In this respect, black ministers in Boston were far more fortunate than those in the South, where white society often curbed their activities with local restrictions and sometimes open hostility.[47]

Those who remember the role played by black ministers and churches during the civil-rights movement of the 1950s and 1960s can more easily understand their function and importance in the antislavery and civil-rights struggles during the antebellum period. As CORE, SCLC, and SNCC used southern black churches in the 1960s as staging areas for freedom rides, sit-ins, and voter registration drives, black and white abolitionists and reformers held their meetings and rallies and assembled supplies for fugitive aid in black churches. The foot soldiers in the battle against racism have traditionally been churchgoers.[48] Black working people were among the marchers in Montgomery in the 1960s and among those attempting to rescue the fugitive Anthony Burns in 1854. Although documentation of widespread working-class involvement in the black church is problematic, since the churches were often informal and casual about maintaining membership lists or minutes, what little information exists is convincing. Black people, at all social and economic levels, turned to the black church and its ministers for a range of services which the broader society could not afford them.

The church was not only a source of spiritual and political leadership; it also provided a cultural center. Musical concerts and dramatic productions were routinely held in the church. Musical training and rehearsals occupied several evenings during the week. On Monday evenings, William F. Bassett taught music fundamentals to adults and children. On Wednesdays, the church choir held its rehearsal and sometimes musical concerts. On other nights of the week, the church provided a place for the rehearsals of the Amateur Band, directed by barbers Peter Howard and James G. Barbadoes, the Social Harmonic Society, and the various youth choirs. With so much going on at the church, it was little wonder that on several occasions the various black literary and debating societies, like the Boston Philomanthean Society or the Young Men's Literary Debating Society, were forced to meet in the rooms of the black school.[49]

The church was also an important meeting place where community members could make social and economic contacts. Archaeological evidence suggests that meals were served at the African Baptist Church. Church suppers may have been popular social occasions. Since the church drew its members from all segments of the black population, workers and potential employers often met there. This was especially true for workers migrating to Boston.[50]

It was always an honor for members of the congregation to entertain their minister in their own home. This was especially the custom when out-of-town guests visited. Jehial Beman was likely to be invited to the homes of those he served in the North End. Leonard Grimes spent much time socially with the members of his fugitive slave congregation.

The church was even important in the lives of those single black seamen and laborers who steered clear of "the preacher" on Saturday night, because they knew that if they were observed drinking or gambling he "would have a sermon on it" for Sunday morning.[51] Like most other blacks, these men often developed strong relationships and lasting attachments to the church and other churchgoers. Often boarding houses advertised their proximity to the church as an attractive feature. This was true of some North End boarding houses as well.

Thus, the church played an important and varied role for black Bostonians. The black minister was a natural leader, politically and socially as well as spiritually. The church was a place of worship, a social and cultural center, a political meeting place, and a hiding place for fugitives. The congregation provided a financial and social base for aiding the poor and a pool from which political activists could be drawn. The structure and function of the church provided a training ground for potential community leaders. Blacks unable to participate in Boston's political structure, forbidden access to the city council or the school committee or the multiplicity of bureaucratic positions which were traditional outlets for political ambition, turned to the organized black church or to the associations of their community. Thus church offices became important, prestigious, and sought after. Such positions filled many of the status needs of black people in the same ways sociologists have suggested that social and political organizations function within the wider society. Cyrus Foster was proud to be called Deacon Foster, and George Washington used his church title whenever possible.

The church was the major black institution outside the home for most black people of all ranks and all stations. Through their church, blacks protested injustice, pressured an often immobile state and local government, and provided for community needs. The church was a place of education and a place where blacks found spiritual and emotional comfort. Historically, the church was a sustaining force in black society. It offered a sanctuary to which exhausted blacks could come to draw new psychological and emotional strength. In 1960, a white writer, John Griffin, darkened his skin for an experimental taste of American society from the black man's perspective. Humiliated, frightened, psychologically and emotionally exhausted, Griffin at one point found it necessary to recuperate for several days at the home of white friends before continuing his experiment. Historically, black Americans have recuperated in fellowship with one another, fellowship often connected with the church.

The importance of the black church cannot be overemphasized. It sustained and nurtured those it served. In some ways it filled vital gaps left by a racially discriminatory society. It acted to counter the image of blacks often imposed from without black society. As C. Eric Lincoln says, "Black religion . . . cuts across denominational, cult and sect lines to do for black people what other religions have not done: to assume the black man's humanity, his relevance, his responsibility, his participation, and his right to see himself as the imge of God."[52] Those who fail to understand the central role of black religion and the church in the lives of black people fail to understand an important source of the inner strength which forms a major theme in black history.

5/Leaders and Community Activists

Many community members were engaged in reform and protest activities in the pre–Civil War years. It is difficult to provide an inclusive list of community activists, since those who were not officers of organized groups seldom appear in historical records; few membership lists from black organizations have survived. Those immediately identifiable as activists are those highly visible individuals whose names appeared in newspaper accounts of organizational functions or those whose names are available through personal correspondence. It is far easier to discover the active roles of blacks who worked in conjunction with William Lloyd Garrison and other white reformers than to identify black activists who worked exclusively among blacks. It is also easier to identify those black activists of higher occupational status than to discover the roles of unskilled workers.

Some indication of activism among workers at the lower occupational levels can be found in Civil War pension records, newspaper accounts of group direct action, and some church records. Even these sources may not discuss many of those less visible activists who were important supporters of reform and social protest, since many were active spontaneously or covertly, attached to no formally organized group. This makes an accurate assessment of such individual activities as the underground railroad especially problematic. The underground railroad attracted the broadest spectrum of blacks. Since its activities and membership were often secret, it is difficult to demonstrate the extent of individual participation.

Despite the shortcomings of available data, an attempt has been made to characterize the black activists of antebellum Boston. All told, 129 individuals have been identified from various records.[1] Their names were checked against the federal census for 1850 and 1860, city tax records, city directories, and vital statistics in an effort to discover some of the characteristics of these activists. Undoubtedly these characteristics will be biased towards the most stable, economically secure elements of the community. Evidence of active participation of those below that level must be regarded as especially significant.

Most activists were men, and 71 percent of these men were married. They tended to be in their mid-forties, with an age range from 21 to 79 years. During the decade between 1850 and 1860, activists were generally upwardly mobile in terms of occupation. In 1850, 58 percent of activist men were from the unskilled, semi-skilled, or unemployed group. The skilled and entrepreneurial group constituted about one-third of activist men, which was an overrepresentation of their proportion among black Bostonians. Professionals were greatly overrepresented among activists; almost all were involved in a broad range of community activities. This involvement of professionals is less significant than might be assumed, however, because there were so few blacks in this occupational category.

By 1860, the percentage of activists who were skilled and entrepreneurial workers had grown to 59 percent. This reflects both the upward mobility of some activists and an increase in the number of skilled and entrepreneurial workers active in community reform and protest. Many in this group were attracted by the efforts to integrate and reform public education and the increase in aid to fugitive slaves after the new, stronger federal fugitive slave law of 1850.

Between 1850 and 1860, there was an increase in southern-born and mulatto activists. Although activists were more likely to be northern born throughout the period, the percentage of southern-born activists rose from 34 percent to 42 percent during the decade. The percentage of mulatto activists also rose from 27 percent of the total number of activists to 58 percent during the same ten-year period. The proportion of southern-born and mulatto Negroes among activists exceeded their proportion in the black population of the city in both 1850 and 1860.[2] The rise in the activism of these two groups was related to their increase as a proportion of the population. Both the southern-born and mulatto Negroes were also more likely to be skilled workers.[3] The involvement of large numbers of blacks in efforts to protect and free fugitives held special significance for many southern-born blacks. The presence of a growing southern-born black population was certainly important in the increased activity of the black underground during the 1850s. Southern-born blacks were often leaders in the activities of the underground.

One such black leader was Lewis Hayden. Born a slave in 1811 in Lexington, Kentucky, Hayden escaped from slavery with his family in 1846. He was aided by a white minister, Calvin Fairbanks, who was jailed for his part in the escape. After spending some time in Detroit, the Haydens made their way to Boston. Shortly after his arrival, with the aid of friends, Hayden established a clothing store on Phillips Street. As his business prospered he was able to save $650, which was apparently enough to secure the release of Fairbanks from jail.[4]

Hayden was in many ways typical of black Boston's leaders in the 1850s. He was a small businessman, a migrant from outside New England who had been active with black groups elsewhere. Hayden had led a group in Detroit in the building of the brick structure that housed the Colored Methodist

Society of that city. He had been an abolitionist who apparently made a number of trips south, where "he engaged in stirring up a slave insurrection in Louisiana."[5] Hayden's activism and leadership in Boston represented a continuation of this work.

His home was a meeting place for many of those involved in reform and protest and served as an important station on the underground railroad. Hayden was a member of the Boston Vigilance Committee, a group that aided fugitives. His name was frequently mentioned in the records of that organization as taking part in most of its important activities.[6] On one occasion, author Harriet Beecher Stowe visited his home and found thirteen fugitive slaves on the premises. Hayden also hosted John Brown and his sons during their visit to the city in the mid-1850s and aided Brown in raising funds and troops for his ill-fated raid on Harpers Ferry in 1859.[7]

Hayden's role as black reform leader placed him in a position of liaison between white reformers and the black community. It was often his role during underground activity to coordinate actions of black and white activists or to organize blacks for some specific task. Hayden was very much a leader of lower-level black workers. In instances such as the attempted rescue of fugitive Anthony Burns in 1854, his companions were the seamen, the laborers, and the unemployed of black society.

Hayden was a man of great energy who achieved leadership in a relatively short time largely through the force of his personality and his active participation in a broad range of community projects. Like most black leaders, he realized the value and necessity for concerted action in dealing with the pressing problems of slavery and racial prejudice. On one hand, he encouraged racial unity and self help, but on the other, he was willing to act in conjunction with committed whites. He was a successful businessman, but his business seemed to take secondary importance to his social and political concerns. He was well able to support his family and in many ways conformed to the American ideal of the small businessman, independent, self-sufficient, and competitive. Yet many of his friends were not middle class, indeed most of those who shared his household were unskilled workers. To these people and to other blacks in need Hayden provided financial aid and comradeship.

Like successful white businessmen of the late nineteenth century, Hayden, to the extent of his ability, engaged in philanthropy. He provided money for many community programs. After his death, his wife Harriet bequeathed several thousand dollars to Harvard College to found a scholarship fund for poor and deserving black medical students.[8] Hayden's contributions were, however, not limited to giving money. His leadership was direct, often placing him in physical danger and on at least one occasion leading to his arrest.

While Hayden's activism was motivated, at least in part, by his personal experience in bondage, other blacks who had never been in slavery were equally as active. Robert Morris was one of Boston's most influential activists, a position he attained largely through his unique position as one of the city's few black lawyers. Morris' grandfather, Cumons Morris, was enslaved in Africa and brought to Ipswich as a boy. His father, York, was freed by the Massachusetts court decision that abolished slavery in the state in 1781. York moved to Salem, where he married Nancy Thomas and fathered eleven children before he died at the age of 49. Robert Morris was born on June 8, 1823, lived with his family for the first thirteen years of his life, and then went to work as "table boy" for the King family. The Kings were a wealthy white Boston family, and it was while in their employ that Morris met the wife of Boston attorney, Ellis Gray Loring, who soon hired him. Morris served the Loring family a number of years and impressed them with his quick wit and intelligence. When the white youth who worked in Loring's law office as a "copyer" gave up the position, Morris was given the job. He performed so well that he became Loring's law clerk and student. During this period Morris was also active in Boston's black community. He became a member of the Boston Lyceum and of the African Methodist Episcopal Church, where he was superintendent of the Sunday School.[9]

Morris married Catherine Mason shortly after his twenty-first birthday, and passed the Massachusetts bar examination in 1847. His success was a source of pride for the entire black community. In his first case, a suit brought by a black man against a white man for "services rendered," the opposing attorney treated Morris with disrespect in a private session before the formal court appearance. This unpleasant experience reinforced his determination to succeed in law. When this case came to court, the room was filled with black spectators. After the presentation of arguments, the jury deliberated for a short time before returning a verdict favorable to Morris' client. Morris recalled the enthusiasm of blacks at the decision and his own deep satisfaction. "My heart bounded up, and my people in the courtroom acted as if they would shout for joy."[10]

Although both Hayden and Morris were widely respected in the community for their commitment, it is clear that their orientation and style of leadership were very different. Morris gave freely of his legal talents but was less likely than Hayden to lead direct collective action. On one occasion, the escape of a fugitive was effected, in part, because Morris arranged for black rescuers to gain access to the courtroom where the fugitive was being held. Hayden, however, headed the group that rescued the fugitive.[11]

Much of the contrast in leadership styles between these two men may be accounted for by differences in their personalities and the roles and status of their respective professions. Hayden was a shopkeeper in the black community. Most of his contacts were there, and he depended largely upon blacks for his business. His origins and his identification were with black lower classes. Although Morris had also risen from humble roots, much of his life and all of his legal training had included the important influence of upper-class whites. His law practice was also partially dependent on white clients. Most of them were Irish, despite the notorious antipathy between blacks and Irish immigrants. Indeed, so many of his cases involved Irishmen that in some circles Morris was known as the "Irish lawyer" (presumably "black Irish").[12]

During the 1850s, at the urging of his wife, Morris joined the Catholic Church, an unusual religious affiliation for nineteenth-century Boston blacks. It was also during the 1850s that Morris moved out of the black community, a move made easier, no doubt, by his professional standing in the city. Whites and blacks alike recognized Morris as a superior lawyer. Many judges agreed that "by his tact and good nature he had won many cases where, if tried by almost any other attorney, the verdict of the jury would have been reversed." He was said to have a wit that on more than one occasion enabled him to "laugh" the jury into a favorable decision. Yet, Morris used his legal talents not only to achieve prominence but to provide effective leadership for his community.[13]

He was a member of the Boston Vigilance Committee's finance council and provided important legal services to the black underground.[14] There can be little doubt of his strong racial pride and sense of responsibility to the black community. Many of his black clients were from "among the humble, the actually poor [as well as] the middling classes." Edwin Walker, son of David Walker, bore witness to Morris' feeling for the black community, recalling that Morris had helped him in gaining admission to the bar and advised him, "Don't ever try to run away from our people. . . . Do you ever wear gloves? If you do, take them off and go down among our people."[15]

He became a leader in a movement to recognize the contribution to America made by blacks, helping to establish a monument to the memory of Crispus Attucks, the first black American killed in the prerevolutionary struggle of the late eighteenth century. Morris also led the crusade to institute a black military company in Boston in the early 1850s.[16] Some of the reforms in which Morris engaged were directed at the integration of public facilities. On many occasions he attended various performances presented at theaters known to practice segregated seating. Sometimes he was forced to leave, and thereafter instituted legal action against the theater managers. He also worked to open Boston's lecture rooms to blacks.[17]

The ranks of black activists included a number of blacks who shared Morris' double commitment to integration and collective black action. One important example was William Cooper Nell. Nell was a native of Boston, born on Beacon Hill in 1817. Political activism had been an important part of his family life and he was affected by the role of his father, William G. Nell, as "race leader" and organizer during the 1820s. In these early years, emphasis was placed on the development of black group activity. His father was one of the founders of the black antislavery group, the Massachusetts General Colored Association, in 1826. By contrast, his son became a leader in the integration movements of the 1830s and 1840s.[18]

William Cooper Nell learned about the burdens of segregation early in his life. He attended the segregated Smith School in the basement of the African Meeting House. An excellent student, he stood with a number of white students in the city as eligible to receive the Franklin medal awarded by the school board for scholarship. Because of his color, he was denied the medal and was not invited to a special dinner given in honor of medal winners except as a waiter. This experience profoundly affected Nell's decision to dedicate his life to the elimination of all racial barriers.[19]

He displayed leadership qualities at an early age. At age sixteen, Nell was secretary of the Juvenile Garrison Independent Society, a group of black youth organized for education, community service, and self-help. He showed exceptional ability as a speaker and writer. In October 1833, Nell's address before the second anniversary of the Juvenile Garrison Independent Society was found so inspiring that it was printed in the *New England Telegraph.* In 1834, Nell was featured in an oratorical exhibition for the antislavery cause. Although Nell was a modest and unassuming youth, Garrison recognized his talents as he worked as an errand boy for the *Liberator.* Against substantial opposition, Garrison made Nell an apprentice in the *Liberator* office at a time when "no colored boy could be apprenticed to any trade in any shop where white men worked." The white community was sure that "no nigger could learn the art of printing and it was held to be evidence of [Garrison's] arrogant folly to try the experiment."[20]

William Cooper Nell, unlike his father, worked side by side with many dedicated white reformers. As a result of this experience, Nell became an ardent integrationist, leading the fight for integration of Boston's public schools, urging the abolition of all-black organizations like the Massachusetts General Colored Association and even going so far as to encourage the abolition of black churches. In 1843, Nell attended the National Negro Convention, which was held in Buffalo. While admitting that the organization had been of substantial value to blacks, he believed that it should not remain an exclusively black organization. He asserted that once racially separate groups had been valuable, but that that time had passed. Nell urged blacks to abandon "all separate action" and become "part and parcel of the general community."[21]

Like Morris, Nell believed that blacks, given the opportunity, could compete successfully in the wider society and would benefit from being judged as individuals. Yet at the same time, he clearly saw the need for black group action based on the mutual concerns of the race. Nell's emphasis upon integration did not prevent his support of separate black organizations when they performed necessary services for the black community neglected by integrated groups. In 1842, when the Freedom Association, a black group, was founded to protect fugitive slaves, Nell became an active member and remained so until 1846, when the Committee of Vigilance, an integrated group, was organized for the same purpose. Nell clearly placed the needs of the black community ahead of his disapproval of separate black action. He favored integrated action because he believed it to be the most effective and most generally beneficial to the black community.[22]

Nell felt a responsibility toward his fellow blacks, as his leadership clearly showed, but he was not of the black masses in the same way that Hayden was.

Many of his close associates were white abolitionists or prominent blacks. Like Morris, Nell built a strong following among black working classes for his integrationist activities, especially during his leadership in the struggle to integrate Boston's public schools. Yet there was clearly a different tone to Nell's activism, which involved less confrontation than that of Hayden and even fewer direct political contacts with the masses than that of Morris.

One important source of Nell's integrationist zeal was his close association with William Lloyd Garrison and other white abolitionists. He hoped that if blacks could overcome legal and extralegal segregation, they would be able to share American opportunity. He also believed that separate black organizations could only serve to perpetuate racial prejudice and discrimination. Before Garrison and the New England Anti-Slavery Society, there was simply little opportunity for interracial action.

It is often difficult to determine the relationship between prominent black activists and members of the black community. Sometimes it is helpful to link issues pursued by a particular activist with those of special concern to the community. If this is done it becomes obvious that Hayden, Morris, and Nell were all committed to antislavery and the protection of fugitive slaves. Yet Nell's extreme dedication to integration might have caused some ambivalence among the black masses of the city. Moreover, Nell's orations, even during the militant 1850s, lacked the appeal to racial pride and unity which by then even moderate-minded black audiences were coming to expect.

One leader who was especially popular with black audiences was John Swett Rock. Even though Rock was not a long-term resident of Boston, he became very influential with many Boston blacks. He differed greatly from Nell; he was less moderate in approach, less committed to integration, and less optimistic about the extent to which white allies could be depended upon.

Born in Salem, New Jersey, in 1825, Rock began his career teaching and studying medicine. His medical study was interrupted by ill health, and he finally gave up medicine in favor of dentistry. Rock was also an amateur historian, concentrating largely on American and black history. In 1849 he was called upon to speak before the Twelfth Annual Meeting of the Pennsylvania Anti-Slavery Society. His interest in antislavery and in general social reform grew during the next few years. While successfully practicing dentistry in Philadelphia, Rock became deeply involved in social action. He instituted a night school for blacks, became involved in the city's antislavery movement and in a number of other social projects. He also resumed his medical study, graduating from American Medical College in 1852.[23]

In 1853, when Rock decided that Boston's more "liberal atmosphere" would be better for his medical practice, he arrived with good credentials in social reform and community action. In Boston he not only practiced medicine and dentistry but also became an effective lecturer for temperance and antislavery. Like Morris, Rock felt a sense of responsibility to and pride in his race. He was vocal in his effort to have it understood that, "I not only love my race but am pleased with my color." He often spoke of his duty and his pride to "concentrate my feeble efforts in elevating to a fair position a race to which I am especially identified by feelings and by blood." Not only was he personally dedicated to racial solidarity and pride, he also saw them as prerequisites to racial improvement. "We can never become elevated," he told fellow blacks, "until we are true to ourselves." This meant more than "brilliant speeches." For Rock this entailed hard work, "each man in his place, determined to do what he can for himself and his race."[24]

Like Morris and other black professionals of his day, Rock believed that educated and wealthy blacks had a particularly important role to play. He thought they should operate within and without the black community to "wield a power that cannot be misunderstood" in aiding their fellows to improve themselves.[25] Unlike Nell, who expressed a faith in eventual white acceptance of educated or otherwise respectable blacks, Rock's position was a more militant one which emphasized a racial strategy similar to that dubbed "black power" during the 1960s. Rock encouraged black capitalism, not to prove anything to whites, but to bring to the black community the benefits and power of money and business success. More than Nell, Rock emphasized the responsibility of successful blacks to the community's poor. Like Morris, Rock saw the necessity of not setting himself apart from the community. However, he apparently never developed the personal relationships that Hayden had established among poor blacks.

Rock, like other black professionals, served as an important role model and source of pride for many in the community. He also provided needed medical services to his fellows. He saw to the medical needs of fugitives and of the general black community until failing health forced limitations on his activities. When in 1858 Rock traveled to Paris to receive surgical treatment, the members of the Twelfth Baptist Church held a farewell reception in his honor. The medical treatment he received in Europe was apparently quite effective, for his health was much improved by February of 1859. Thereafter Rock returned to the United States, studied law, was admitted to the Massachusetts Bar in 1861, and established offices on Tremont Street in Boston. Rock later became the first black man admitted to practice law before the United States Supreme Court in 1865, and the first black man to be received on the floor during a session of the United States House of Representatives.[26]

At the time of his death in 1866, Rock had spent most of his forty-one years serving and leading his race. He was able to secure the confidence of Boston's blacks partly because of his reputation as a community organizer in Philadelphia, and partly because of the much-needed dental and medical services he provided. The pride felt by many blacks in a black professional also aided his assumption of a leadership role.

Hayden, Nell, Morris, and Rock are examples of important local activists. They were joined by a number of small businessmen like barbers Peter Howard and J. J. Smith, both of whom were important members of the black underground, or John T. Hilton, a hairdresser who, together with Hayden, was very active in the African Masonic Lodge.[27]

For many blacks, the antislavery movement provided a chance not only for leadership within the local community but for prominence on a national and even international scale. One such notable black abolitionist was Charles Lenox Remond. The son of John Remond, who was born on the island of Curaçao and naturalized as a citizen of Massachusetts in 1811, Charles Lenox Remond became one of the first paid, full-time antislavery speakers. John Remond had become a lifetime member of the Massacusetts Anti-Slavery Society in 1835, and Charles became an active touring speaker for the American Anti-Slavery Society during the mid-1830s. In a letter to his Boston friend Thomas Cole in 1838, Charles Lenox Remond expressed his optimism and enthusiasm for his work. He was encouraged, he explained, by the changes he saw taking place across the free states and expressed his belief that support for slavery and racial discrimination was "falling." Such optimism allowed Remond to maintain a strong belief in the possibility and benefits of successful integration of blacks into the wider society.[28]

By 1840, Remond had gained sufficient stature in antislavery circles to be appointed as an American Anti-Slavery Society delegate to the World Anti-Slavery Convention in London. He was joined by white delegates William Lloyd Garrison, Nathaniel Peabody Rogers, and Lucretia Mott. Although Remond was a man of growing prestige, he was treated with contempt by the captain of the ship that transported the delegates to England. During the trip he was confined to steerage because of his color. A crew member, however, befriended Remond and provided him with better accommodations.[29]

Black leaders generally found considerable acceptance among European antislavery groups, and Remond was no exception. Of his popularity as a speaker Garrison wrote, "our colored friend Remond . . . is a great favorite in every circle." "Surely," he continued, "if dukes, lords, duchesses, and the like are not ashamed to eat, sit, walk and talk with colored Americans, the democrats of our country need not deem it a vulgar or odious thing to do likewise." Remond so impressed British royalty that "the Duchess of Sutherland . . . signified her wish to see him at her palace." While abroad, most American blacks found that for the first time in their lives they were treated with respect. For most, Europe was an extremely pleasant and refreshing experience. It was not surprising that Remond extended his European tour beyond its original length. In August 1840, when Garrison and other delegates returned to the United States, he remained in Britain speaking and raising support for the American antislavery struggle.[30]

On his return to the United States eighteen months later, he brought with him the "Great Irish Address," a communication signed by 60,000 Irishmen urging their Irish brethren in America to support abolition and black equality. Although conditions in the United States insured that this communication would not be generally supported by Irish Americans, it did provide favorable propaganda for the cause of abolition.[31]

Remond's popularity may be gauged by an incident which occurred in Lynn, Massachusetts. When Remond was asked to speak before the Lyceum in Lynn, some members expressed opposition. Whereupon "a majority united in the formation of another institution . . . in order that they might hear his speech."[32]

The rise of militant white abolitionism after 1830 and the employment of black antislavery orators provided opportunities for blacks to address white audiences as national and international figures. Their prominence among blacks often was not locally based, and the issues they addressed were not limited to local issues. Remond, for example, did not live in Boston but in Salem, Massachusetts, a town to the north of the city. Therefore, he was not in a strict sense a member of Boston's black community. He held no membership in any of the community's churches, and his role may be seen as distinct from that of local community leaders. Remond's influence was, nevertheless, considerable among Boston's blacks largely because of his national reputation and his close affiliation with Garrison. Although not a community organizer in Boston, Remond became involved in community affairs. He was chosen to address the Massachusetts House of Representatives in 1842, in support of various petitions protesting segregated railroad accommodations within the state.[33]

Remond was only one of a number of leaders who became prominent in the national abolition movement. The most influential black abolitionist speaker during this period within Boston's black community was Frederick Douglass. Like Remond he was not a community organizer in Boston, nor did he live in the city during most of his residence in Massachusetts. Yet, because of his dedication to the cause of black people and his national reputation, he cannot be overlooked in any discussion of Boston's black activists. Born Frederick Augustus Washington Bailey, a slave in Talbot County, Maryland, in February 1817, Douglass escaped to New York in 1838, finally making his way to New Bedford, Massachusetts. There he first read the *Liberator,* which, with its editor, William Lloyd Garrison, "took a place in [his] heart second only to the Bible." He attended local antislavery meetings and traveled to Nantucket, Massachusetts, in 1841 to hear Garrison.[34]

At this meeting, Douglass was persuaded to relate his personal experiences as a slave. He was thus launched on a long and eventful career as an advocate of freedom and equal rights for his people. Douglass proved to be such an effective speaker for the cause that in short order he had gained national and international fame. Until the early 1850s, Douglass was a staunch Garrisonian, joining with Remond, Nell, and other black abolitionists.[35] Douglass remained influential in Boston's black community even after his split with Garrisonian abolitionists in the early 1850s. By 1847, Douglass had determined to publish an antislavery newspaper. Considering Boston at first as a location for his new press, Douglass finally settled on Rochester, New York. Feeling that his venture should be undertaken independently, Douglass ignored Garrison's objections to the new publication. Garrison's was not the only objection. Many white abolitionists could see no need for another antislavery paper and argued that the venture was doomed to failure. They also believed that the editorship of such a paper would take too much of Douglass' time and restrict his usefulness as an antislavery speaker. However, Douglass interpreted their opposition to his paper as racial prejudice and persevered with even greater determination.[36]

A later source of friction between Douglas and white abolitionists was his close association with Julia Griffith, his white secretary and assistant. Many felt that such an association between a black abolitionist and a white woman could do the antislavery cause great harm. Indeed Douglass did experience some public embarrassment, and Julia Griffith was "very grossly insulted on account of going about with Douglass."[37] The situation was exacerbated and ugly rumors of an affair spread when it was learned that Julia Griffith had loaned Douglass a considerable sum of money and held the mortgage on his home, which supported his newspaper.[38] Personal attacks by those he had considered to be friends saddened and angered Douglass. They also provided the basis (along with growing ideological differences concerning the feasibility of political antislavery action) for a formal and bitter split between Garrison and Douglass.

In 1848, Douglass complained that Massachusetts' white abolitionists were trying to sabotage his editorial venture by boycotting his newspaper. The answer was quickly given, as before, that there were already too many antislavery papers, and Douglass' complaints were labeled "utterly without reason or excuse."[39] Douglass was called an ingrate—ungrateful for all that abolitionist friends, especially Garrison, had done for him. This charge was particularly odious to Douglass because of its paternalistic implications. By 1849, there could be little doubt that the split was indeed serious. Anne Weston, a white abolitionist, reported that at an antislavery meeting at which Douglass was lecturing, he was "very cool to us."[40] Garrison recognized that "with Douglass, the die [seemed] to be cast, and lamented, "the schism [seemed] unavoidable."[41]

In contrast, Boston's black community supported Douglass' venture. Many defended his action, arguing that the establishment of a newspaper would not necessarily restrict Douglass' effectiveness as an antislavery lecturer. It was pointed out that Garrison himself combined the two activities quite successfully. It was also argued that many who did not subscribe to any antislavery paper might subscribe to one edited by a black man "to satisfy themselves of the ability of a colored man to sustain" such a publication. It was predicted that blacks "would joyfully give him their support in preference to any other individual because he was better known to them than any other." Some blacks were angered by the attempt to discredit and suppress Douglass' publication out of what they felt to be the "selfishness of some . . . leading abolitionists."[42]

Douglass' influence among Boston's blacks was tested in a confrontation with William C. Nell. Nell, a long-time Garrisonian, had joined Douglass' staff in Rochester in 1851, but as conflict with Garrison grew, Nell found himself caught between the two warring factions. By late 1852, he was back in Boston siding with Garrison and, according to Douglass, trying to destroy the influence of *Frederick Douglass' Paper.* Nell retaliated, calling Douglass ungrateful to Garrison and a "contemptible tool" of anti-Garrison forces. In the fall of 1853, Douglass and Nell appeared before a black meeting in Boston to debate the issues of the conflict. Ostensibly, the meeting had been called to discuss the feasibility of the formal endorsement of Douglass' newspaper by Boston's black community. Speaking first, Nell denied that Douglass was worthy of community support, maligned him for his recent conduct, and defended white abolitionists against false criticism.[43] At this time, Nell was in the midst of a school integration struggle that was supported by many blacks.

Nell had long been admired by the black community for his oratorical ability, but he proved no match for his opponent. The force and persuasiveness of Douglass' argument were irresistible. Garrison's popularity and influence notwithstanding, Boston blacks enthusiastically endorsed Douglass' newspaper, dealing Garrison and his followers, many of whom were prominent local black leaders, a stunning defeat. Obviously, Douglass' break with Garrison had not significantly diminished the former slave's influence with Boston's black community.[44]

Thus may be seen the power of national black leaders like Remond and Douglass. Yet, local leadership was not diminished by their appeal. Boston's blacks had rejected Nell's argument in the debate but certainly not his leadership. In 1855, when Boston's public schools were finally integrated by law, the black community acknowledged Nell's dedicated leadership in a public testimonial held in the black church on Southac Street. By 7:30 P.M. on December 17, the church was crowded "by a finely appearing and evidently intelligent audience, all of whom appeared to take a lively interest in the proceedings."[45] The meeting included many of Boston's most prominent black citizens, and local leadership was well represented. The list of testimonial officials indicates that in 1855 Nell had lost no respect as a result of his confrontation with Douglass two years earlier. Moreover, the audience and the testimonial officials were representative of the entire black community and reflected broad support for Nell. For example, among those listed as meeting vice-presidents were Peter Hawkins, a laborer, and waiters William H. Logan and Robert Johnson.[46]

The continued influence of both Nell and Douglass with the city's black community is not surprising in view of their distinct roles. There were few blacks who commanded Douglass' national following. Although national leaders were a source of inspiration and pride, most activities were local, requiring regular presence and attention. Local activists like Nell were important grass roots organizers of the black community. Theirs was the often tedious job of sustaining community action.

Although the majority of known activists during the antebellum years were men, women played an important role in community activism. They were underrepresented among identifiable activists, being a quarter to a third of all activists, but this proportion of female activists is significant in the context of nineteenth-century society. Black women carried on activities which made much of the community work possible, particularly fund-raising. Through the church, in independent bazaars and community fairs, black women collected thousands of dollars. Sometimes black women worked with whites, as in the Anti-Slavery Bazaar that became an annual fund-raising event supporting the antislavery campaign.

They also belonged to the Boston Female Anti-Slavery Society, established in the mid-1830s. The members of this organization included many of the most prestigious women in the city. Black members represented the upper echelons of Boston's black community and included women like Susan Paul, life member of the Massachusetts Anti-Slavery Society and daughter of Thomas Paul. Susan Paul was an officeholder in the Boston Female Anti-Slavery Society. In 1838 she was chosen as one of the vice-presidents for the Second Annual Anti-Slavery Convention of American Women, which was held in Philadelphia.[47] She recruited a Garrison Junior Choir, which became a regular attraction at antislavery gatherings, served as secretary to Boston's all-black temperance organization, and later was active in the regional black temperance group formed in 1835.[48]

Susan Paul was concerned not only about injustices suffered by her race but also about those suffered by her sex. She was a speaker for the women's rights movement, but for her, as for many black women, the cause of racial justice won her first allegiance. She realized the connection between the existence of slavery and the persistence of racial discrimination toward free blacks. Writing to Garrison in 1834, she made clear her belief that the latter condition was inextricably bound to the former.[49]

Other black women became assets to the cause, participating in a variety of roles. The wife and the sister of Charles Lenox Remond, Sarah Parker Remond and Caroline Remond Putnam, were not only active in organized abolitionist groups, but acted individually to protest racial segregation at such public places as Boston's Howard Theater. Sarah Remond was one of those involved in the bizarre effort to free Henry "Box" Brown, who escaped from slavery in a box mailed to Philadelphia via Railway Express. Black women played important roles in providing shelter, medical aid, and food for fugitives in hiding within the community.[50]

Black women even participated in rescuing fugitives. They played key roles in the rescue of Eliza Small and Polly Ann Bates, fugitives from Baltimore who were captured in Boston in 1836. In this successful rescue, a group of women rushed into the state Supreme Court and took the fugitives from their captors.[51] Generally, women involved directly in fugitive slave rescues were from the working class, including washerwomen and domestic servants. Middle-class women were more likely to take part in fund-raising and organizational leadership. For black women then, as for black men, economic and social status influenced the nature of their community activism.

Yet middle-class women were active in the underground railroad. The records of the Boston Vigilance Committee reveal that many women provided aid to fugitives. The list included the daughters of the Reverend Samuel

Snowden, Isabella and Holmes, Mrs. Charles D. Williams, whose husband was the proprietor of a popular retail clothing shop, and Jane Putnam, wife of one of Boston's wealthiest black hairdressers. Many wives and daughters of Boston's black leaders were themselves active not only in antislavery organizations, but in the black church and community groups as well.[52] Unfortunately, organization records and newspaper accounts identify these women only in relation to male family heads. This makes information specifically related to black women difficult to gather except through husbands and fathers. It also reveals something of the attitudes toward women within the black community.

Although black women suffered from the sexist attitudes of their men as did most nineteenth-century women, black society was more tolerant of women in active roles as social protestors than was the society at large. The antislavery movement offered to women, both black and white, a platform for community recognition outside of the home; but the black community and leaders were more willing to accept female abolitionist speakers than were whites. In 1840, while attending the World Anti-Slavery Convention in London, Charles Lenox Remond rose to speak in protest against the exclusion of female delegates. He then participated in a boycott of the convention staged by a number of abolitionists, including William Lloyd Garrison.[53] Frederick Douglass was an advocate of women's rights and missed few opportunities to praise women for their valuable work in the antislavery cause. The Seneca Falls Convention for women's rights, held in 1848, selected Douglass to give the major address. He distinguished himself at the convention as the only male present to endorse Elizabeth Cady Stanton's resolution calling for women's suffrage.[54]

By the time of the Civil War, activism and social protest had become traditional among blacks in Boston. Many of these families could count three or more generations of active social protest.[55] Slavery and racial discrimination and the common realization that their effects must be resisted had created a socially active community in which individual differences of style and strategy, reflecting diverse backgrounds and experiences, complemented each other in pursuit of the common goal.

6/Segregation, Discrimination, and Community Resistance

In antebellum Boston, blacks were segregated into a few highly concentrated areas of the city, restricted to "Jim Crow" accommodations on public transportation, isolated in schools that were rapidly deteriorating and scholastically inferior, excluded from juries, and seated apart in white churches, lecture halls, and places of entertainment. They held the worst jobs at the lowest pay. Friends were rare among the white elite and working classes, native and foreign. Crude racial insult and injury often passed over into subtler forms of condescension and contempt in more polite circles. Black Boston faced incredible obstacles with little more than faith to sustain it.

Jim Crow dogged black Americans wherever they traveled in the northern states. Since public discrimination made few distinctions in social or economic class, a black doctor or celebrity might as easily be faced with the humiliation of Jim Crow as a seaman or dock worker. In many ways, the pressures of hostile white society forced blacks of varying backgrounds to share an experience most nonblacks could hardly comprehend. In Boston where slavery was not available to clearly delineate the superior status of whites, this discrimination was evident in any situation in which whites and blacks made contact. In public places, blacks were either segregated or completely excluded. Frederick Douglass spoke of being turned away from a menagerie on the Boston Common, a revival meeting in New Bedford, an eating house in Boston, and an omnibus to Weymouth, Massachusetts. He had been forcibly ejected from public trains several times because he refused to take a place in the "Negro car." On one memorable occasion he purchased a first-class ticket on the Eastern Railroad from Boston to his home in Lynn, Massachusetts. He subsequently refused to leave the first-class car to take a seat in the Jim Crow accommodations as provided in the regulations of the railroad company. The conductor and several men tried to force him out and did so with great difficulty. Douglass recounted, "they however found me much attached to my seat, and in moving me I tore away two or three of the surrounding ones, on which I held with a firm grasp, and did the car no service in some other respects." He caused so much confusion and difficulty that the railroad superintendent ordered all passenger trains to bypass Lynn, much to the consternation of its residents.[1]

Traveling on any public facility could be a frustrating and humiliating experience for blacks. The public stages either refused to admit them or forced them to stand or to ride outside.[2] Blacks traveling by boat experienced similar difficulty. Charles Lenox Remond reported that he was confined to the deck during a boat trip from Boston to New York City. This was apparently the practice irrespective of climate, as Remond recalled that on one such occasion he very nearly froze to death.[3]

Blacks were also excluded from or segregated in many places of public entertainment. In 1847, Julian McCrae purchased tickets to a Boston theater but was forcibly excluded because of his color. When he sought redress through the courts, the judge ruled only that McCrae be reimbursed for the price of the tickets.[4] In a similar case of discrimination, William C. Nell, Sarah Parker, and Caroline E. Putnam were denied their reserved seats at a Howard Theater performance. Nell protested when theater manager Palmer ordered them to the gallery, a section reserved for blacks. Police officer Philbrick then tried to eject the party from the theater. In the ensuing struggle, Sarah Parker's dress was torn and her shoulder injured. She then brought assault charges against Palmer and Philbrick. Testimony during the trial revealed that the Howard was the only theater in Boston that "observed the color line," one fact among many which indicated the relatively liberal atmosphere in Boston compared to other northern cities. The defense claimed that the whole episode had been staged to test the discriminatory policies of the theater, and therefore, the complaining parties involved were simply interested in creating a disturbance. The court found for Sarah Parker in the amount of one dollar.[5]

Not only did blacks face discrimination in places of entertainment, they sometimes met insults and violence from individual whites. Blacks were not safe in some parts of the city. Remembering his youth, Wendell Phillips recalled that black boys were hunted and attacked on the Boston Common by roving bands of white youths. Such attacks were not limited to black youth. In 1854, Cyrus Foster was attacked on a downtown street at noon by an "intoxicated Irishman, who pushed the Deacon off the sidewalk and, otherwise, insulted him." The attacker, however, found Foster, even at his advanced age, quite capable of defending himself, for "the Deacon administered summary punishment, with a vigor and promptitude worthy of his military career." Foster's attacker was subsequently arrested.[6] Blacks were not usually willing to submit to such insults mildly. On another occasion, a black laborer was walking on Cambridge Street at the foot of Beacon Hill when two white men insulted him with a number of racial epithets ending with, "there goes another nigger." At this point, the black man who had been carrying a heavy load put his burden aside and challenged the two men. After a brief conversation, they apologized and departed.[7] In the first decade of the nineteenth century, Prince Hall had complained about the "daily insults met in the streets of Boston." By mid-century the situation was much the same.

Sometimes whites played humiliating jokes on the black community, ridiculing black institutions and leaders. Before 1800, black leaders protested satirical newspaper sketches of the black Masons. Sometime later a number of posters appeared in Boston advertising the "Babolition of Slavery Grand Selebrashum By de Africum Shocietee." A number of handbills were printed purporting to be accounts of a parade followed by a celebration conducted by the African Society and the black Masonic Lodge. The account was written in a manner that was supposed to depict a black dialect, with a generous sprinkling of misspelled words and grammatical errors. The total description was obviously intended to picture black organizations as incompetently run, farcical imitations of white organizations. Blacks were portrayed as semi-literate, drunken, lazy inferiors for whom meaningful, effective leadership responsibility was impossible.[8]

There is no way of knowing how widely these sheets were circulated, but it is clear that among white Bostonians racial stereotyping was common. Perhaps some measure of the psychological effect of this kind of bigotry is reflected in the comments of William C. Nell, who grew up and attended school in Boston during this period. As a boy in Lyman Beecher's church in 1831, he was asked by his Sunday School teacher about his plan for adulthood. Nell, replied, "What is the use of my trying to be anybody? I can never be anything but a nigger anyhow."[9] Significantly, Nell was a child of an economically successful family and the son of a prominent black community leader. It would seem that a boy with his ability and background might have a more optimistic outlook and a better self-image. That he did not may indicate the extent to which prejudice and discrimination had robbed him of self-esteem and usual middle-class aspirations. Yet, Nell did grow up to be "somebody" and although whites like Oliver Johnson, his Sunday School teacher, and William Lloyd Garrison influenced Nell's career, it was the support of the members and institutions of the black community which was instrumental to his success—a fact that Nell never forgot as he served his community in return.

The experiences of Frederick Douglass, Charles Lenox Remond, William C. Nell, Cyrus Foster, and others were typical of those blacks of every class who lived in or visited Boston or the surrounding towns. By 1840, pressure from the black community and from some white abolitionists in the form of petitions and public demonstrations forced some changes in the policy of segregation. In August of that year, Thomas Cole, a black hairdresser, reported that railroad accommodations between Boston and Newport, Rhode Island were "tolerably good" for blacks. Apparently, there were seats for blacks in first-class cars, although they remained separated from whites.[10] Not satisfied with this partially improved arrangement, blacks with their white allies continued their protest with more petitions to the state legislature.

In February 1842, Charles Lenox Remond addressed the Massachusetts House of Representatives supporting these petitions. Not raising the question of social equality directly, he emphasized, "we all claim the privilege of selecting our society and associates but—one man does not have the prerogative to define rights for another." He spoke of being separated from white traveling companions and asked, "If R. M. Johnson [then Vice-President of the United States, living out of wedlock with his black housekeeper and their two children] . . . should be traveling from Boston to Salem, would the State of Massachusetts be prepared to sanction the separation of . . . him from his wife and daughters?"[11] Although the Massachusetts Legislature failed to act, continued protest and rising public support forced railroad companies "voluntarily" to integrate their trains. Although there were some dramatic victories in the drive for equality, racial discrimination in Boston proved a persistent and well-established adversary. Indeed, its durability apparent in the city's contemporary racial confrontations provides a continuity in Boston's ethnic relations.

One victory that blacks cautiously endorsed but did not actively participate in was the repeal of Massachusetts' law against interracial marriage in 1843. William Lloyd Garrison spoke out against the law in 1831, but blacks made few public comments concerning the drive for its repeal until the early 1840s. The law's removal from Massachusetts' statutes was largely the result of a petition drive sponsored by white Boston abolitionists.[12] The lack of direct and substantial black participation in this campaign is significant, since in other such protests blacks were conspicuous. In 1843, a meeting of blacks held at the African Baptist Church endorsed a weak and extremely general resolution that supported the law's repeal but never mentioned the law by name. Although blacks favored the removal of the statute, the tone and concentration of this meeting made it clear that they realized the extreme sensitivity of this issue.[13]

One of the most spectacular black-sponsored protest drives was aimed at the integration of Boston's public schools. Separate black schools had been established as private and later as public institutions after the turn of the nineteenth century. Although Boston's educational system was not legally segregated, few black children attended school before 1800. The experience of those who did was characterized by discrimination, mistreatment, and public ridicule from white students and teachers. As a result of this treatment, blacks, led by Prince Hall, petitioned in 1787 and again in 1800 for the establishment of a separate black public school. Failing in this, they organized the private African School in 1798. Initially students gathered in the home of Primus Hall, Prince Hall's son. By 1806, classes taught by Elisha Sylvester, a white schoolteacher, were meeting regularly in the basement of the newly built African Meeting House. Black parents, concerned most with the quality of their children's education, accepted the services of the white teacher until qualified black instructors could be found. Two of the school's best-known teachers were Thomas Paul, Jr., and John Russwurm, graduate of Bowdoin College and one of the first black college graduates in the United States.[14]

Financial support for the school was provided by parents and the black community. In 1815, Prince Saunders, one of the early black teachers at the school, convinced a white merchant, Abiel Smith, to make a substantial contribution to black education. Smith willed securities worth in excess of four thousand dollars to the city of Boston for the education of black students. Shortly after this grant, the African School was renamed the Smith School in honor of its benefactor. By 1820 the city was providing two hundred dollars annually for the education of black children. This amount plus a twelve-and-one-half-cent tuition charge per week per child paid by parents sustained the school.[15]

In 1820 and 1831, the city established two public black primary schools in addition to the older Smith School. Although the city had accepted some financial responsibility for black education by the early 1830s, black children, as a rule, received an inadequate education. Their schools did not generally meet the standards of white schools either in facilities or in curriculum. "The school committee forbid the colored children from learning grammar—they would not allow any but the white children to study grammar." This condition prevailed in direct violation of the spirit of the Law of the Public Schools, which specifically stated that "in every town containing fifty families or households, there shall be kept one school for instruction of children in Orthology, Reading, Writing [and] English Grammar."[16]

Black schools were not only inadequate in facilities and curriculum but were also poorly located for many families. The only two public primary schools for blacks were located in the West End on Belknap Street and on Sun Court. One family living in East Boston was compelled to send their children to school by ferry—a costly inconvenience. Families in the North End had similar problems. Although, at one point, the city offered to provide transportation for black children living a great distance from the black schools, inaccessibility of black schools was one factor in the community's support of integrated neighborhood schools. In addition to these problems, many teachers in black schools were ill-prepared to accept their educational responsibilities.[17]

In 1844, William C. Nell, John T. Hilton, and Jonas Clark, a clothing dealer, organized to integrate public education. In 1846, petitions were sent to the Primary School Committee asking for the abolition of city-supported black schools and the integration of all Boston public schools. In its deliberations, the school committee questioned the mental and physical capability of black children to compete with white students. They reasoned that "the distinction is one which the Almighty has seen fit to establish, and it is founded deep in the physical, mental and moral natures of the two races. No legislation, no social customs, can efface this distinction."[18] How could the committee be so bold as to grant such petitions which seemed to violate laws of God and nature? They could not; the petitions were denied.

Agitation on this question continued, and in 1849 the Negro School Abolition Society was formed which, with the aid of influential white abolitionists, applied pressure in various ways to achieve school integration. By this time the physical facilities of the schools had deteriorated beyond the point of usability and safety. A special committee report described the Smith school in stark terms: "The school rooms [were] too small, the paint [was] much defaced, and every part [gave] evidence of the most shameful negligence and abuse. There [were] no recitation rooms, or proper places for overclothes. . . . The yards, for each division, [were] but about fifteen feet square, and only accessible through a dark, damp cellar. The apparatus [was] so shattered and neglected that it [could not] be used until it [was] thoroughly repaired."[19]

More petitions were sent to the school committee, and blacks picketed the Smith School in a largely successful effort to discourage black attendance. Average attendance dropped from 263 in 1840 to 51 in 1849.[20] They also instituted a suit against the city under an 1845 statute which allowed any child unlawfully excluded from public school to recover damages. The statute further stated that students should attend the school closest to their residence unless special provision had been made. Parents applying to the school committee were to be issued a ticket of admission to the appropriate school. Accordingly, Benjamin Roberts, a black printer, applied to the district Primary School Committee in the name of his daughter, Sarah, age five, who passed five white schools on her daily journey to the black school. He was denied an admission ticket on the grounds that special provisions had been made for colored students at colored schools. After a number of appeals, Sarah finally entered the school nearest her home without an admission ticket. After she was ejected by a teacher, her father brought action against the city of Boston for unlawful exclusion under the 1845 statute.[21]

Roberts retained Charles Sumner, an abolitionist who was later United States senator from Massachusetts, to present Sarah's case before Chief Justice Lemuel Shaw. Sumner was assisted by Robert Morris. Sumner pleaded Sarah's case eloquently, using arguments paralleled over a hundred years later in a landmark United States Supreme Court decision in the case of *Brown* v. *Board of Education of Topeka.* Although the Smith School had undergone substantial renovation "including an entire remodeling of the building" just prior to the hearing of Roberts' case, Sumner argued that the all-black school remained inferior. He charged that racially segregated schools and equality of education were mutually exclusive. Segregation and discrimination in public education, he asserted, were not only unconstitutional but were socially and emotionally damaging to both black and white children.[22]

"The school," Sumner explained, "is the little world in which the child is trained for the larger world of life. It must, therefore, cherish and develop the virtues and the sympathies which are employed in the larger world." Segregation of children according to race in these early years of their lives, he went on, would implant within them a sense of caste distinction, which would make social intercourse among the races difficult or impossible at a later age. Such a situation, Sumner contended, would preclude "those relations of equality which our constitution and laws promised to all."[23]

The Court, refusing to judge the educational, social, political, and moral consequences of school segregation, ruled in favor of the right of the school committee to set educational policy. The charge that Sarah had been denied access to public schools was rejected on the grounds that the city had provided a school for her and other colored children. Shaw acknowledged that black children in the commonwealth were entitled by law to "equal rights, constitutional and political, civil and social." The issue, he explained, was "whether the regulation in question, which [provided] separate schools for colored children, [was] a violation of any of these rights." The court reasoned that since political and legal distinctions were made on the basis of sex, racial distinctions, as well, could be legitimately made in education.[24]

It was also the opinion of the court that segregation did not perpetuate class distinctions, but that such segregation was demanded by the deep-rooted prejudice which could not be altered by law. Justice Shaw's argument became the legal precedent for the 1896 Supreme Court decision in the case of *Plessy* v. *Ferguson,* which established the segregationist doctrine of "separate but equal." Sarah was denied access to an integrated education, but this defeat did not halt the integrationist forces. Two months later they were planning a statewide petition drive.

Although Nell and the Negro School Abolition Society were persistent and conspicuous and were widely supported by blacks, there was not complete agreement within the community that black schools should be abolished. There were some among Boston's blacks who saw in "race schools" the potential for black control of the education received by their children. After all, they reasoned, had not the establishment of separate schools originally been a response to the concern felt by many black parents that the conditions of racial prejudice and intolerance in public education damaged black children? What kind of education could a black child receive from a white teacher who accepted the concept of racial inferiority? If black children were to be educated, they concluded, it must be by black teachers in a black school.

This group was led by a clothing store owner, Thomas Paul Smith, a laborer, Joseph Russell, and a minister, James Simmons. They claimed a following of at least 10 percent of Boston's black population, and hoped to rally great community support around the question of black pride generated by community control of black schools and the push for hiring black teachers. In 1849, 170 people, including several clergymen, signed a petition asking that "race schools" be maintained for those who favored separate education.[25]

One important issue on which most blacks agreed was the necessity to replace and upgrade the teaching staff at the Smith School. In the mid 1840s, an increasing number of black parents were becoming incensed at the racism, apathy, and brutality of many of the white teachers and of Abner Forbes, the white headmaster. Forbes' neglect of his responsibilities, his use of abusive language, his disrespect for both his students and their parents, and his excessive use of corporal punishment led to demands by many blacks that he be removed.[26] The school committee, however, did not respond. The problems with the staff at the Smith School continued and, in some cases, the morality as well as the professional competency of its teachers was questioned. The charge of immoral conduct against Smith School teachers caused quite a scandal. William Bascom, who had been headmaster for a short time, was accused of indiscreet behavior towards a number of the female students. Four former pupils testified that on several occasions Bascom had displayed "lewd conduct" of an unspecified kind toward them. It was also revealed that James G. Barbadoes, black abolitionist and hairdresser, and two students had observed Bascom entering a house of prostitution during school hours. This alleged misconduct enraged many blacks on both sides of the school integration question. For blacks favoring the maintenance of the Smith School, this incident was seen as further evidence of the need for qualified, and presumably morally sound, black administrators and faculty.[27]

Continuing pressure for the hiring of black teachers, and the hope that such action might blunt the thrust of the school integration movement prompted the Boston school committee to replace several white teachers with blacks at the Smith School. In this way, the committee created the illusion of black control of black education. In reality it never relinquished power over general policy, hiring practices, salaries or funding. To forestall further community criticism concerning the administration of the Smith School, the school committee asked Thomas Paul, Jr., who was living in Providence at the time, to become the new headmaster in 1849. Paul, a graduate of Dartmouth College and an experienced teacher, was well qualified for the position. He accepted the offer. As a result of the school committee's effort to "turn hostility into race pride," the leader of the group of blacks who philosophically favored separate education now had a vested interest in the maintenance of the black school. Thomas Paul Smith was the nephew of Thomas Paul, Jr., making it entirely possible that Smith's concern for his uncle's position affected his efforts on behalf of separate education.[28]

Despite the hiring of Paul, Nell and the other integrationists were successful in organizing a protracted boycott of the Smith School that reduced black attendance dramatically. Blacks who participated in the school boycott, which lasted eleven years, were well organized, holding frequent meetings which provided mutual support and communication.[29] There was also an alternative school opened in a black church, in which several blacks including at least one black minister instructed black children. Some blacks, like John T. Hilton, who could afford to establish residences outside the city did so, taking advantage of integrated schools in several of the towns outside

Boston. Deacon Roberts and Jonathan Cash, explained that they had withdrawn their children from the Smith School because of its inadequate curriculum and irresponsible faculty. For many blacks who saw education as one of the only avenues to success, a quality education for their children was essential.[30]

After a number of petitions aimed at applying pressure on the school committee produced little progress, integration forces turned their attention to the state legislature. The Massachusetts' legislature in 1855 was dominated by the "Know-Nothing" (American) party. This nativist, anti-Catholic group was in close contact with the Free Soil party. Seven of the eleven Massachusetts' Know-Nothing congressmen had been Free Soil men until 1854. Although Massachusetts' governor, Henry Gardner, had been a Whig, many important state offices were held by old Free Soilers, and Henry Wilson, a radical Free Soiler, was elected to the senate with Know-Nothing support. This legislature also acted with antislavery elements of the state to extend the personal liberty law in 1855, making it illegal for Massachusetts' officials or facilities to be used in apprehending fugitive slaves. This law had also been a factor in efforts to censure Judge Edward G. Loring for his role in the return, in 1854, of a fugitive slave from Virginia.[31]

Given the antislavery character of the state legislature in 1855, it was natural that black leaders might look to it for aid in their efforts at school integration. Working with friends in the legislature, such as Charles W. Slack, they were able to lobby successfully for the passage of legislation abolishing separate schools. The greatest opposition to the bill came from whites in Boston, probably because Boston contained by far the largest concentration of the state's blacks and because it was mainly Boston schools that would be affected by the bill. Finally, Governor Gardner signed the bill into law in April 1855.[32] Ironically, the Fugitive Slave Law of 1850 and federal efforts to return fugitives from Boston to bondage heightened antislavery sentiment and gave rise to the forces which accomplished the integration of Boston public schools.[33]

The school integration victory was an occasion for great rejoicing in the black community. Celebrations were held for months after the event. On December 17, a grateful black citizenry paid tribute to William C. Nell, the man who had dedicated himself to securing for black children that equality in education he himself had not enjoyed.[34] For more than fifteen years he had organized and encouraged the protest against separate schools.

In this effort, Nell had been joined by many important black businessmen. In light of the assertions of some that "few colored men, in their business associations have independence sufficient to practice fidelity to principle," it is important to note that many black businessmen were active in the cause of school integration.[36] George Putnam, a hairdresser and co-owner of "Putnam and Clark Salon," who had moved out of Boston before integrated education became a fact, had been instrumental in gathering petitions. In this effort he had been assisted by his wife and the wife of Charles Lenox Remond, Jonas W. Clark, Lewis Hayden, John B. Bailey, a gymnasium owner and Harvard boxing coach, and many others. A list of those gathered on December 17 in honor of Nell and the triumph of school integration would serve as a directory of Boston's black businessmen, but significantly, it also included a number of unskilled laborers and seamen. The celebration was, much as the integration campaign itself had been, a community affair. Nell, the guest of honor, was hailed as the "Champion of Equal School Rights" and presented with a gold watch "from the colored citizens of Boston for his untiring efforts in behalf of Equal School Rights." School integration had been a personal victory for Nell and for a great number of blacks throughout the community.[36]

As segregated transportation, public accommodations, and education were important areas of community action and protest, so discriminatory hiring practices and job competition aroused serious concern. Blacks throughout the antebellum period suffered from chronic unemployment and underemployment. Even whites dedicated to the cause of abolition were not likely to employ blacks at any but the most menial levels. Some of the city's leading blacks, responding to the need for job stability and technical training, instituted business ventures to train and employ blacks in trades.

Hosea Easton and a "number of other colored men of master spirits and great minds" formed an iron manufacturing company. Easton was a master blacksmith, and he conducted a training program for the company's employees. The company also operated a "regular school for youth connected with the factory" and in keeping with the values of respectable nineteenth-century society, black and white, instituted a "strict moral and economic policy." Temperance, thrift and moral conduct were emphasized as virtues which led to eventual success. Although "thousands of dollars" were invested in the business it eventually failed, due to "repeated surges of the tide of prejudice," according to Easton.[37]

In 1838, Benjamin Roberts established a printing office in the city for the employment and training of blacks. He made two attempts, in the 1830s and in the 1850s, to establish an antislavery journal but failed each time, perhaps because of competition with the *Liberator.* Although he was successful in maintaining a small print shop, his employees and trainees were few because of the limited scale of his business. Roberts' shop was supported largely by printing work done for black institutions such as the church, the Masons, and the literary societies. There was also work from the Vigilance Committee and a number of small local abolitionist groups. Yet, this venture could aid only a few of the many black workers in need of more and better jobs.[38]

Black businessmen, such as Roberts and Easton, attempted to fill the employment gap by offering jobs to blacks in need. Coffin Pitts' clothing store or Peter Howard's barber shop could provide at least temporary employment, but blacks realized that temporary measures would never solve the long-term problem. Some blacks, such as Nell and Lewis Hayden, used their influence with white friends willing to employ blacks. William Lloyd Garrison was especially noted for lending his aid in finding jobs. The Reverend Jehiel C.

Beman attempted a more formal approach through his employment agency. Although these efforts helped, none could meet the spiraling need that worsened with the approach of mid-century.[39]

By the late 1840s, the already limited job market for blacks was threatened by a wave of white immigration. Although Boston had received some immigrants throughout the first half of the nineteenth century, its limited opportunities in both agriculture and industry had tended to keep the city's foreign population smaller than those of New York or Philadelphia. Those immigrants who did settle in Boston before the 1840s were largely French, Scottish, German, English, and Italian. There were some Irish who came to Boston in the 1830s, but they, like most of the city's immigrants during this period, were small groups who settled with comparative ease among native Bostonians. In 1845, potato rot destroyed great portions of Ireland's vital food crop, and the 1846 repeal of the English Corn Law brought to an end Ireland's favorable position in the British trade system. The disastrous economic conditions in Ireland caused a mass emigration, most of it to the land of opportunity in America. Before the tide of emigration abated in the mid 1860s, 2.5 million Irishmen had landed on American soil. The number of Irish entering Boston increased from 443 in 1836 to a high of 65,556 in 1846.[40]

These immigrants often reached the city with no funds, shelter, or job prospects. Many had been poor farmers in Ireland and had few skills useful in an urban environment. They became the chief economic competitors of blacks. Positions traditionally open to blacks, such as house servant, cook, waiter, porter, and laborer were often filled instead by immigrants "whose hunger and whose color [were] thought to give [them] a better title to the place."[41]

By 1850, over 7,000 laboring jobs were being filled by Irish workers. In all, 87 percent of the city's laboring jobs in that year were being filled by foreign-born workers, while blacks held only 1.5 percent of those jobs. Even given the small percentage of black workers, considering that the vast majority of blacks were unskilled workers, their percentage of the laborers was very low. By 1860, there was a decline in black laborers, while the number and percentage of foreign-born laborers increased. Foreign-born workers filled over 80 percent of the jobs as domestic servants, while blacks filled less than 2 percent.[42] Most discouraging was the steadily deteriorating job situation for black seamen. The sea had traditionally offered employment for blacks, not only in Boston, but in most American port cities. The year 1850 found growing pressure from new Irish immigrants in this area as well. By 1860, the percentage of Irishmen filling jobs on ships sailing out of Boston had almost doubled, so that they were nearly one-quarter of the city's seamen. Combined with a slight rise in the number of other foreign-born seamen, over half of the city's mariners were immigrants by 1860. Between 1850 and 1860, there was a decline in the number and percentage of black seamen.

The only trade in which blacks maintained a precarious hold during the last two decades of the antebellum period was that of barber and hairdresser. There was a rise in the number of foreign-born barbers and hairdressers in Boston between 1850 and 1860, increasing from one-fifth to one-third of the profession. Although blacks were able to maintain a hold on over one-third of these jobs, foreign-born barbers and hairdressers were increasing at a much faster rate.

As immigrant competition pushed many black workers from traditional unskilled fields, few blacks had or could acquire training necessary for skilled positions. The percentage of black skilled workers remained virtually unchanged between 1850 and 1860. The failure of earlier training ventures did not deter those to whom the need for a black trade school was obvious. Such a school could train black craftsmen, who could in turn take on black apprentices, providing a route to skilled work. In America, blacks asserted, men were valued for what they could contribute. "The individual must lay society under obligation to him, or society will honor him only as a stranger and sojourner."[43]

To counter the competition for unskilled work, Frederick Douglass advised blacks to "Learn Trades or Starve." Professional education and academic scholarship would not, as he saw it, provide adequate employment for blacks whose communities could not support educated clergy, lawyers, and teachers. The black man's only hope, Douglass explained, was to train for highly skilled occupations, which would put him in demand both inside and outside his community.[44] The crush of immigrant competition was felt not only in Boston but in most eastern cities. Thus the response of blacks was both national and local. At the National Negro Convention in 1853, a committee was appointed to raise funds and choose a location for the construction of a manual training school for blacks.[45]

Some blacks argued that the establishment of such a school was too costly a project, since the majority of blacks would not participate, and that it would be a capitulation to segregation. This criticism notwithstanding, Douglass drew up a detailed plan for the "American Industrial School" to be established near Erie, Pennsylvania, on a two-hundred-acre farm. Faculty and student selection was to be made irrespective of race or sex—an attempt to quiet criticism leveled by integrationists.[46]

Funding for the institution was the most immediate and pressing problem. Initially, supporters attempted the sale of stock at ten dollars per share. But this venture was not successful, mainly because black supporters could not generally afford to purchase stock and white abolitionists, especially Garrisonians, were not appeased by what appeared to be an afterthought to integrate the school. The failure of the project was insured when in 1854, Harriet Beecher Stowe, antislavery author of *Uncle Tom's Cabin,* refused to contribute promised funds from her European antislavery fund-raising tour. Garrisonian influence was no doubt a factor in her refusal.[47]

This project was not a popular one among Boston's blacks who favored the end but not the means—a school which could be seen as an acceptance of educational segregation. At a time when the city's blacks were embroiled in the struggle to integrate public education, they could not generally be persuaded to support the venture. The hope of providing trade education for blacks remained a dream, to be taken up again after the Civil War and later, most successfully, by the educator and advocate of racial self-help, Booker T. Washington.

The intense competition from newly arriving immigrants and the dissatisfaction of many blacks with the education provided for their children contributed to a 18 percent drop in Boston's black population between 1840 and 1850. Never again during the antebellum period did the black community reach its 1840 level. Significantly, this decade saw the greatest influx of Irish immigrants.[48] In this same ten-year period there was an increase in the black population in the towns surrounding Boston. Many blacks who left Boston in search of education and employment during this period entered these surrounding towns.[49]

Many blacks who lost jobs turned to the community for support. Repeatedly, black leaders in the 1850s called upon blacks to aid one another. Blacks were urged to patronize black businesses, to utilize black labor and to unite for the preservation of the community. Black fraternal organizations, like the Prince Hall Masonic Lodge and the Odd Fellows, initiated charity drives. According to census data, there was also an increase in the practice of taking in boarders.

The mid-1840s and the 1850s was a time of economic crisis for Boston's blacks. It was a time when the community spirit that had sustained black people in slavery—facilitating the establishment of organizations in the early years of the century and fostering collective protest—came to the fore again. In organized protest drives and in informal individual protest, blacks in Boston continually announced that they would not acquiesce to oppression. Whether in the fight to ride with dignity on the public transport, to eat in the public restaurants, to seek entertainment in the public theaters, or to educate their children in the public schools, blacks reaffirmed their resolve to struggle toward the rights of equal citizenship. The rising tide of immigrant competition which found blacks sorely handicapped by generations of disadvantage was but another challenge to the cooperative spirit which was an essential element in the fabric of black community.

The dehumanizing forces of prejudice and discrimination were countered by a determined struggle to improve their condition. Contemporary scholars have investigated the society of the southern black slave and have discovered the many ways that slaves managed to resist the intended effects of the slave system. Blacks in Boston obviously had more freedom and opportunity. Yet they too were an oppressed people, relatively powerless in their urban environment. For them, as for the slave, religious faith was an important means of coping with the frustrations of daily living. In a seemingly hopeless situation, religion held out both hope for the future and the promise of strength. The knowledge of the morality of their struggle against the sin of human bondage, gave blacks and their white allies the assurance of the power of the righteous.

Not all blacks united for the good of the community. As in slavery, there were those "no-'counts" in black Boston who took advantage of other blacks. In 1859, when Bill, a fugitive from Louisiana, passed through Boston, he was victimized by a black man who sold him a train ticket, supposedly to Canada, for four dollars. In reality, the ticket was only good for transportation to Lawrence, Massachusetts. In addition, the fugitive was given a slip of paper that he was told to put on the front of his cap. Later, the train conductor informed him that the paper said "fugitive slave." With the help of the underground railroad, Bill eluded his pursuing master in New Hampshire and made his way to safety in Canada. Bill had fallen prey to one black Bostonian who did not exhibit the spirit of the community.[50] Those whose response to poverty was to engage in swindling, robbery, or prostitution were not approved by those who sought the moral uplift of blacks.

Some Boston blacks, like some southern slaves, used positions of trust with whites to influence matters important to the black community. Often white allies were called upon to help to find jobs for blacks. When Lewis Hayden's clothing store failed in 1858, he obtained a job as a messenger for the state. Working at the State House, Hayden was the first, it was said, to urge his white abolitionist friend, John A. Andrew, to run for governor of Massachusetts. Governor Andrew was a powerful ally of blacks during the Civil War years.[51]

With the freedom to organize, blacks in Boston had more resources than the slaves with which to fight off the attacks on self-esteem that continually plagued them. Black societies and churches provided positions of status and respect for members of the community. Those few blacks who achieved professional careers provided important role models for ambitious black youths. Many blacks, no doubt, continued to have the kind of fatalistic and discouraged attitude displayed by William C. Nell, who, as a boy, had questioned the practicality of his aspiring to "be somebody." Yet for the oppressed and the powerless, the successes and the visible cooperation of blacks from diverse backgrounds in progressive community efforts were signs of hope, promising a better life in an otherwise dismal future.

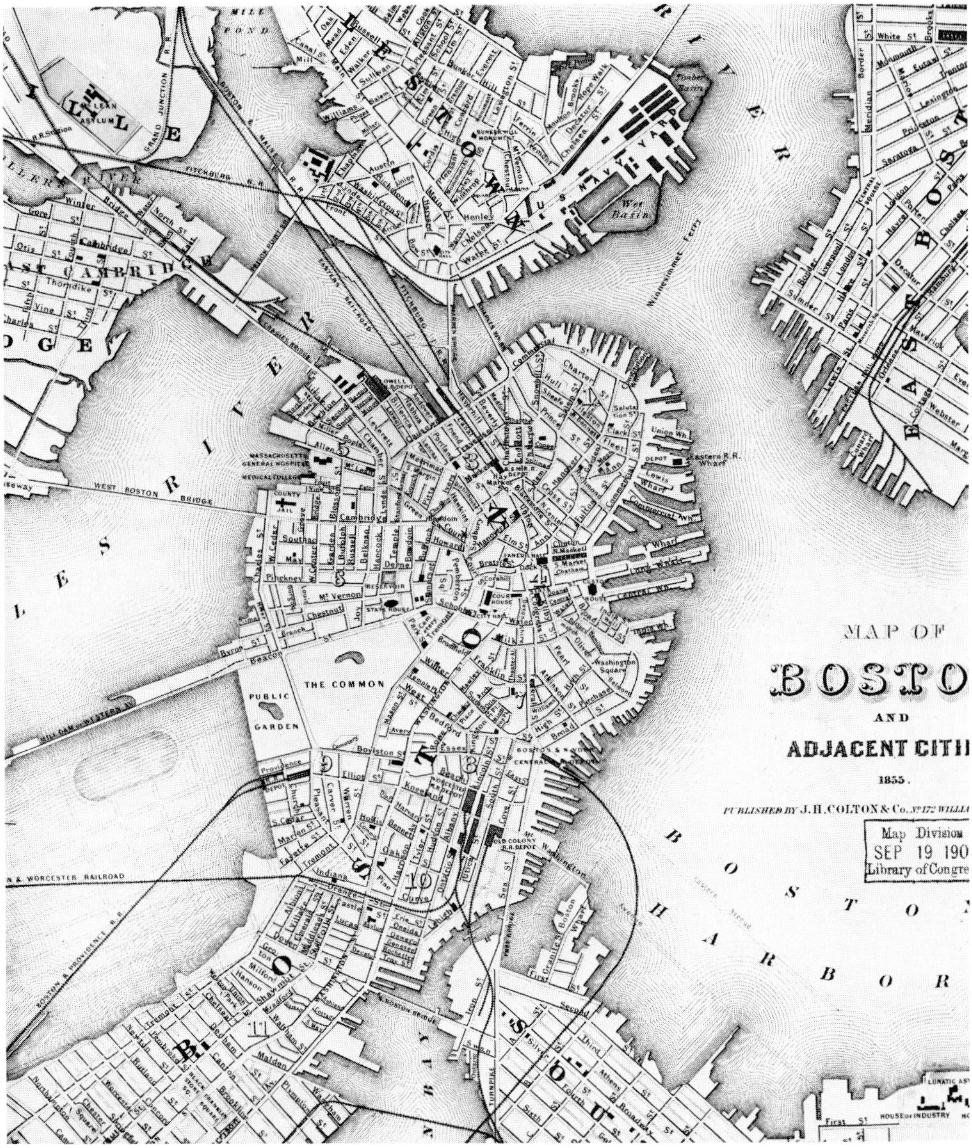

MAP OF
BOSTO
AND
ADJACENT CITII
1855.
PUBLISHED BY J.H.COLTON & Co.
Map Division
SEP 19 190
Library of Congre
THE COMMON
PUBLIC GARDEN
WEST BOSTON BRIDGE
MASSACHUSETTS GENERAL HOSPITAL
MEDICAL COLLEGE
COUNTY JAIL
STATE HOUSE
COURT HOUSE
RESERVOIR
U S NAVY YARD
West Basin
FITCHBURG R.R.
GRAND JUNCTION R.R.
BOSTON & WORCESTER RAILROAD
BOSTON & PROVIDENCE R.R.
OLD COLONY R.R. DEPOT
Eastern R.R. Wharf
Central Wh.
Long Wh.
India Wh.
Union Wh.
Lewis Wharf
Commercial Wh.
Washington Square
Winnisimmet Ferry
Timber Basin

BOBALITION
Of Slavery.

Kernel Duebill, chah! I scratch um out and begin agin, I mean GENERL ORDER.

Bosson, Uly 14teenth 18 hundred and 30 tu.

Head Quarters, Hum Lane, fut house where the cellar is up stairs.

To Captin Lookpate, squier, Greeting

Sir.—De ardus task gain debolbe on me to conform you dat I gain point you shief Marshall ob dis bressed day, and I spect you gubern youself cordingly. I tink you better set up all night fore, dat you get all um customer boot brush fore de time cum for de grand processun to start.

You will see dat dey be derange in de follerin order:—De sages and onerabel members ob de BobalitionSocietee firs nex cum de invited guest, mung dem de onerabel Smico Smashpipes from de Iland ob Moonshine. Den cum de stranger ob destincshun – nex de Barbers wid dare proprate bages, de razer strap and dare lather-box, den de Boot-brack wid jug ob bracking in dare right hand and boot-jack in turrer one—and last cum de sweep wid dare usual bage ob oner.

Dis mos splendid processun will mobe as soon as it start, (unles sum axident happen) from Crow strete percisele at nine o'watch, P. M. in de fore noon, little fore or little arter exactly to a second. You will be tickular when dey march to mobe dat dey keep zact step wid de moosick both foot togedder, and dat de platoon keep in zact strate semicircular line perpendicularly, and dat dey hold up um head like man out ob bebt, and walk horizontalle as dey can Dey will recumlec dat large number ob grate milumtary carakter is spected to witnes our marchin, mung de mos extinguish, I would tickularle menshun de North-square Silver-heels, de Millpond Mud-larks, de Copps-Hill Grave-diggers and de Neger-Alley Cadetts. De hole under de escort ob de gallant Captin Snippo Snarlhead's cumpane ob Independent Terribles.

Signed in my elbow chair,
POMP PETERS, President,
CEZAR GARBO, Sec'ry.

Toasts.

De Day we celumbrate.—May he neber be darken wid de shades ob southern ignorance. *3 cheers, 1 pop gun.*

De Orator ob de day.—He beat Massa Cicero and Pop Emmons widout speakin single word, and gib um odds wid both he hand in he briches pocket.

Moosick on de Jews Harp.

American Genius.—He bery curious feller, de bes ting he eber do for me he make basket wid two partments, one to pick up de chip in, de udder to hold um cole vittel.

49 laff, 9 grin and quarter.

De Cold Water Societee.—Wonder what de poor fish do when dey drink all um water up. 339 sober look.

Arter dis toast wad drunk, Simon Snubnose, Poet Laureat to de Duke ob Dandylion sung de followin song:

To all merry fellers – [hic] here's a long life,
And plentee ob good ting [hic] to feed ob—
Let us be cleber and (hic) free from all strife,
A ting we hope we're not in need ob. (hic)

Cum pas round de bole, de ful floing bole—
What is de coloured man so fraid ob?
While he's protected—(hic) hand, heart and sole,
By a Garrison that good stuff is made ob.

Our brudders at de souf (hic) wid wat'ry mouf,
Wood stare (hic) to see (hic) us drink such whisky,
But I'm de chap (hic) dat likes brackstrap,
It makes me feel so (hic) nice and frisky. (hic! hic!)

Bolunteers.

Our brack brudders at de souf.—How we feel under um jacket for um—fore we stand de nonsense, we wood get um libing by takin um kink out ob pigs tail and eat noshin but alamode leather-apron and fryed wool! Moosic—Solo on de base drum.

De Ole Made.—What de ole boy do de brack raskallee stupid ole bachelor mean, why he no sho heself industrius, and not let de poor tender blossum widder and fade way like sun-flour in January on north side de hous? 27 pop gun & haff.

De Fair Sex.—May dare virtues neber be discumboblicated by de arts ob de cruel spoiler. 97 hard sneeze, 1 pop gun

As soon as dis toas wad drunk, Sambo Snags begin sing de followin plaintiv lines:

When Jubly Phillis stoup to follee,
And not mind what Pompey say—
He harte waz sad and melumcolly—
Den he not wish sea nudder day!

Sam Sharpshins he cum one night
And cauz Missa Phillis to elope—
Now do you tink dis waz rite?—
Dat bery nite Pomp's harte waz broak.

Now he wander trew de treet,
Be de wedder hot or cool,
And ebery one dat he mete,
Tink he born de nat'ral fool.

Sam Sharpshins Missa Phillis wed,
And Missa Phillis wed to him,
But Sam's nose is growin red,
And Phillis' eyes are growin dim!

Arter de cumpanee wipe way de teer dat gush warm from de eye-brow, dey all fill um glas wid two-center of strike-dady, which quite cumpose um.

Neger Hill.—He no more what he useter was, dan my ole boot-jack like hole regiment ob horrid accidents.

Moosic on de banjo, jews-harp & punpkin-vine.

Dis las toas waz drunk in slantindicular sition, each one havin on pair ob cock-eyed spectacles. As good luc wood hab um, no axumdent take place cept de onerabel Titus Numskull ob Musquash Place hab he red silk briches bery much spoil by de upsetting ob boiling pot full ob skillegalee in he lap.—Deacun Grizzle he like to be choke wid skulpin, which he so carles as try swallow wid de head on.

On de hole dare waz no mistake in de rangements cept Pomp Peters de presumdent ob de day drink hole bottel ob Rochelle—he tink um sum new strange kind ob mead.

☞ *Printed for the especial edification and instruction of all full grown children. It is also tho't to be a remedy for the cholera.*

Antiblack Satirical Handbill Circulated in Boston, 1830. (*Reproduced from the collection of the Library of Congress*)

DECLARATION OF SENTIMENTS

—OF THE—

COLORED CITIZENS OF BOSTON,

ON THE FUGITIVE SLAVE BILL!!!

Per adjournment, the Friends of Freedom rallied at Belknap Street Church, on Friday Evening, October 5th, 1850, a vast concourse, including Fugitives and their Friends were in attendance,—the organization was completed as follows:—

LEWIS HAYDEN, *President.*

JOHN T. HILTON,
WILLIAM CRAFTS,
HENRY WATSON, } *Vice Presidents.*

WILLIAM C. NELL,
ISAAC H. SNOWDEN, } *Secretaries.*

The President stated that the present was an adjourned meeting from that of last Monday, and trusted the Vigilant Friends had come prepared for definite action on the Fugitive Slave Bill. Though the people were Seventeen Million Strong, he trusted to influences, such as might emanate from these meetings for its Nullification,—the party were now augmenting who knew their rights, and knowing, dare maintain them.

Robert Morris, Esq., called for the Report of the Committee, which was submitted by William C. Nell, as follows:

The Fugitive Slave Bill, (exhibited in its hideous deformity at our previous meeting,) has already in hot haste commenced its bloody crusade o'er the land, and the liability of ourselves and families becoming its victims at the caprice of Southern men-stealers, imperatively demands an expression, whether we will tamely submit to chains and slavery, or whether we will, at all and every hazard, Live and Die freemen.

The system of American slavery, the vilest that ever saw the sun, is a violation of every sentiment of Christianity and the antipodes of every dictate of humanity.—The slaveholder's pretensions to a claim on human property, are of no more weight than those of the midnight assassin or the pirate on the high seas. "God made all men Free,—free as the birds that cleave the air or sing on the branches,—free as the sunshine that gladdens the earth,—free as the winds that sweep over sea and land,—free at his birth,—free during his whole life,—free to-day,—this hour—this moment."

The Massachusetts Bill of Rights declares that ALL MEN are born free and equal, and have certain natural, essential and inalienable rights, among which may be reckoned the right of enjoying and defending their liberties.

The example of the Revolutionary Fathers in resisting British oppression, throwing the tea overboard in Boston Harbor, rather than submit to a three-penny tax, is a most significant one to us, when Man is likely to be deprived of his God-given liberty.

Among the incidents of that seven years' struggle for liberty, and to which the page of impartial history bears record, is the fact that the first Martyr in the attack on residents was a colored man. Crispus Attucks by name, who fell in State Street on the 5th of March, 1770. In that conflict, as also in the war of 1812, colored Americans were devoted and gallant worshippers at Freedom's shrine; and pre-eminently at New Orleans, they were warranted in believing that when the victory was achieved, they, as all who fought shoulder to shoulder, would be invited to the banquet. But lo! the white man's banquet has been held, and loud peals to liberty have reached the sky above; but the colored American's share has been to stand outside and wait for the crumbs that fell from Liberty's festive board. And to cap the climax at this advanced hour of the nation's prosperity, and the spread over all Christendom of a sentiment of liberty, fraternity and equality, the colored man, woman and child, bond and nominally free, are hunted like partridges on the mountain, if their hearts aspire for freedom.

The American people glory in the struggle of 1776, and laud the names of those who made the bloody resistance to tyranny. The battle cry of Patrick Henry of Virginia—"GIVE ME LIBERTY, OR GIVE ME DEATH,"—and that of General Warren, "MY SONS SCORN TO BE SLAVES," are immortalized, and we are proud in not being an exception to that inspiration. It warms our hearts, and will nerve our right arms, to do all, and suffer all for Liberty.

The laudation and assistance volunteered by the United States to the Poles and Greeks, and South Americans in their struggles for freedom,—the recent manifestations of sympathy with the Blouses of Paris,—the oppressed of Italy, and with Kossuth and his band of noble Hungarians, are so many incentives to the victims of Republican American despotism, to manfully assert their independence, and martyr-like, die freemen, rather than live slaves; confirming also, our pre-determined resolution to abide the issue made with us by the slave power—counting our lives not worth preserving at the expense of our liberties.

In connection with what has been previously adopted, the committee would submit the following preamble and resolutions:

Whereas, the Fugitive Slave Bill is unconstitutional, and in direct conflict with the higher law enjoined by our Saviour, "whatsoever ye would that men should do unto you, do you even so to them."

Whereas, from time immemorial, unrighteous enactments have been nullified by all who feared God rather than man; by Moses the deliverer of Israel, against wicked Pharaoh, and Daniel who welcomed incarceration in a den of Lions, rather than perjure his own soul in obedience to the tyrant's mandate.

Whereas, St. Paul expressly declares that he who will not provide for his own household, is an infidel, having denied the faith.

Whereas, the history of nations attest numerous instances where the gallows stake and gibbet have been welcomed when security of life and limb might have been purchased by obedience to inhuman statutes.

Whereas, Thousands in the land from every class and profession in life, without exception, are eagerly registering their vows to oppose this infamous enactment, at whatever cost of money, reputation or life.

Whereas, Sustained as we are, by examples of Mosaic and Christian practice, and from the history of civil society from the earliest ages; encouraged by the voices of our brethren from the East and the West, from the North, and even the tyrant's domain, the bloody South (where many true hearts beat for freedom). But above all, and independent of any suggestions, counsels or examples, guided by our own promptings for the freedom of ourselves and families, (by which we mean, of course, all those in any way exposed to danger from the slave power) and believing that Resistance to tyrants is obedience to God, we are now

Resolved, To organize a League of Freedom, composed of all those who are ready to resist this law, rescue and protect the slave, at every hazard, and who remember that

"Whether on the scaffold high,
Or in the battle's van,
The fittest place where Man can die,
Is where he dies for Man."

Resolved, That in view of the imminent danger, present and looked for, we caution every colored man, woman and child, to be careful in their walks through the highways and byways of the city by day, and doubly so, if out at night, as to where they go—how they go—and who they go with; to be guarded on side, off side and all sides; as watchful as Argus with his hundred eyes, and as executive as was Briareus, with as many hands; if seized by any one, to make the air resound with the signal-word, and as they would rid themselves of any wild beast, be prompt in their hour of peril.

Resolved, That any Commissioner who would deliver up a fugitive slave to a Southern highwayman, under this infamous and unconstitutional law, would have delivered up Jesus Christ to his persecutors for one-third of the price that Judas Iscariot did.

Resolved, That in the event of any Commissioner of Massachusetts being applied to for remanding a fugitive, we trust he will emulate the example of Judge Harrington, of Vermont, and "be satisfied with nothing short of a bill of sale from the Almighty."

Resolved, That though we learn that bribes have already been offered to our Judiciary to forestall their influence against the panting fugitive, we would not attempt any other offset, than to remind said officers that

"Man is more than Constitutions—
He'd better rot beneath the sod,
Than be true to Church and State
And doubly false to God;"

that should he, in the emergency obey God rather than the devil, by letting the oppressed go free, he will have done his part in wiping out from the escutcheon of Massachusetts the foul stain inflicted by Daniel Webster in promoting, and Samuel A. Eliot in voting for this Heaven-defying law.

Resolved, That though we gratefully acknowledge that the mane of the British Lion affords a nestling place for our brethren in danger from the claws of the American Eagle, we would, nevertheless, counsel against their leaving the soil of their birth, consecrated by their tears, toils and perils, but yet to be rendered truly, the "land of the free and the home of the brave." The ties of consanguinity, bid all remain who would lend a helping hand to the millions now in bonds. But at all events, if the soil of Bunker Hill, Concord and Lexington is the last bulwark of liberty, we can nowhere fill more honorable graves.

Resolved, That we do earnestly express the hope that the citizens of Boston will rally in Faneuil Hall, and send forth in the ear of all christendom their opinion of the infamous Fugitive Slave Bill, and of their intention to disobey its decrees; their voice, uttered in the Cradle of Liberty, will assure us as nothing else can, whether they are to be reckoned on the side of liberty or slavery—whether they will vouchsafe to us their aid, or will assist the manthief in hurling us and our little ones into interminable bondage.

Resolved, That this meeting would invite the clergymen in this city and vicinity to dedicate a day or part thereof, in presenting to their people by prayer and sermon, their Christian duty to the flying fugitive, and also in acceding to requisitions of this atrocious Bill.

Resolved, That as in union is strength, and in this crisis a combination of power is all-important, this meeting recommend the calling of a New England Convention of the friends of Liberty to operate against the Fugitive Law, and to devise ways and means for consolidating their resources here on the soil.

Resolved, That the doings of this and preceding meeting be published for wide circulation.

The report was accepted, and the resolutions adopted by a unanimous vote.

John T. Hilton, in an eloquent and earnest speech advocated the resolutions—remarking that twenty-five years ago he eulogized, as the greatest talent in the country, Daniel Webster for his efforts on Plymouth Rock on the slavery question, and he regretted exceedingly that that talent should have been used in favor of the odious bill. He was no longer to be trusted by the friends of liberty, for he had done more evil, and committed more sin than a thousand such men as the late Professor Webster ever did. This speaker concluded his remarks which were listened to with marked attention, by saying that when his services should be wanted in defence of their rights, he would desire no greater office than to lead them on to battle and to victory.

Joshua B. Smith, hoped no one in that meeting would preach *Peace*, for as Patrick Henry said, "*There is no Peace.*" He narrated with much feeling the increased consternation of his much loved friend—a Fugitive Slave. Since the passage of this infernal bill a near relative of his claimant having been repeatedly seen skulking around his place of business, evidently anticipating the hour of successful seizure, but that he had done his utmost to dispel the agitation of his friend, bidding him at the outset show himself a man,—*If Liberty is not worth fighting for it is not worth having.* He advised every fugitive to arm himself with a revolver—if he could not buy one otherwise to sell his coat for that purpose. As for himself, and he thus exhorted others, he should be kind and courteous to all, even the slave dealer, until the moment of an attack upon his liberty. He should not be taken alive, but upon the slave catcher's head be the consequences. When he could not live here in Boston a freeman, in the language of Socrates, "*He had lived long enough.*" Mr. Smith in conclusion made a demonstration of one mode of defence, which those who best know him say would be exemplified to the *hilt*.

Robert Johnson proclaimed that the meeting was largely composed of actors, and not speakers merely, they were men of over-alls—men of the wharf—those who could do heavy work in the hour of difficulty. He administered a timely caution to the women, who, in pursuit of washing and other work, visited the hotels and boarding houses, that they should be on the constant look-out for the Southern slave catcher or the *Northern accessory*, and as they valued their liberty be prepared for any emergency. [This word to the *wise* women and others, was greeted with lively demonstrations; some remarking that the spirit exhibited by the women some years since, in a slave rescue from the Supreme Court, was yet alive and ready for action.] He would have it a well understood point in our creed of vigilance, in no case to be ourselves the aggressors; in this it was all important to be cautious; we will not go to the depots or elsewhere after the slave hunter, but when he rushes upon our buckler—*kill him.*

Dr. Dan'l Mann spoke of the present state of affairs as affecting us all, white men as well as colored, and detailed many liabilities to which the Fugitive Slave Bill exposed both. He was opposed to war and the spirit of war, but the existing crisis was one that superceded the ordinary, scruples:

"Though space and law the Stag we lend
Ere hound we slip or bow we bend,
Who cares how, where or when
The prowling Fox is trapped or slain!"

R. B. Rogers—would have the Fugitive and his friends remember that it was with the United States Government they were to contend, and that their position in resisting this obnoxious law was that of *Rebels*,—a name however which he did not hesitate to accept, if loyality to the constitution made him false to humanity. He urged the colored people to strive in securing the moral strength of the community in their favor as a potent lever for their enlargement; but would nevertheless assure them that in the event being forced upon them of a personal contest for Liberty, *God was their helper.*

Mr. Garrison—Though a non-resistant himself and determined with the help of God to live and die such, would yet call upon all to be consistent with their own principles, reminding them that William Tell, and George Washington were among the glorious names in the world's annals of patriotic devotion to the shrine of Liberty; but after all, the fugitives in this city and elsewhere would be more indebted to the moral power of public sentiment than by any display of physical resistance. In appreciation of their resolution, invoking the religious sentiment in behalf of the poor fugitive, he would submit an address to the clergy;—its reading was called for and produced a marked sensation upon the meeting, and on motion was unanimously incorporated with the minutes. Mr. Garrison also read an extract from Rev. Henry Ward Beecher's late tribute for the fugitive, pledging himself in a characteristic manner to succor and defend him at every conceivable sacrifice. The applause which this demonstration received would have abundantly convinced its noble hearted author that his proffered aid had not fallen upon ungrateful soil;—many prayers ascended to the fugitives' God, for blessings upon him who would thus commit himself unreservedly for the victims of American Slavery.

Father Hanson—would tell our oppressors that in condemning resistance on the part of the colored people, they were denouncing the examples of Washington and Jefferson, and all Martyrs of Liberty. He concurred with Mr. Garrison and others in a reliance upon moral power, but the meeting well understood that in a crisis for *Liberty or Death*, the speaker would not be quietly led like a lamb to the slaughter.

Charles List, Esq.,—was glad that the fugitives were prepared to defend themselves, and that they solicited a Faneuil Hall meeting of Boston citizens, where they may learn whether their lives and liberties can be secured in the land of the Pilgrim Fathers, or whether men catchers may make hunting grounds of the streets of Boston, driving them at the approach of an inclement season to seek in a foreign land, that safety and refuge from oppression which they cannot find here at home.

Wm. G. Allen being called upon declined in favor of C. C. Briggs, of Vermont, the fugitives' friend. Mr. Briggs responded in thoughts that breathed and words that burned for Liberty; testifying to his pride in being a son of the Green Mountain State, where the sentiments of the people had rendered unnecessary any law relative to slavery. He would yield to no man in efforts to befriend and protect the victim of this inhuman law; and though he would caution all against any injudicious movements by way of resistance, yet he could not but express the opinion that those who would not defend, to the death, their Wives, Sisters and Families from the slave hunter were totally unworthy of a position in civil society.

Rev. Elijah Grimson urged calling upon the Mayor, and police authorities of Boston for defence. [This was generally opposed, knowing that the city officers were not required by the law to arrest the fugitive, and believing that the police force wese not at all ambitious of hunting slaves, the appeal was negatived by an overwhelming vote.]

Charles Lenox Remond—having received word of the meeting at his home in Salem left in express haste to be present and though at a late hour, in obedience to a hearty call, gave vent to one of his best efforts; his zeal to reach the meeting, and his liberty inspiring eloquence was loudly and gratefully appreciated. He alluded to the fact that the infamous provisions of the Slave Bill made all colored persons fugitives, imposing on them the necessity of unceasing vigilance. Numbers are nothing in a good cause;

"Thrice armed is he who hath his quarrel just."

The idea of leaving our homes and firesides was in every sense a mistaken one; the Old Bay State should be our Canada. Boston is the Thermopylæ of the anti-slavery cause. Let us be ready in the trial hour to insure its analogy with that classic spot rendered so illustrious by Leonidas and his Spartan Band, or like the more modern but not less significant—Bunker Hill. The history of our country's struggles for Liberty had never been disgraced by a *colored* Arnold; if then we have not proved traitors to the white man, in God's name shall we not prove true to ourselves? He believed that the Fugitive Slave Law had been enacted in great part at the instance of the hand maid of slavery, the Colonization Society in the wicked hope that the fear of being recaptured into bondage would move the colored man to emigrate to Liberia. But this feature only made the whole more damnable, and was to be opposed at all and every point. After rebuking the colored people for lack of anti-slavery character, he declared that he would not yield to any institution or individual that would abridge his liberties or his efforts for the fugitive, and was happy in believing that the colored citizens of Boston would do their whole duty and defend themselves.

Dr. Bowditch moved a general circulation among the masses of the address to the clergy.

The meeting was further addressed by Messrs. Spear, Pierce, Pickett, and others.

On motion the Address to the Clergy was adopted by acclamation and ordered to be published.

After a hymn of Liberty the gathering separated mutually pledging, as did Hannibal, "*Eternal Hostility to Slavery!*"

LEWIS HAYDEN, *President.*

WILLIAM C. NELL, *Secretary.*

Address to the Clergy of Massachusetts.

We, the trembling, prescribed and hunted fugitives from chattel slavery, now scattered through the various towns and villages of Massachusetts, and momentarily liable to be seized by the strong arm of government, and hurried back to stripes, tortures and a bondage, "one hour of which is fraught with more misery than ages of that which your fathers rose in rebellion to oppose,"—most humbly, importunately, and by the mercies of Christ, implore you at this distressing crisis, to "lift up your voices like a trumpet" against the Fugitive Slave Bill, recently adopted by Congress, and designed for our sure and immediate re-enslavement.

You claim, in a special sense, to be witnesses for God — the ambassadors of Him who came to bind up the broken-hearted, to proclaim liberty to the captives, and the opening of the prison to them that are bound. As you would be clear of the blood of all men, it is for you to give to the down-trodden and the oppressed your deepest sympathies, and to hold up to reprobation those who "frame mischief by a law." It is for you to declare the supremacy of the eternal law of God over all human enactments, whether men will hear or forbear.

After years of unrequited labor, of enforced degradation, of unutterable and inconceivable misery, we have succeeded in making our escape from the Southern house of bondage, and are now attempting to lead quiet and peaceable lives in this Commonwealth, and by expanding our faculties and cultivating our moral nature, to "glorify God in our bodies and spirits, which are His." By the recent law of Congress, it is made a highly criminal act to shelter us from the slave-hunter, or to refuse to participate in our capture, at the command of the appointed Commissioners.

Now, therefore, by the solemn injunction of a Christian apostle, "Remember them that are in bonds as bound with them," we implore you, from your pulpits to denounce that iniquitous law!

By the command of Christ, "Whatsoever ye would that men should do to you, do ye even so to them," denounce the law!

By all the horrors and iniquities compressed into that system of slavery, which Wesley has justly styled "the sum of all villainies," denounce the law!

By the cherished memories of Pilgrim Fathers and Revolutionary Sires, denounce the law!

By your warm approval of your country's Declaration of Independence, denounce the law!

By your belief in the scriptural affirmation, that by one God are we all created, and that he "hath made of one blood all nations of men to dwell on all the face of the earth," denounce the law!

By all the woes and warnings pronounced by the prophets against those who refuse to hide the outcast, and bewray him that wandereth—who decree unrighteous decrees, and write grievousness which they have prescribed, to turn aside the needy from judgment—denounce the law!

Thus will you exalt the Christian religion, oppose the mightiest obstacle that stands in the way of human redemption, exert such a moral influence as shall break the rod of the oppressor, secure for yourselves the blessings of those who are ready to perish, and hear the thrilling declaration in the great day of judgment, "Inasmuch as ye did it unto one of the least of these, my brethren, ye did it unto me."

Blacks Protest the Fugitive Slave Bill, Handbill, 1850. (*Reproduced from the collection of the Library of Congress*)

The African Meeting House, Smith Court, about 1860. (*Courtesy of the Society for the Preservation of New England Antiquities*)

Boston Courthouse under Guard after the Capture of Thomas Sims, Fugitive Slave, 1851.
(*Reproduced from the collection of the Library of Congress*)

The Charge of the 54th Massachusetts Colored Regiment at Fort Wagner, South Carolina

John Rock Admitted to Practice before the United States Supreme Court, 1865. (*Reproduced from the collection of the Library of Congress*)

Disruption of John Brown Memorial Meeting at Tremont Temple, 1860. *(Reproduced from*

7/The Integration of Abolition

Historians have traditionally dated the militant antislavery movement in Boston from 1831, when William Lloyd Garrison began to publish the *Liberator*. This view, however, ignores important antecedents to Garrison's efforts. Abolitionism in Boston dated from the late 18th century and was almost entirely a black endeavor during the early years. It was carried on through the black church, the Prince Hall Masons, and several other black associations. By 1826, a group of blacks had formed the Massachusetts General Colored Association, the most significant pre-Garrisonian abolitionist group in Boston. Many in this group, including its best known member, David Walker, became outspoken advocates of immediate emancipation and racial equality.

Before 1830, black abolitionists in Boston found little sympathetic support among the city's whites. In 1831, however, William Lloyd Garrison established himself and his newspaper as a strong ally of those who believed in liberty and freedom for all Americans. In the 1820s Garrison, a native of Newburyport, Massachusetts, had edited a number of reform-oriented newspapers in Massachusetts and Vermont and had sponsored at least one campaign for the liberation of black slaves in the nation's capital. This young man in his mid-twenties had been an antislavery advocate in Baltimore before coming to Boston. He had worked as a co-editor with Quaker abolitionist Benjamin Lundy on the *Genius of Universal Emancipation*. During these early years Garrison had supported the American Colonization Society's program for gradual emancipation and the colonization of black Americans on the west coast of Africa. By 1831, Garrison had become an advocate of immediate emancipation and was increasingly distrustful of the aims of the American Colonization Society. Garrison attributed his changed attitude to the influence of his "colored friends."[1]

The *Liberator* was an antislavery organ, but it was also a journal for black Americans. It contained obituaries and public announcements from black communities throughout the East and letters and articles concerning black problems written by blacks from as far away as Colorado and California. The *Liberator* also served the local black community, announcing political and social events and articulating political concerns, providing inspirational literature for spiritual and moral guidance, and carrying advertisements for blacks seeking jobs or housing. It provided valuable information for blacks contemplating travel, detailing social and political conditions and the types and extent of discrimination which might be expected under almost any circumstance. Although the *Liberator* strongly reflected the viewpoint of its editor, it performed an invaluable service to the blacks of Boston, aiding the development of the community which had begun almost a half century before.

The *Liberator* had an undeniable influence on Boston itself, helping to establish the city's reputation as a stronghold of antislavery sentiment and a haven for fugitive slaves. In at least one respect, however, the *Liberator* handicapped the development of the black community. Its service as a community newspaper and the intense loyalty engendered by its editor probably retarded the development of a black press in Boston. Except for two abortive attempts, Boston did not have a black-owned and operated newspaper during the antebellum period. In 1838, Benjamin Roberts, "a young man of enterprise and character," established the *Anti-Slavery Herald*. The paper was intended to be an antislavery journal by and for blacks. Only a few issues were printed, however, and the enterprise soon failed. Although the specific reasons for the failure are not altogether clear, it seems reasonable, considering the heavy subscription of blacks to the *Liberator* and the relative lack of financial resources within the black community, that Boston's blacks lacked the means to support a second newspaper. The problem of a limited and poor audience was one faced by the black-oriented press in general. For this reason many black newspapers were relatively short-lived.[2]

Also, Roberts received some opposition from some white Garrison supporters. Amos Phelps, a minister and abolitionist, provided a letter of recommendation for Roberts in his efforts to establish a printing office in May 1838, but by June he had asked for its return. A rift had developed between Roberts and some white abolitionists over the militant tone of the newspaper. Roberts was charged with organizing the paper out of self-interest and not antislavery principle. He answered these charges with countercharges of abolitionist hypocrisy. The whole venture, Roberts asserted, had been undertaken in an effort to improve the information available to the black community and ultimately improve the mental and physical condition of black people. He charged that prejudice caused "professed abolitionists" to attempt to "muzzle, exterminate and put down the efforts of certain colored individuals affecting the welfare of their colored brethren."[3]

Although there is no evidence that the black community rose to Roberts' defense, neither was he ostracized. He continued to play a significant role in the struggle for integration and abolition in the 1840s and 1850s. In 1853 Roberts attempted to establish a black newspaper under the name *Self*

Elevator, but again the venture was short-lived, for although by the 1850s Roberts had become well known in the community, the *Liberator* was already too well established and Garrison too well loved to allow for a competitive sheet.[4]

That Boston had no black press is significant, for although the city's blacks could depend upon a few out-of-town black newspapers like *Freedom's Journal* (later *The Colored American*) and the *North Star* for national news, most local news was sifted through the editorship of William Lloyd Garrison, a friend to be sure, but not a member of the black community. Some blacks rightly complained that all points of view were not fairly represented in the *Liberator*. Garrison was an integrationist who often ignored views favoring independent action for the black community.[5] Of course, a black integrationist might have been no more fair to black separatists than was Garrison himself.

Perhaps the most valuable contribution which might have been made by a black newspaper would have been in the areas of employment, training, self-esteem, and racial pride. The *Liberator* did employ some blacks, yet it did not emphasize black employment or training. Although William C. Nell held a responsible position for a number of years and seemed to be next in line for general agent or "chief man" of the *Liberator*, in 1853 he was passed over in favor of Robert F. Wallcut, a white man and a comparative newcomer to the firm. If there had been a black newspaper in the city, no doubt blacks would have held a greater variety and number of positions.[6]

William Lloyd Garrison himself was an important link between the black and white societies of Boston. He was instrumental in building an alliance between developing white abolitionist sentiment and veteran black abolitionists. It was at Garrison's urging and after he had laid considerable groundwork that fifteen white men gathered in the office of Samuel Sewall on November 13, 1831, to discuss the formation of a regional antislavery society. A month later another such meeting was held and a committee was appointed to draft a constitution for the proposed organization.[7]

Blacks, realizing the significance of an abolitionist group which included some of Boston's most prominent white citizens, offered the African Meeting House on Belknap Street as a location for the gathering. It was there, on the evening of January 6, 1832, that the young William C. Nell stood in the snow to witness the formal creation of the New England Anti-Slavery Society. Although the twelve signatories of the preamble to the society's constitution were white, perhaps a quarter of the seventy-two who signed the constitution itself were black.[8]

The fiery articles and editorials of the *Liberator*, the inspiring speeches of its editor, and the professed purposes of the new antislavery organization all encouraged blacks. The New England Anti-Slavery Society pledged itself to work not only for the abolition of slavery, but also for the improvement of the condition of free blacks. The influence of some prominent white Bostonian antislavery men made Boston one of the most important centers of antislavery activity in the country. Despite the discrimination and prejudice with which black Bostonians contended, the community was aware of the comparative liberalism of the city. In 1819, in a speech before the African Society, Paul Dean, a white minister of the First Universal Church in Boston, had struck a responsive chord with his contention that the Commonwealth of Massachusetts provided considerably more protection and equality to its "colored" than most any other state in the union. Although Dean was more optimistic in 1819 than most blacks were in 1831, the presence of enthusiastic white abolitionists was encouraging.[9]

While most white abolitionists were received with appreciation and honor by the black community, Garrison held a special place in the hearts of blacks. His vehement denunciations of the institution of slavery and those who supported it and his willingness to work for racial justice and equality in Boston were significant factors in explaining his special importance to the black community. It was, however, his willingness to associate with blacks as human beings on the basis of social equality which made Garrison almost unique. He listened to and seriously considered arguments put forth by the black community at a time when many whites believed blacks incapable of rational and intelligent argument.[10]

Many blacks found Garrison not only a willing co-worker in the cause of freedom but a good friend as well. He was a guest in the homes of blacks on a variety of occasions. As a young child, the black abolitionist William J. Watkins first met Garrison when he was a houseguest of Watkins' father in Baltimore.

In 1833, Garrison was honored at the home of George Putnam, a black hairdresser in Boston, and was presented with an inscribed silver cup in appreciation for his service to the black community. The cup was presented on behalf of a group of Garrison supporters which included seamen and waiters as well as teachers and ministers. Garrison was popular among the various segments of the black community.[11] Blacks realized the danger to which Garrison exposed himself in their behalf. On October 21, 1835, Garrison was mobbed in Boston by a number of white "gentlemen of property and standing" who broke into a meeting of the Boston Female Anti-Slavery Society where Garrison was speaking. After an exciting chase, during which a black carpenter attempted to hide him, Garrison was captured and assaulted by the mob. Blacks were among those who came to his aid, rescuing him in a daring carriage escape The next day John B. Vashon, a black abolitionist who had witnessed the incident, visited Garrison, presenting him with a new hat to replace the one lost during the attack. Garrison expressed regret that their dinner engagement for the previous evening had been interrupted.[12]

More than most abolitionists, Garrison was hosted by blacks while on speaking tours and business trips. Blacks were also houseguests of the Garrisons. After dining at the Garrison home, Charlotte Forten reported that not only was the evening enjoyable but that Mrs. Garrison was "one of the loveliest persons I have ever seen, worthy of such a husband."[13]

Garrison also used his influence to aid individual blacks in need and in so doing provided a valuable service to the community. Henry Mitchell worked as a journeyman on the *Liberator* for two years. When his services were no longer needed, Garrison contacted a friend, Oliver Johnson, to secure this "capable compositor" future employment.[14] Garrison provided similar services for Edmund Quincy Putnam, son of George Putnam.[15] He also arranged shelter for those in need. Nathaniel Paul had married a white English woman and, because of the violent reaction of many whites, was unable to find a place to live. Garrison arranged for Mrs. Paul to live in Northampton at the home of George W. Benson, Garrison's father-in-law, for one year while Nathaniel Paul was on a speaking tour. The lady was to do suitable work to help defray some of the cost of her support, and Garrison was to provide the remainder.[16]

Blacks deeply appreciated Garrison's respect for and aid to their community and in return they opened their halls and churches to him when he could find no other platform in the city. They subscribed in great numbers to his *Liberator*, and in its early days when the newspaper suffered financial difficulties blacks provided the funds which allowed it to continue. When in 1833 Garrison traveled to England soliciting funds for a manual training school for black youth and speaking against African colonization, about half the contributions financing the trip came from the black community.[17] He was revered as more than a good and faithful friend. He was, in the words of one former slave, "the Moses raised up by God, to deliver his modern Israel from bondage."[18] "Mr. Garrison," recalled William C. Nell, "has at times, been supposed to be a colored man because of his long, patient and persevering devotion to our cause."[19]

Garrison was not oblivious to the warmth and admiration shown him by blacks. He valued his black friends and took pride in his position of respect among them, particularly in his special place among Boston's blacks. After a speaking engagement before a black audience in Philadelphia, he wrote that although the audience had been large, "the colored Philadelphians as a body, do not evince that interest and warmth of attachment which characterize my Boston friends."[20] His black support must have been especially striking in light of the considerable hostility which so many whites in northern cities, as well as on southern plantations, felt toward Garrison and his antislavery work.

In 1831, the state of Georgia offered a reward of five thousand dollars for Garrison, and there were many in Boston who might well have desired to rid the city of his influence. Aware of the danger to which Garrison was exposed, blacks tried in a variety of ways and with substantial success to provide for his protection. Black bodyguards armed with clubs followed him from his office to his home each evening. Because of Garrison's commitment to nonviolence, guards had to be careful that he not detect their presence.[21]

There were important areas of disagreement between Garrison and many of his black admirers, primarily centering on his rejection of the political process as a means to antislavery ends and his commitment to the philosophy of nonviolence. Garrison arrived at his opposition to slavery as part of a radical analysis of American society. His philosophy of nonresistance was opposed to coercion in all forms. Individual freedom should be maximized, he believed, and should not be abrogated by slavery's lash or by governmental proclamation. He interpreted the United States Constitution as a coercive document which protected the rights of slaveholders. Garrison's refusal to participate in politics reflected his disillusion with America's government.

Most blacks did not share his analysis of American society. They saw the evil of slavery in more directly racial terms, with their opposition rooted in the experience of discrimination and racial oppression. Instead of the restructuring of society that Garrison called for, blacks demanded that society be reformed. They wanted the American ideals of freedom and justice to be applied to racial policies, creating racial parity. These differences in analysis were reflected in differences in strategies. Garrison's reliance on moral suasion was dictated by his commitment to nonresistance and nonviolence. Blacks had no such limiting philosophy and were likely to use any means which seemed most practical.

Garrison's goals were radical, moving beyond racial equality to more general equality. The goal of blacks for equal opportunity was inherently more moderate. It was extending this opportunity to blacks which was radical in the American context. Most blacks may not have understood how attaining racial equality would fundamentally change the society or what changes might be necessary before it could be attained. Since practicality guided their activism, they adopted a wide range of strategies from petitioning the government and political organization to the use of violent civil disobedience.

Politics was a potentially powerful weapon for blacks in New England. As late as 1860, this region, with the exception of Connecticut, was the only area which extended equal suffrage rights to blacks. Although antebellum black protest in the state had depended more on the petition than the ballot, about 50 percent of the eligible black voters paid their poll tax in preparation for the exercising of their right.[22] In New York and Pennsylvania, by contrast, black suffrage was limited by law. New York blacks struggled during the antebellum period to overcome a state constitutional ruling in 1821 that disqualified all blacks with landed property worth less than $250. In Pennsylvania a similar fight proceeded after a state constitutional convention added the word "white" to the list of voting qualifications in 1838. This struggle for political rights grew in intensity after 1840 and involved state and local protest across the country, from New Jersey to California.[23]

In Boston, blacks held special political meetings and advertised in newspapers as early as the mid-1830s, urging fellow blacks to vote for Whig candidates in state elections. Despite Garrison's personal preferences, he did not condemn blacks who sought to cast a vote against slavery. Instead, he urged that blacks not vote for any particular party, but for individual candidates with antislavery concerns.[24] The emphasis on black political action was encouraged by the development, during the 1840s and 1850s, of political parties seeking to limit the extension of slavery. Eight black clergymen were instrumental in the establishment, in 1840, of the American and Foreign Anti-Slavery Society, an organization which opposed Garrison's stand against political action for antislavery purposes. This new political wing of the abolition movement joined with the Liberty party, dedicated to antislavery principles.

Blacks in Boston generally remained faithful to Garrison in this split at least until the late 1840s. In 1843, the National Negro Convention meeting in Buffalo, New York, endorsed the Liberty party platform. Two influential Garrisonians, Charles Lenox Remond and Frederick Douglass, cast dissenting votes.[25] Remond was especially opposed to black support for any party because he agreed with Garrison that the Constitution was itself proslavery. Within five years, however, the attitude of many black Garrisonians had changed. Remond abandoned his nonvoting position to cast a ballot for Stephen C. Phillips, the Free Soil candidate for governor of Massachusetts in 1848. Phillips' support for larger appropriations for black schools drew a number of black votes.[26]

In the early 1850s, Douglass broke with Garrison partly over the political question and became the Liberty party nominee for secretary of state of New York. By 1850, William C. Nell, a long-time Garrison supporter, also disagreed with Garrison's political stance and was nominated by the Free Soil party for the Massachusetts legislature. Robert Morris found it impossible to resist urging fellow blacks to use their vote in the fight to integrate the city's public schools. Although he thought of himself as a political independent, he was nominated by the Free Soilers for mayor of Boston.[27] Even Garrison saw the Free Soil party as an encouraging sign of antislavery progress. He remained firm, however, in his personal opposition to participation in a political system which he believed protected slaveholders.[28] The bond between Garrison and the black community went far deeper than adherence to a mutually held philosophy or ideology. Nell, for example, retained affection for him and six years later attempted to raise funds to purchase a home for the Garrison family.[29]

In the 1850s Boston's black community moved in substantial numbers toward political action. In December of 1852, public meetings were held under the auspices of the Colored Citizens of the Free Soil party. William J. Watkins, Garrisonian and former agent for the *Liberator*, urged that every eligible black voter support the Free Soil party. Robert Johnson, a waiter, encouraged blacks to pay taxes, as he was doing for the first time in many years, in order that they might vote for Free Soil candidates.[30] While rejecting Garrison's nonpolitical philosophy, blacks assembled in these meetings continued to express their personal admiration by giving him a unanimous vote of confidence. Four years later, on August 26, 1856, black Bostonians held a mass meeting, and passed a resolution vowing their support for Republican candidates. They resolved "that we the Colored Citizens of Boston will support . . . John C. Fremont . . . as President of the United States and William L. Dayton of New Jersey as Vice-President." Acknowledging that the Republican party was not an antislavery party they added, "We do not pledge ourselves to go further with the Republicans than the Republicans will go with us."[31] Among those present at this meeting was Coffin Pitts, an original member of the Massachusetts General Colored Association and Garrison's co-worker since the early 1830s.

Garrison accepted this defection from his leadership with remarkable grace. Except for his condemnation of the Liberty party's weak antislavery stance and some rather cutting denunciations of Douglass after their split in the early 1850s, he never directly attacked his black Boston supporters for their deviation. Clearly, political disagreement did not disturb the personal relationship between Garrison and Nell, Remond, Pitts and others throughout this period. Recent scholarship indicates that there may not have been such a clear difference of principle between Garrison and political abolitionists as has been heretofore assumed. If this is so, it might help to explain the continued good relations between Garrison and politically active blacks.[32]

Not only did many blacks in Boston find it difficult to work within the bounds of Garrison's political approach, but they also found his pacificism constraining. Most blacks never really accepted pacifism as a principle even though there were instances of nonviolent protest by individuals.[33] Since the late eighteenth century, when Prince Hall had counseled patience in the struggle against slavery and discrimination, local and national events had prompted a growing militancy in the black community. By the mid-nineteenth century, this militancy erupted in the open and sometimes violent defense of fugitive slaves and defiance of federal laws.

One year after the founding of the New England Anti-Slavery Society, there was a move to combine the activities of this and the older black abolitionist group, the Massachusetts General Colored Association. On January 15, 1833, Joshua Easton, representing the black organization, presented the following communication to the first annual meeting of the New England Anti-Slavery Society:

> The Massachusetts General Colored Association cordially approving the objects and principle of the New England Anti-Slavery Society, would respectfully communicate their desire to become auxiliary thereto. They have accordingly chosen one of their members to attend the Annual Meeting of the Society as their delegate, (Mr. Joshua Easton of North Bridgewater), and solicit his acceptance in that capacity.
>
> Thomas Dalton, Pres.
> William G. Nell, V. P.
> James G. Barbadoes, Sec.[34]

This communication was accepted by the society. The Reverend Samuel Snowden of the African Methodist Episcopal Church was elected as a counselor to the New England Anti-Slavery Society. Under Garrison's influence the society also adopted resolutions pledging itself not only to the abolition of slavery in America, but also to work toward the improvement of the condition of free blacks and to counteract "the measures and principles of the American Colonization society."[35]

This latter resolution was a particular concern of Boston blacks. While they were working to integrate the abolition movement, the separatist solution of colonization was hotly debated. The American Colonization Society, formed in December 1816 in Washington, D.C., directed its efforts "to colonize, with their own consent, on the coast of Africa, or such other places as Congress shall deem expedient, the people of colour in our country, already free, and those others, who may hereafter be liberated by the humanity of individuals, or the laws of the States."[36] Although by the 1830s blacks generally, and Boston's blacks especially, emphatically rejected this colonization program, a few influential blacks had supported such a plan. Paul Cuffe, a black Quaker from New Bedford, Massachusetts, was an important proponent of African colonization in the early years of the century. He was the son of Cuffe Slocum, a native African who had been brought to Massachusetts and sold as a slave in the eighteenth century. His mother, Ruth Moses, was of local Indian descent.[37]

By the time of his death in 1759, Slocum had been emancipated and had acquired a one-hundred-acre farm in Westport, Massachusetts. Paul Cuffe became a seaman, making his first sea voyage at age sixteen, and eventually acquired his own vessel. In 1811 he visited the British African Colony of Sierra Leone, which had been organized by former slaves in the late eighteenth century. He was so impressed with the colony that he became a strong supporter of African colonization for blacks. Cuffe attempted unsuccessfully to secure Congressional support for the transportation of American blacks to Sierra Leone. In 1815 after the wartime restraints on shipping were lifted, Cuffe at his own expense transported nine families, comprising thirty-eight individuals, to the West African colony. He then provided Robert Finley of the American Colonization Society with encouraging accounts of the colony's potential.[38]

In the summer of 1812, Cuffe communicated with the African Society in Boston asking for their support in his colonization venture. On August 3 he received a letter from that organization indicating some support and the willingness of several members to travel to Africa.[39] In a petition to the president and Congress in 1813, Cuffe reported that his proposal to form a colony was making strong headway.[40] He was overly optimistic, however, in his account of the "zeal" with which Boston blacks received his back-to-Africa plans. There was opposition from some blacks who expressed the fear that American blacks once in Africa would take advantage of African natives and become slave traders. This opposition was great enough to frustrate Cuffe's plans to settle significant numbers of Boston's blacks in Africa.[41]

Another supporter of African colonization was John Russwurm. In 1829, Russwurm helped to found and edit *Freedom's Journal* in New York City, the first black newspaper in the United States. His pro-colonization position brought such opposition from blacks that he was forced to resign from that position. In 1829, Russwurm migrated to the African colony of Liberia. There he found a self-governing colony that had been established by the American Colonization Society earlier in the decade. The colony was run by "colored men exercising all the duties of office . . . many fulfilling their important trusts with much dignity. It was a republic in miniature." Russwurm quickly established himself as a colonial leader and became superintendent of the colony's six schools and later governor of the province of Cape Palmas.[42]

Despite the activities of Cuffe, Russwurm, and other prominent blacks, the opposition of Boston's blacks to African colonization, which became progressively more vehement during the early nineteenth century, was indicative of the sentiment of other free black communities. In 1816, shortly after the African Colonization Society had announced its plans for transporting free people of color to Africa, a wave of protest swept through free black communities throughout the North. In January, 1817, a mass meeting of more than three thousand blacks at Philadelphia's Bethel Church unanimously condemned African colonization. Many blacks viewed the colonization society as a racist organization seeking to degrade and separate their race.[43]

Evident in the opposition of free blacks to African colonization was a deep feeling of loyalty to and responsibility for their brethren in slavery. In the 1820s, free blacks, who pointed out that their removal from America would strengthen slavery by expelling its most active adversaries, were instrumental in William Lloyd Garrison's conversion to anti-colonization.[44] Further, it was charged that slaveholders would exile disruptive slaves, leaving the more submissive slaves in bondage. This accomplished, slaveholders might find slavery a much less frustrating institution. In 1832, Garrison issued one of the strongest denunciations of African colonization to date, calling its advocates enemies of immediate emancipation, apologists for slavery and slaveholders, and "disparager[s] of free blacks." He accused them of conspiring to increase the value of slaves.[45]

Blacks were not only concerned with the plight of slaves who would remain in America. They were also adamant in their insistence that, as native Americans who fought and died to establish the nation in the American Revolution and to defend it in the War of 1812, they had a right not only to be allowed to remain in the United States, but to receive the full protection of its laws and the full benefits granted to all its citizens. Many blacks viewed colonization as an attempt to deny those rights and to exile them to a land in which few white Americans would wish to reside. In Boston, Robert Roberts, James G. Barbadoes, John T. Hilton, Coffin Pitts, and Thomas Cole called for a meeting of the black community on February 15, 1831, to consider the question of African colonization. As a result of this and subsequent meetings in March, resolutions were passed condemning the Colonization Society as "a clamorous, abusive and peace-disturbing combination," and denouncing those supporting the society as "false prophets." These resolutions were passed unanimously.[46]

In their comments denouncing African colonization blacks revealed typically American views of Africa. It was evident that some blacks, like most Americans, viewed Africa as an uncivilized jungle continent inhabited only by savage cannibalistic natives and dangerous wild animals. Glowing reports of progress and prosperity communicated to American blacks by those who settled in the Liberian colony did not allay the fears or alter the stereotypes of the African continent for most of black America. Blacks persisted in the belief that they would not fare well in "any [such] tropical climate."[47] Significantly, the church known since its founding in 1805 as the African Baptist Church changed its name in 1837 to the First Independent Baptist Church of People of Color of Boston "for the very good reason that the name African is ill applied to a church composed of American citizens."[48]

The removal of "African" from organizational names was not universal among blacks in Boston after their denunciation of African colonization. In 1838, the African Methodist Episcopal Zion Church was organized and the African Methodist Episcopal Church, founded twenty years earlier, retained its original name. Yet, most black organizations formed after 1830 did not use "African" as a descriptive title. One black literary society was termed the Adelphic Union and another the Boston Mutual Lyceum. Other black groups bore names like the Attucks Quartet and the Histrionic Club, a drama group. A black military company formed in 1854 was called the Massasoit Guards.

Yet, black opposition to emigration was not so simple as it appeared at first glance. At a time when most blacks rejected African settlement, there was wide support among blacks in Boston for the Wilberforce Colony in Canada. The wife and children of William C. Nell resided for a time at Wilberforce.[49] Boston blacks also supported the efforts of the National Convention of the Free People of Color to purchase Canadian lands for black settlement. Yet it was the Reverend Hosea Easton, a member of the Boston delegation to the convention in 1832, who recommended that the convention reject African colonization—a recommendation that was accepted.[50]

Boston's blacks were not alone in their acceptance of Canadian colonization and rejection of African colonization. A meeting of blacks in Brooklyn, New York, in 1831 approved a resolution which summed up the preference of blacks generally for Canada over Africa. In a telling statement, they left no doubt that in their eyes Africa was not a fit place for black Americans and that Canada was a "place far better adapted to our constitutions, our habits, and our morals."[51]

A Columbia, Pennsylvania, meeting in the same year agreed "that we will support the colony at Canada, the climate being healthier, better adapted to our constitution, and far more consonant with our views than that of Africa."[52] For all their physical separation from white society, most blacks clearly shared the American opinion of Africa.

The unwillingness of blacks in Boston to accept emigration as a solution to their problems remained strong throughout the antebellum period. During the 1850s, there was a rebirth of colonization spirit in New York, Philadelphia, and other northern cities. Boston's blacks never favored such separation, partly because of the influence of William Lloyd Garrison and other whites, but mostly because of the exceptional progress black Bostonians had made by the 1850s.

By 1855, Boston's public schools had been legally desegregated; many, certainly not all, public theaters and places of entertainment were open to blacks, and as early as 1843 the Boston Lyceum, one of the nation's first, admitted patrons irrespective of color. By the early 1850s, travel accommodations for black Bostonians journeying within the state were greatly improved. In 1849, Frederick Douglass reported that "not a single railroad can be found in any part of Massachusetts, where a colored man is treated and esteemed in any other light than that of a man and traveler." Although blacks did not vote or hold office in the state and city in significant numbers, partially because of tax requirements, their right to do so had been acknowledged for decades.[53]

This relatively liberal situation in Boston contrasted sharply with that in other towns in New England or cities generally across the North. In New York, for example, blacks in 1858 lost a court case to integrate public transportation in the city. Blacks complained in that year of "continued harassment in public conveyances." Cities like Philadelphia and Providence lagged behind Boston in the integration of public schools. Before 1860, only five states (Maine, Rhode Island, New Hampshire, Vermont, and Massachusetts) admitted blacks to equal suffrage rights; and in Illinois, Ohio, Indiana, Iowa, and California blacks were prohibited from giving testimony in cases where one of the principals was white.[54]

Boston blacks acknowledged that their city was superior to other locations, providing a measure of racial tolerance. They were, however, quick to add that this was no cause for apathy, as conditions in the city did not approach racial equality. Blacks criticized those who believed "because we have the right to vote, and enjoy the privilege of being squeezed up on an omnibus, and stared out of a seat in a horse-car, that there is less prejudice here than there is farther South."[55] Racial intolerance in Boston remained the common attitude. Blacks still found it hard, even by 1860, to find decent lodging and to secure a job with status and wages commensurate with skill and experience. One black spokesman estimated that "it is five times as hard to get a house in a good location in Boston as it is in Philadelphia, and it is ten times as difficult for a colored mechanic to get work here as it is in Charleston."[56] Considering the limited and competitive job market and the high degree of residential segregation in Boston, this comment may have been only a slight exaggeration.

These criticisms notwithstanding, the realization of substantial progress was important in distinguishing black Bostonian attitudes from the pessimism of New York's Henry Highland Garnet, or the dedication to "race action" of Pittsburgh's Martin Delany. Yet, Boston blacks were not committed to integrated action when it did not serve the needs of their community. The black institutions, the church, and mutual aid and social organizations spoke to the concerns of Boston's black people—those of antislavery and racial equality and opportunity. Sometimes white allies were not fully attuned to black needs.

Although the city's black groups merged with the white antislavery movement in 1831, in many respects this merger was more structural than ideological. With the notable exceptions of Garrison, Wendell Phillips, and a few others, white abolitionist ideology was substantially different from that of blacks. For many whites, the exclusive goal of antislavery was the abolition of slavery. It is true that the stated purposes of the New England Anti-Slavery Society and the American Anti-Slavery Society aimed to improve the "character and condition of the free people of color, to inform and correct public opinion in relation to their situation and rights, and obtain for them equal civil and political rights and privileges with the whites," but often these were seen as secondary and less important objectives.[57] Blacks often complained that white abolitionists "supposed their antislavery mission was ended when they had publicly protested against slavery, without being careful to exemplify their principles in every day practice."[58]

Blacks, on the other hand, sought to abolish slavery not only to free those in bondage, but also as a necessary step toward racial equality. For them slavery perpetuated the larger evil of racism which infected the country and plagued the lives of all blacks, free and slave. Black abolitionists were concerned and actively involved in the movement to end the discrimination and injustice which free blacks faced, and to otherwise improve the lives of black people. David Walker, for example, was involved in militant attempts at gaining superior education for black children and movements to establish black churches and improved opportunities for black employment.

Black leaders throughout the antebellum period were equally concerned with antislavery and with community improvement. While William C. Nell worked for Garrison and the *Liberator*, he was a community organizer in a variety of projects. Benjamin Roberts, who printed posters for the New England Anti-Slavery Society and the Boston Vigilance Committee, was a leader in school integration drives and in a project to train black printers. This plural involvement was typical of may black abolitionists. For white abolitionists involvement was of a different order. Although committed to ending the institution of slavery, many were not themselves free from the racism upon which that institution was based. Many white abolitionists, believing blacks to be intellectually inferior, would employ them only in the most menial of jobs. For some, blacks as a group were general incompetents whose misfortunes called for the benevolent aid of whites. This paternalism was reflected in the comments of antislavery advocates, like James Russell Lowell, who believed that although blacks by virtue of their strongly religious and gentle natures had much to contribute to white western civilization, whites with superior intellect and general ability must provide encouragement and guidance.[59]

This conception of black character was shared by white clergymen such as James Freeman Clark, who believed that blacks possessed "a native courtesy, a civility like that from which the word gentleman had its etymological meaning, and a capacity for the highest refinement of character."[60] Yet for Clark the guidance of kind white men was also essential to proper black development. Even Charles Sumner, the fiery antislavery senator, was not free from the kind of paternalistic racism that allowed him to believe that emancipation would not bring about black rebellion because of the essential meekness, gentleness, and forgiving nature of blacks.[61] Many whites feared and resented the rise of urban capitalism, the crude electioneering in American politics, and by the mid-1840s, the rapid growth of a poor immigrant population. For them the image of loyal, patient blacks was a comfort, symbolizing stability in a society of declining traditional values.[62]

Perhaps the most ironic indignity suffered by Boston's black society was the prejudice and discrimination displayed by white abolitionists. Some early abolitionist groups excluded blacks from membership. Later, when blacks were admitted to Garrisonian-dominated antislavery societies, many white members tried to insulate themselves from the black membership. It was customary for separate sections to be provided for blacks at some antislavery meetings. Blacks breaking this seating pattern were likely to incur the anger of white abolitionists. Although significant as ideological symbols to many white abolitionists, there was generally no rush to embrace blacks as social equals.

In 1841, when Charlotte Coleman attended the February meeting of the Boston Female Anti-Slavery Society, she seated herself in the "white" section of the hall. Although she was apparently allowed to remain there throughout the meeting, within a few days she received a note from one of the white women, Mrs. Elisha Blanchard, expressing displeasure of her bold act. Mrs. Coleman was informed that antislavery whites were anxious to aid blacks in any proper manner, but that traditions must not be violated. Mrs. Blanchard disapproved of Mrs. Coleman's actions but was quick to add that "colored people were very well in their place." On another occasion a white abolitionist was "astonished at the impudence of the colored people in going to [reform meetings] and taking their places anywhere."[63] There were some white abolitionists who expressed a desire to support black equality within antislavery organizations, but they were generally opposed by other more tradition-oriented members. In 1838, a convention of antislavery women resolved that white abolitionists should make a greater effort to associate socially with blacks. This resolution caused a furor within antislavery circles, and many asked blacks to repudiate it.[64] With the exception of William Lloyd

Garrison and a very few others, there was little if any social contact between most black and white abolitionists.

Antislavery work was a soul-purifying experience for many white abolitionists. For others it served the very practical aim of avoiding slave competition with free labor. This latter Free Soil group opposed the expansion of slavery beyond the boundaries of the old South, but would not tamper with the institution where it existed. They must be distinguished from those who called for the abolition of slavery throughout the nation.[65]

There were white abolitionists who were also willing to work locally to improve conditions within Boston's black community. Caroline Weston, a member of a prominent and wealthy Boston family, donated many of her evenings to the Belknap Street School, where she taught adult night classes. She also helped secure employment for blacks, particularly those new to the city.[66] Maria Weston Chapman was instrumental in 1835 in the planning of the Samaritan Asylum when black children were refused admission to Mr. Tracy's Essex Street Orphan Asylum.[67] Also willing to aid the black community with funds and influence were white antislavery advocates such as Amos Phelps, a prominent minister, Richard Henry Dana, and Ralph Waldo Emerson. Yet, even among these friends of the black community, the influence of America's racial climate was readily visible. Emerson, for example, had publicly expressed the view that if Boston could prosper economically only as a "slave port," he would wish to see the city returned to wilderness. He was one of those who, in 1849, opposed the membership of Frederick Douglass in the Town and Country Club, a white literary society. This incident profoundly affected Emerson, as it brought him to recognize his own prejudice.[68]

Blacks recognized only too well the varying degrees of commitment of white abolitionists. While those who worked closely with blacks and associated with them outside the movement might in time come to view blacks as equals, most white reformers never freed themselves from the grip of racial prejudice. They never saw blacks as capable of filling important leadership roles in the antislavery struggle. They saw that former slaves, like Frederick Douglass, might be extremely useful as antislavery speakers, but never considered that blacks might actively participate in the formation of abolitionist strategy. Yet, blacks did influence antislavery strategy in Boston in many ways. Black leaders, understanding the sensitivity of many white abolitionists on the subject of their own racism, played upon abolitionist guilt to pressure many reform-minded whites toward a more militant antislavery position. Blacks generally took the lead in underground railroad activity, leading more conservative whites toward a more active antislavery role.

Boston blacks felt about white abolitionists much as they felt about white Republicans. Although white aid was gratefully accepted and was certainly needed, blacks would have carried on the struggle alone, as they had prior to white aid, if necessary. This was never necessary in Boston, for, under Garrison's leadership and that of white reformers such as Wendell Phillips and Thomas Wentworth Higginson, whites and blacks were able to work together throughout the antebellum period. By 1860, both could look back on a campaign for freedom that had much success locally and would soon bear fruit nationally with a strike against slavery.

8/The Fugitive and the Community

The participation of blacks in action to abolish slavery and overcome racial injustice intensified the feeling of community among Boston's black people. One of the most important activities involving large segments of black population was aiding fugitive slaves. Sometimes fugitive aid in Boston was an individual effort, but more often it was a group concern. In 1827, John and Sophia Robinson were convicted of withholding a five-year-old black child, Elizabeth, from her white guardian whom they feared would sell her into slavery. The Robinsons, who were part of no organized antislavery group, received four months in jail for this act, but the child was never recovered, having "disappeared into the black community."[1] A similar case arose in 1836, when blacks were successful in convincing the court to withhold a six-year-old black girl from Mary Slater of Louisiana. Mrs. Slater's husband was owner of the child's mother, and Mrs. Slater had claimed the right to return the child to Louisiana. Individual blacks, most of whom were not involved formally in organized abolitionist action and whose names do not appear on membership lists of local antislavery groups, were instrumental in bringing this action and in sheltering the child.[2]

After 1830, organized action became more important. In the mid-1830s, collective legal actions were organized to protect black seamen travelling to slave states. Partially as a result of Denmark Vesey's plotted slave revolt in 1822, black seamen arriving in the port of Charleston, South Carolina, were held in local jails for the duration of their stay in the city. This practice was designed to prevent contact between the city's slave and free black population and blacks from other areas. City officials viewed the outsiders as the carriers of radical abolitionist material and the fermenters of local black unrest. In 1824, the South Carolina law was declared invalid by the Supreme Court. The court decision was supported by United States Attorney General William Wirt, but the practice was not discontinued.[3]

Many in the black community were particularly vulnerable to the threat of southern incarceration, since about 20 percent of black workers were seamen.[4] This issue brought many of these most transient blacks into organized protest, perhaps for the first time. Seamen sometimes became involved as a result of a personal request from a friend in need, as in the case of John Tidd. Tidd, a seaman serving aboard the *Union*, found himself in a New Orleans jail after his "freedom papers" and clothing had been confiscated. Arthur Jones, proprietor of Tidd's boardinghouse, and other tenants joined the larger community in a long-term effort to aid Tidd and others in his situation.[5]

Despite vigorous protest, black sailors continued to be imprisoned. In 1844, the Massachusetts legislature sent Samuel Hoar, a distinguished Boston lawyer, to South Carolina in an effort to reach some legal solution to the problem. The South Carolina legislature passed a resolution directing that Hoar be expelled from the state. The resolution was enforced by a hostile mob which threatened to burn down the hotel in which he was lodged.[6] In July 1844, a black seaman from Boston brought suit against his captain who had deducted jail costs levied against the ship from his wages. The federal court found no reason to force the seaman to finance his own imprisonment and granted his suit. The court, however, did not question the constitutionality of these laws.[7]

Blacks often employed the orderly process of petition to secure freedom for their fellows, but the increasing use of direct action to rescue fugitive slaves gave perhaps the clearest indication of the growing importance of Boston as a center for militant abolitionism. These rescue attempts directly violated state and federal laws. Under the Fugitive Slave Act of 1793, a slaveholder or his representative could, without a warrant, seize a fugitive and, after satisfying a judge that he was a slave, a statement of repossession was issued. The slave was then returned to his master. Since the fugitive was not allowed to plead in his own defense, once he was located by his master his recovery seemed a fairly simple procedure. The black community of Boston conspired, as did blacks in other cities, to make such recovery difficult or impossible. In the process of protecting fugitives, Boston's blacks strengthened the bonds of their community as blacks of all classes stood together in a community effort.

In this effort there were many dramatic episodes. Blacks sheltered Eliza Small and Polly Ann Bates, fugitives from Baltimore, when they arrived in Boston in the 1830s. When, in the summer of 1836, they were captured by slavehunters and brought before the judge to be returned to their master, blacks acted to save them. On a given signal, a group of black women rushed into the courtroom, whisked the runaways out of the building to a waiting carriage, and escaped the city. In this action a key role was played by a black cleaning woman "of great size," who subdued an officer of the court long enough for the rescue to be effected. This daring rescue, which caused great excitement and raised spirits in the black community, came to be known as the Abolition Riot. Neither the fugitives nor the rescuers were ever captured.[8]

To many whites this act seemed a flagrant breach of law and order, but to the black community it stood as a victory over injustice. Hosea Easton commented that "a highway man or assassin acts upon principles far superior" to those of a slavehunter.[9] Charles Lenox Remond, who in 1839 was optimistic about the progress of antislavery and antidiscrimination sentiment in the North, three years later called for "more radicalism," commenting that abolitionists had been "altogether too fearful of martyrdom," too indefinite, and "too slow in their movements."[10] During the next two decades, blacks quickened their movements and heightened their militant direct action as their community came under increasing federal attack.

On October 20, 1842, a fugitive slave, George Latimer, was arrested in Boston and was to be returned to his master in Norfolk, Virginia. Quickly the word of his capture spread through the black community, and a group of blacks led by Henry G. Tracy attempted unsuccessfully to rescue him, assaulting a Boston constable in the process.[11] This incident excited community feeling against the police. Signs appeared denouncing the police as "Human Kidnappers," while blacks joined the legal efforts of white abolitionists to form Latimer aid committees throughout the state. After efforts to gain Latimer's release by a writ of habeas corpus failed, mass meetings were held to protest his capture. The *Latimer and North Star Journal*, protesting the impending return of the fugitive, was issued every other day, petitions were circulated, and Douglass and Remond addressed fund-raising meetings. Blacks gathered with white abolitionists and separately at the black Baptist Church on Belknap Street to protest Latimer's imprisonment and to unanimously approve all efforts which might lead to his release. Finally, blacks helped collect funds which were used to purchase Latimer's freedom.[12] Yet, even after the fugitive was a free man, the Latimer committees continued working, gathering 64,526 signatures on a petition that weighed 150 pounds. This petition was presented to the Massachusetts legislature and resulted in the passage of the 1843 Personal Liberty Act. This law forbade Massachusetts officials or facilities from being used in the apprehension of fugitive slaves, and represented a major victory for abolitionist forces.[13]

Blacks did not, however, depend totally upon the new law for the protection of fugitives. They established the Freedom Association in 1842 for the stated purpose of providing fugitives with food, clothing, shelter, and other aid which might be necessary to assure their freedom. The membership of this black organization was widely representative of the community. The leadership included two women and at least two traditional Garrisonians, Henry Weeden, a tailor, and William C. Nell. The activities of the Freedom Association were clearly illegal, and at times violent, a fact which did not deter the black Garrisonians. Yet, members saw the Freedom Association as legitimate antislavery work. Funds for its operation came from black contributions. The group sponsored juvenile music concerts, charging a small admission that netted some funds, and substantial amounts were collected through black churches.[14]

Blacks continued to act in defense of fugitives throughout the 1840s. In 1846, a fugitive who had smuggled himself aboard a ship arriving in Boston harbor from a southern port was discovered by the crew. Despite gallant efforts to resist capture, he was finally returned to slavery. This incident angered both black and white abolitionists. By 1846 white abolitionists were ready to join blacks in efforts to protect and aid fugitive slaves. On September 24, at Faneuil Hall in Boston, the question was considered in an open meeting. A committee of thirty-five under the chairmanship of Samuel G. Howe, and including Robert Morris and Charles Sumner, was appointed to consider this question. Later a second public meeting was called to hear the committee's report. It was chaired by the aging John Quincy Adams, former president of the United States and civil rights lawyer.[15] Howe, as chairman of the committee, reported its findings, warning against acts of violence and suggesting careful watching of slavehunters, "making them outcasts" in the city. He further stated that the abduction of blacks into slavery was a threat to every man's freedom. Sumner then rose in support of Howe's remarks, but the more militant Wendell Phillips encouraged Bostonians to more direct action than "looking the slavehunters out of Massachusetts." Calling the United States Constitution a farce, he demanded another 1776 to dissolve political bonds with a government which supported slavery.[16]

Theodore Parker, a white minister, accused the speakers of ambiguity and urged that concrete action be taken to establish a permanent forty-man committee of vigilance. This proposal was unanimously accepted, a one-hundred-dollar reward was offered for the earliest information received by the committee concerning captured fugitive slaves, and the medical services of John S. Rock were retained.

Blacks participated as members and leaders of the Committee of Vigilance. Joshua B. Smith, "Prince of the Caterers," and Lewis Hayden were members of the executive committee, and Morris was a member of the finance committee. Of the organization's 168 members, 5 percent were black, a percentage more than double that of blacks in the city's population. Black membership in the Vigilance Committee was not, however, representative of the black community. Without exception, blacks joining the group were skilled, entrepreneurial, or professional workers.[18] Significantly, this seems to have been the pattern of other interracial organizations such as the New England Anti-Slavery Society.

Although this regional society and the national American Anti-Slavery Society included a number of black members and some black officers, blacks involved were overwhelmingly from the middle and upper strata of black society. The majority of blacks—especially poor blacks—involved in aiding fugitives worked in informal all-black groups. These groups were often formed for a particular occasion and quickly disbanded. There was little joint direct action between white abolitionists and black activists, except at the leadership level. Thus, while there was extensive and important interracial cooperation in these efforts, for the majority of blacks abolition and aid to fugitives were racially separate enterprises.

There was some contact between the bulk of black society and the integrated or white abolitionist or fugitive aid groups. Although unskilled and semi-skilled black workers were not members of the Vigilance Committee, all classes of blacks did work indirectly, in most cases through black leaders, with that organization. George Johnson, a seaman, provided board for fugitive Fielding Banks, and was reimbursed $5.50 by the Vigilance Committee for two flannel shirts and other expenses incurred in the process.[19] The records of the Boston Vigilance Committee indicate that unskilled and semi-skilled black workers provided shelter, food, and other aid to fugitives. In these informal ways, blacks of all classes and occupations joined in this important cause.

Many blacks worked independently to aid fugitives, often for personal reasons. Henry L. W. Thacker hid Lizzie Lewis, a fugitive from Washington, D.C., at his home on Southac Street in 1847. Lizzie's father, George, was himself a fugitive from Virginia who had been sheltered by Lizzie in Washington before he came to Boston. In Boston, George, a carpenter, was befriended by Thacker. When Lizzie escaped from Washington to Boston, she found her father's friend ready and willing to shelter her. George, meanwhile, lived in East Boston where he worked in a shipyard. Over the next three years he saved enough money so that, added to the contributions he received from the congregation of the Twelfth Baptist Church, he was able to purchase the freedom of his wife (Lizzie's mother) and five other daughters.[20]

In these informal efforts, many blacks worked through individual relationships with fugitives in need. Black businessmen and professionals provided their wares and skills. Clothing dealers like Hayden, John R. Manley, Jonas W. Clark, and James Scott could be counted on for outfitting fugitives. William Davis, a fugitive from Virginia on his way to Canada, for example, was outfitted for his trip with a coat, pants, vest, "two pairs of drawers," two shirts, one pair of shoes, and one pair of stockings. Printers like Benjamin F. Roberts, who provided one thousand placards warning fugitives to beware of Boston policemen, also participated, as did Morris, who defended captured fugitives, and Rock, who attended ill and injured fugitives.[21] In Boston, most fugitives stayed at stations on the underground railroad which were within the black community. These stations included Peter Howard's barber shop on Cambridge, Leonard Grimes' church, and Lewis Hayden's home on Phillips (Southac) Street.

Although many blacks worked formally or informally with integrated antislavery groups, there was a growing demand by some that an all-black antislavery organization be formed on the model of the old Massachusetts General Colored Association. There was an attempt to form such a group in 1848. On January 24, at a crowded meeting at the old African Baptist Church, Thomas Paul Smith spoke in favor of an all-black antislavery society, but this was blocked by a resolution offered by John T. Hilton, Robert Morris, William Wells Brown, ex-slave and abolitionist, and Edward B. Lawton, a waiter.[22] Black opposition to independent organization may be seen as a reflection of Garrison' influence. Those blacks who worked against separate black groups were usually Garrisonian integrationists. Thomas Paul Smith, as evidenced by his stand for separate black schools, favored "race" organizations and institutions. Most blacks in Boston, however, were integrationists.

In cities more removed from Garrison's influence, in which integrated protest had been less successful than in Boston, blacks were much more disposed to independent organization. At the 1848 National Negro Convention in Cleveland, various local committees were appointed to organize vigilance groups "so as to enable them to measure arms with assailants without and invaders within."[23] In their insistence on integrated organization, Boston blacks were clearly out of step with other black communities, such as those in New York City and Philadelphia, where blacks worked through separate organizations for abolition and local concerns. When there was a move in 1853 to maintain the National Convention of Colored People as a distinctively black movement, some, including Bostonians, questioned the wisdom of racially restricted national conventions.[24]

In time of crisis, the black community displayed a united front; procedural differences tended to be set aside in favor of joint action. Social distances among strata were diminished, with a blurring of class distinctions. Informal institutions were espeically important in this process. Many black barbers, for example, became social and political links, connecting customers of various social levels. Such was the case in 1850, when President Millard Fillmore signed into existence a new, more extensive fugitive slave law. The law had been part of the controversial Compromise of 1850, and was the most comprehensive statement by the federal government to that time on the rights of slaveholders in reclaiming fugitives. It provided that "Any person obstructing the arrest of a fugitive or attempting his or her rescue, or aiding him or her to escape, or harboring and concealing a fugitive, knowing him to be such, shall be subject to a fine of not exceeding one thousand dollars, and be imprisoned not exceeding six months, and shall also forfeit and pay the sum of one thousand dollars for each fugitive so lost."[25] No longer were fugitives to be brought before judicial officers for determination of status. Now federal commissioners made such determination; thus, a judicial process was made an administrative process. Further, commissioners were paid a greater amount if blacks were found to be slaves than if they were judged free—a fact which seemed to encourage the kidnapping of free blacks.[26]

In Boston this law outraged both white abolitionists and the black community. It was denounced as unconstitutional, inhuman, and un-Christian. Many fugitives, some of whom had lived in relative security for months or years in Boston, understandably felt new fears of capture. Because of the abolitionist sentiment among many whites in the city and the determination of the black community to protect its own, Boston had been considered a haven for fugitives. "Perhaps in no community of the North did fugitive settlers feel themselves more secure than in Boston."[27] Theodore Parker estimated, in October 1850, that there were between four and six hundred fugitives in the city. Although there is no way to judge the accuracy of this estimation, there is little doubt that fugitives were a significant portion of Boston's black population.[28] Many fugitives responding to the new law fled for the safety of Canada. The black church felt the exodus immediately. The African Methodist Episcopal Church lost eighty-five members, the African Methodist Episcopal Zion Church lost ten members from its small congregation, and the Twelfth Baptist Church lost more than one-third of its members. The latter almost lost two deacons, whose freedom was finally purchased by the congregation. Wendell Phillips estimated that in just fifteen days, from mid-February to early March 1851, one hundred blacks fled the city.[29] George Lewis, who had by 1850 gathered his family in Boston, fled to Canada with the aid of the Vigilance Committee. He had lived in the city for five years.[30]

Blacks unwilling to be intimidated vowed that "no man will be taken from Massachusetts" and redoubled their efforts to protect those fugitives who remained in the city. Nell urged fugitives to stay and resist.[31] The protection of fugitives became one of the most significant issues in the 1850s around which community activism was organized. The successes, frustrations, and failures encountered by blacks in their endeavor intensified community spirit, unity, and purpose. During that decade, federal laws and rulings played an increasingly important role in what blacks perceived as a direct assault on their liberty and citizenship. Boston blacks, like those in New York, Philadelphia, Buffalo, and other northern cities, reacted strongly tq the increased pressure of federal law. Even among Garrisonian blacks, the events of the 1850s spawned a growing militancy.

Although there had been some moves away from the pacifism of William Lloyd Garrison before 1850, they were always tentative and often discouraged by black leaders. Starting in 1850 with the passage of the fugitive slave law, blacks regularly departed from Garrisonian principles when circumstances required more militant action. At a public meeting held in October 1850, Nell cautioned black citizens to be watchful while on the streets of Boston lest they become prey to slave kidnapers. Blacks, however, were not cautioned against the use of violence in defending themselves or their fellows against slavehunters. Indeed, Nell urged blacks to act in that situation "as they would rid themselves of any wild beast." Nell also condemned anyone who would "deliver up a fugitive slave to a southern highwayman under this infamous and unconstitutional law," implying that the community should take action against anyone who would do such a thing.[32] At a meeting at Faneuil Hall, abolitionists vowed to stand with fugitives regardless of the new law, and Douglass warned that should "this law be put into operation . . . the streets of Boston . . . would be running with blood."[33] Such militancy was indicative of the mood of the community, which was translated into action throughout the decade.

One of the most dramatic successes in the campaign to protect fugitives occurred early in 1850. William Craft and his wife, Ellen, had escaped slavery in Macon, Georgia in 1848 following an ingenious plan which became legendary in the annals of the abolitionists. Ellen, light enough to pass for white, posed as a white gentleman, while the darker William played the role of body servant. In this disguise they made their way to Pennsylvania where they met black abolitionist William Wells Brown, who convinced them to undertake an antislavery speaking tour. After spending a year in Boston addressing abolitionist meetings, they toured Scotland and England for six months, accompanied by Brown, relating their story to sympathetic audiences. The Crafts, returning to Boston in the fall of 1850, participated in abolitionist meetings held in the city to protest the fugitive slave law.[34]

The Crafts were the first of Boston's fugitives to be sought by slavehunters under the new law. The Crafts' owner, Dr. Robert Collins, had been following their activities in the abolitionist press, and when they returned to Boston he dispatched two agents to effect their capture. On October 26, these agents arrived in Boston and obtained warrants for the Crafts' arrest. Excitement raced through the black community. The presence of slavehunters was announced from the pulpits of the city's black churches. They were kept under constant surveillance and faced continual harassment. William Craft, vowing not to be taken, armed himself with two guns and a knife, and the Vigilance Committee made it clear that slavehunters were not welcome in the city. The fugitives were hidden in the homes of various committee members, moving frequently to avoid capture.[35]

At one point Ellen was concealed in Brookline, Massachusetts, while William took refuge in Hayden's home on Beacon Hill. Hayden's home was converted into a veritable fortress, with doors and windows double locked and barred. Inside, Craft and Hayden were joined by Hayden's son and a number of armed black men. Hayden confronted the slavehunters on the steps of his barricaded home. Two kegs of gunpowder had been placed on the front porch and, while the slavehunters watched in disbelief, Hayden iit a torch threatening to blow up his house, himself and anyone attempting to enter, rather than surrender the fugitive. This and similar incidents served to convince the slavehunters that the Crafts could not be taken without considerable violence, for which they were not prepared. Finally, after continuous harassment, the slavehunters withdrew from the city. Even so, it was thought advisable for the Crafts to leave Boston, and the Vigilance Committee arranged for their passage to England.[36]

The deliverance of the Crafts raised the hopes and confidence of the black community. The role played by the whites of the Vigilance Committee also raised black confidence in the willingness of that organization to act on behalf of fugitives. Yet the job of protecting fugitives had only begun, and within a few months another fugitive stood in need of aid. Fred Wilkins was a fugitive from Norfolk, Virginia, who had escaped and made his way to the safety of Boston. There he had taken the name Shadrach and obtained a job as a waiter at Taft's Cornhill Coffee House. He worked there until February 15, 1851, when he was seized by United States Marshal Devens and taken to the federal courthouse, still in his waiter's apron.[37]

News of Shadrach's capture spread rapidly. A number of lawyers from the Vigilance Committee, including Morris, volunteered their services. The federal commissioner was persuaded to allow a court recess so that Shadrach's defense could be prepared. Just as the recess was called, the proceedings were interrupted as Morris suddenly opened the courtroom doors to a group of fifty blacks led by Hayden. Quickly they burst into the courtroom, seized Shadrach, bore him to a waiting carriage, and escaped to the black section of the city. So sudden was the rescue that no pursuit was attempted.[38] That evening Hayden transported Shadrach to Concord, Massachusetts, where Francis Edwin Bigelow, a white blacksmith, waited to see the fugitive safely on his way to Canada. Some of Shadrach's rescuers, however, did not escape.

Repercussions of this incident were felt far beyond the city of Boston. On February 18, 1851, President Fillmore denounced the rescue and in a special proclamation ordered that federal charges be brought against those involved. Morris and Hayden were defended by two white lawyers, Richard Henry Dana and John P. Hale. The trials were lengthy and arduous, but in the end Hayden's jury was unable to reach a verdict and Morris was acquitted. Years later Dana learned that at least two jurors had refused to convict the defendants. One of these jurors was Francis Edwin Bigelow of Concord.[39]

The rescue of Shadrach involved the efforts of many, black and white. The Vigilance Committee contributed funds to pay former slave George Latimer to keep Shadrach's owner under surveillance and to cover the cost of the carriage used in the rescue. The impetus for the rescue, however, did not come from an organized group. As John A. Andrew recounted, Shadrach's rescue was "the result of an extemporaneous effort, energy and enthusiasm of one old man, a personal friend of Shadrach, who stimulated by his own stubborn zeal the few with whom he came in contact to follow him in his determination to save his friend."[40]

The response of the black community, supportive throughout the trials, was enthusiastic. Dana and Hale were praised for their efforts as defense attorneys. As a token of appreciation Dana was awarded an eight-volume set of Henry Hallam's *Constitutional History of England*, "a history marked by . . . the virtue of courage of great lawyers."[41] This New Year's gift, presented by "several colored citizens of Boston," was accompanied by a note of appreciation from Morris.[42] Two more white men were added to the growing list of those considered friends by blacks in Boston, as spirits ran high in the wake of a successful community effort.

Rescue attempts were not all successful, however; there were some heartbreaking failures. After Shadrach's rescue, federal authorities became increasingly security conscious in dealing with fugitives, making further rescues more difficult. The next attempted rescue involved a fugitive named Thomas

Sims. Sims was a boy of seventeen years, of medium, slender build, and with a color as "black as ebony." He had escaped from slavery in Savannah, Georgia, but had not been able to obtain the freedom of his wife, held in that city. Sims had slipped ashore in Boston Harbor after stowing away on an incoming ship.[43] He took odd jobs and lodged at a boardinghouse catering to black seamen on Ann Street, in Boston's North End. He had been a brick maker in slavery and had been given an opportunity by his master to buy his freedom, but he ran away before payment was completed. Sims was known to local police authorities as a drinker and a gambler but otherwise quite harmless.[44] He was involved in a quarrel with a black sailor over a white woman, and some said that the sailor notified Sims' master of his whereabouts. White abolitionists, however, reported that Sims was located through letters he sent to his wife.[45]

On April 4, 1851, Thomas Sims was arrested and told that he was suspected of theft. Knowing himself to be innocent, he accompanied the police officer peacefully. Upon learning that he had actually been arrested as a fugitive slave, Sims resisted, wounding one officer in the hip with a knife. He was subdued and taken before Commissioner George T. Curtis. To forestall another rescue, the courthouse was encircled with heavy chains and extra police officers were stationed inside and outside the building.[46] Although to some the participation of the mayor and city marshal seemed a direct violation of the Personal Liberties Law, city officials defended their actions on the grounds that they were taken purely as an effort to prevent public disturbances. The two officers who performed the actual arrest of Sims were city policemen deputized as federal officers by U.S. Marshal Danvers and the fugitive was incarcerated on the third floor of the federal courthouse.

The role of Boston's police officials in the capture provided additional evidence to the black community that the city police were instruments of community oppression. Banners and signs appeared in the city denouncing police as "slave catchers" and "kidnappers."[47] During the nine days of Sims' imprisonment, large crowds gathered about the courthouse voicing their contempt for the arrest and the part played by Boston officials in it. Many already angered by the arrest were further irritated when police made random searches of crowd members. One black man claimed that he had been assaulted by police officials who detained and searched him illegally.[48] Sims was unsuccessfully defended by Charles G. Loring, Robert Rantoul, Jr., and Samuel E. Sewall of the Vigilance Committee. Finally, when a number of prominent Bostonians had exhausted every legal means to free Sims, blacks laid plans to rescue him.

The Rev. Grimes was sent to instruct Sims that a mattress would be placed outside of his third-floor window and at the appointed time he was to leap to freedom. The plan was thwarted however when federal officials, apparently anticipating some such attempt, placed bars on Sims' cell windows, closing off the last hope of freedom for the fugitive. In the early morning of April 11, 1851, Thomas Sims, still under heavy guard, was marched to Long Wharf and placed aboard the brig *Acorn* to be taken back to slavery in Savannah, Georgia.[49]

Despite the early hour, at least one hundred abolitionists, black and white, followed the prisoner and guards to the wharf in solemn procession. As the *Acorn* sailed out of Boston Harbor, the abolitionist procession made its way back to the offices of the *Liberator*. Many paused for a moment at the site of the Boston Massacre where Crispus Attucks had been killed in the name of American freedom. Many police officers, it was said, "returned to duty on their beats, wondering, in the innocence of their hearts, how one man could own another."[50] The Fugitive Slave Law had been enforced at a cost to the Federal government of $10,000, "the City of Boston about as much or more, and Mr. Potter, the claimant of Sims, about $2,400 . . . " The cost to Sims was not estimated.[51]

Although some $1,800 was raised to buy Sims' freedom in the years following his return to slavery, he remained a slave until he escaped during the Civil War. At that time he was given a pass by General Grant that allowed him to return to Boston.[52]

The return of Sims to slavery was a depressing and frustrating event for the black community and for white abolitionists, yet it served as no other single event of its time to dramatize the inhumanity of slavery and to raise local support for the protection of fugitives. The rolls and treasury of the Vigilance Committee increased as sympathetic whites joined with those whites and blacks who had been early committee members. The sympathetic reaction of many of Boston's police officials, a group not generally abolitionist in sentiment, was indicative of the impact of the Sims capture upon Boston generally. The Sims case also generated greater interest and confidence of blacks in the Vigilance Committee. Hayden opened his home to committee meetings and more blacks attended. The return of Sims was said to have brought disgrace on Boston and "perpetual shame and blot on Massachusetts." The committee vowed that no more fugitives would be taken from the city.[53]

Yet Sims was not the last to be sent back. Washington McQuerry was captured in Boston in August 1853, and although his arrest caused great excitement among black and white abolitionists, all efforts to effect his rescue failed; he, too, was returned to slavery.[54] Perhaps the most famous fugitive slave case in Boston involved Anthony Burns, who had escaped from the home of Charles F. Suttle in Alexandria, Virginia. He had learned to read and write as a slave and was able to make his way to Boston, where he found employment in a clothing store on Brattle Street owned by Coffin Pitts. On Wednesday, May 24, 1854, Burns, on leaving work, was approached by Asa O. Butman, the police officer who had been stabbed by Sims during his capture. Butman was by then U.S. deputy marshal. After verifying Burns' identity, Butman informed him that he was under arrest for robbing a jewelry store. Burns, feeling that there has been some mistake, agreed to accompany him. It soon became apparent, however, that he was being arrested as a fugitive. Burns, six feet tall, broad-chested, and solidly built, resisted arrest. The struggle was overheard by whites in nearby Brigham's saloon and six or seven men rushed to Butman's aid. Burns was quickly subdued and escorted to the federal courthouse, which served as a jail for fugitives.[55]

As soon as he heard of Burns' arrest, Dana volunteered to act as counsel for the fugitive. But Burns, apparently distrustful of the unfamiliar white lawyer, refused the offer. On his first meeting with Burns, Dana described the fugitive as simple and "child-like." Burns explained to the white lawyer that fearing retribution from his master, he did not want to lengthen the proceedings. Dana got the distinct impression that Burns was willing to return to slavery without delay. But after being assured of Dana's trustworthiness by Grimes, Pitts, and Phillips, Burns reconsidered and accepted Dana's offer. The next day Dana again visited the fugitive. This time Burns was described as "self-possessed, intelligent and with considerable force of mind and body." Dana then set about preparing Burns' defense, assisted by Charles M. Ellis and Robert Morris.[56]

Some white abolitionists feared that blacks might turn to violence in an attempt to free the fugitive. John Greenleaf Whittier sought to calm the black community with a plea to "our colored friends to bear and forbear . . . Oh let them beware of violence."[57] A similar call for nonviolence went out from the Vigilance Committee, which advised "no armed resistance; but let the whole people turn out, and line the streets, and look upon the shame and disgrace of Boston. . . . "[58] Two days after the Burns arrest, angry blacks filled the basement of Tremont Temple. "A call was made for persons to come forward and give in their names, that they might be called upon at any moment to discharge not only a responsibility but a dangerous duty"—the rescue of Anthony Burns. A number of black men present stepped forward to enter their names and offer their service.[59]

Meanwhile, at nearby Faneuil Hall, the Vigilance Committee and leading black abolitionists, including Grimes and Morris, were holding a public meeting at which resolutions were presented condemning the arrest. This outrage, they charged, should not be submitted to "tamely." Heated speeches supported resolutions, one of which involved the revolutionary slogan "resistance to tyrants is obedience to God." The method of resistance was left to the individual. At 9:30 that evening the gathering was interrupted by the news that "a negro mob" was storming the courthouse. The meeting was immediately adjourned to the courthouse, where armed blacks led by Thomas Wentworth Higginson, a white minister, and Hayden had laid siege to the west entrance. Members of the arriving crowd joined the attack, helping to man a battering ram, smashing windows, and shouting insults at defenders within. Finally the heavy door gave way long enough for a few at the head of the invading party to slip inside. Finding themselves confronting a number of federal marshals brandishing sabers and billy clubs, Higginson and an unidentified "burly" black man fought their way a few feet into the entrance room of the courthouse. They were driven back, as marshals were reinforced by forces from other parts of the building.[60]

During the most heated part of the fighting, the cry "I'm stabbed" was heard and moments later James Batchelder, a truckman temporarily serving as U.S. marshal, lay dead on the floor.[61] In the resulting confusion the mob hesitated, then withdrew in the face of tenacious battling by marshals determined to hold the building. Although several others on both sides received minor injuries and several shots were fired from the crowd, Batchelder was the only fatality in the assault. Higginson received a "scratch" across the face, doing him no permanent physical damage but making him easily identifiable and forcing him into relative seclusion for a short period. In all, thirteen people, about half of them black, were arrested.[62] The appearance of two military companies restored order but feelings remained highly flammable.

Despite the appearance of spontaneity, the assault on the courthouse was the result of considerable planning and coordination between militant white abolitionists and black leaders. Higginson had arranged through Hayden to have a number of blacks ready to participate in the siege, which was timed to coincide with the Faneuil Hall gathering of the Vigilance Committee. According to the plan, the Faneuil Hall meeting would draw the attention of police while the initial attack was commenced. When the meeting was notified of the siege, Phillips was to issue the call and bring the entire gathering to reinforce the attack, overwhelming guards and freeing the fugitive. Ax handles had been placed in strategic positions to provide ready weapons. The attack failed, in part, because of the hesitancy of many from the Vigilance Committee meeting to immediately join the battle. Higginson accused some in the crowd of cowardice in the face of the need for violent direct action. The attack was also poorly planned, as it was concentrated at the least vulnerable section of the building.[63]

After this incident, security for Burns was redoubled. During his trial he was guarded by the volunteer militia, at least 125 men, described by abolitionists as, "taken chiefly from the vilest sinks of scoundrelism, corruption and crime of the city . . . made deputy marshals for the occasion."[64] Even the nonabolitionist press agreed that these men were "hired bullies, pimps, gamblers and fighting men."[65] A company of Marines from the Navy Yard guarded the courthouse and its entrances. Also called to keep order was an artillery company from Fort Independence and the entire city militia, numbering fifteen to eighteen hundred men. Admission to the courthouse was severely restricted but crowds of seven to eight thousand people, many traveling from rural areas and outlying towns, thronged Court Square outside.[66]

Many walked from as far away as Worcester, responding to the Vigilance Committee's call to the "yeomanry of New England" to come and view the "Mock Trial" of Anthony Burns.[67] By Saturday Boston was bulging with federal and state troops, spectators, and antislavery supporters. Such crowds placed an acute strain on the city's accommodations and resources. The situation worsened when black waiters and caterers, especially those employed by J. B. Smith, himself a fugitive, refused to serve troops brought to the city to guard Burns.[68] Visiting blacks were generally housed within the black community, and white abolitionists made accommodations available to white visitors. Feeling ran high and there was the real possibility of further violence. At least one thousand pistols were sold in Dock Square and vicinity and there were a number of arrests for disorderly conduct on Saturday and Sunday.[69]

Nelson Hopewell, a black laborer, was arrested on Saturday for threatening a white citizen with a knife and John C. Cluer, also black and a known criminal, was arrested for disorderly conduct. Later they were both charged with the murder of Marshal Batchelder during the Friday night raid on the courthouse.[70] William Johnson, a laborer, was arrested on Saturday morning for insulting the mayor of Boston.[71] Marshal Butman, who had captured Burns initially, was the object of black anger in Boston, as he had been when he had visited Worcester on official business. He was stoned by blacks and was driven out of that city. He was also threatened by blacks in Boston.[72]

The spirit of Burns' defenders was not entirely violent. Handbills distributed in surrounding towns urged that those coming to Boston in support of Burns bring no arms. On Sunday morning, four days after Burns' arrest, a letter signed by Grimes and Pitts was delivered to every church in the city. Congregations were urged to pray for Burns' deliverance.[73] Meanwhile, Burns' lawyers devised legal strategy. During the trial, defense counsel argued that the fugitive slave law was unconstitutional.

There was also an attempt to represent the defendant as a person other than that Anthony Burns who had been the slave of Charles F. Suttle of Virginia. In support of this contention, William Jones, an illiterate black day laborer, testified that he had known and worked with the defendant at the Mattapan Iron Works in South Boston during a period before Anthony Burns was supposed to have escaped from slavery in Virginia. Jones' testimony was corroborated by eight other witnesses including a Boston policeman and a member of the Common Council.[74] This testimony was offset, however, by Burns' recognition of his former master, and by the fact that he had addressed Suttle as "master" immediately following his arrest. The federal court refused to rule upon the constitutionality of the fugitive slave law and Burns was remanded to the custody of his master. Blacks, through Grimes and the Twelfth Baptist Church, raised money to purchase Burns' freedom, but Suttle refused to sell him.[75]

On Friday, June 2, nine days after the arrest, authorities spent four hours securing the route for the removal of the prisoner from the courthouse to Long Wharf. A proclamation was issued to the citizens of Boston by J. V. Smith, the city's mayor, urging that people clear the streets and not obstruct or molest any civil or military officer. A regiment of Massachusetts Infantry guarded every street and lane along the way, and General Edmonds, military commander of the operation, gave the order to fire on the crowd if it crossed police lines in a disorderly manner. Supporters of Burns draped buildings along the route in black, and nearly every shop on Court and State Streets was closed. A huge coffin labeled "Liberty" was suspended across State Street and American flags were hung upside down. Burns was marched first to Long Wharf, but the proprietor refused admittance to this procession to slavery. The point of embarcation was then changed to T Wharf, from which Burns was ferried to the steamship *John Tyler* for his return to bondage.[76]

In less than a year Anthony Burns returned to Boston a free man, for Grimes, Pitts, and the members of the Twelfth Baptist Church had collected funds and arranged his purchase. By 1858, he had attended Oberlin Institute and Fairmont Theological Seminary in Connecticut and was traveling in Maine with an antislavery lecture series, "The Great Moving Mirror," promoting his recently published book.[77] Ironically, in April 1855 all indictments stemming from the Burns affair were ruled invalid on the grounds that Commissioner Loring had not been legally qualified to issue the arrest warrant for Burns.[78]

The events of the spring of 1854 in Boston had had a profound effect on the life of Anthony Burns; they had also deeply affected antislavery sentiment in Boston. There was evidence of a more open hostility to slavery and "slave power" among the populace. Douglass, after the Burns affair, examined the morality of antislavery violence in an article entitled, "Is It Right and Wise to Kill a Kidnapper?" He reflected the sentiment of many blacks when he declared, "When James Batchelder . . . abandoned his useful employment as a common laborer, and took upon himself the revolting business of a kidnapper . . . he labeled himself the common enemy of mankind. . . . He had forfeited his right to live." Black militancy, which had been growing steadily for more than twenty years, came of age during the decade preceding the Civil War.[79]

Efforts to protect fugitives were instrumental in galvanizing the community spirit of the 1830s and 1840s into virtual solidarity of action, which cut across class lines as more and more Boston blacks came to agree that "[every] slavehunter who meets a bloody death in his infernal business, is an argument in favor of the manhood of our race."[80] Remond, who had attended the Tremont Temple meeting on the night of the attempted rescue of Burns, approved the willingness of his black brethren to act. "My heart has not been so encouraged for many a day," he said, "as when I witness a large number of the colored men present walk up to that stand, with an unfaltering step, and enroll their names" as those who would risk death in the name of freedom.[81]

Many of those so willing to act on behalf of Burns' freedom had not been, and would not become, members of formally organized abolition groups. Their names are not to be found on the rolls of the New England or the American Anti-Slavery Societies or the Vigilance Committee. Their commitment to freedom and the cause of abolition was not to be found in speeches delivered or public commitments made. Yet they voted for abolition and aid to fugitives with their actions. Most of them were unskilled or semi-skilled workers and in that way were more directly representative of common black society than the black leaders whose sentiments and loyalties are far easier to establish through printed statements.

Those who participated in the initial assault on the federal courthouse were men like Wesley Bishop, a thirty-year-old laborer. He lived in a small apartment at the rear of a private home on James Place in the undesirable North End. Bishop remained at the lower end of the economic scale throughout this period. He stayed in the city at least until 1860, although he changed his addresses frequently. So far as is known, Bishop was not a member of an organized group, save the church, and there is no record of his having expressed any political opinions publicly. Bishop would not appear to be a political activist, yet his actions speak clearly for his concern for the freedom of fugitive slaves. He was arrested during the courthouse assault on a charge of disturbing the peace. He had manned the battering ram in the rescue attempt.[82]

Thomas Jackson was also arrested for disturbing the peace during the Burns incident. Jackson was a forty-two-year-old ex-slave who worked sporadically as a laborer. He and his wife had come to Boston as fugitives in 1852 and were aided by Hayden and the Vigilance Committee. Like Bishop, Jackson had, so far as can be determined, no formal connection with antislavery groups except through leaders like Hayden who provided for Jackson, as for many other blacks, an indirect link with organized abolitionism. That Jackson, a fugitive himself, would take part in this unlawful act is of particular significance, as his capture might well have meant a return to slavery. There was in fact a real danger of Jackson's re-enslavement as a result of his coming to the attention of authorities after his arrest. It was only the quick action of the Vigilance Committee which allowed him to escape to Canada.[83]

Throughout the period fugitives had played an important role in the protection and rescue of other fugitives. The role of prominent fugitives like Hayden has already been noted, but there were others who were less prominent. John Wesley, a twenty-six-year-old fugitive, was charged with riotous conduct in conjunction with the Burns case. It was not at all unusual for fugitives to become active in the positive and direct aspects of rescues but, except for a few who became community leaders, their names never appeared on the rolls of organized groups. Perhaps the fear of being discovered had much to do with this circumstance. This fear, however, was not strong enough to prevent many from participating with free blacks and white abolitionists in direct action.

The protection of fugitives was an antislavery activity of the greatest significance in Boston. It demonstrated most vividly the extent to which the issue of freedom united the black community in common action. To the extent that whites as individuals or as members of the Vigilance Committee were willing to stand with blacks, even against the law, risking life and limb, a bond of trust was built between peoples. Both victories and failures served to strengthen the resolve of blacks and whites in their fight against the fugitive slave law.

Ironically, those cases in which fugitives were actually returned proved most significant in raising the abolitionist consciousness of Boston and in drawing support to the antislavery cause from many who had been unsympathetic. During the Burns trial a petition urging the repeal of the fugitive slave law was placed in the Merchants' News room. Many prominent men who signed it had never before been associated with antislavery.[84] The abolitionists who had previously been treated as dangerous fanatics by the more respectable white community found after the Burns affair that they and their cause enjoyed a new popularity.[85] Thus, the martyrdom of Sims and Burns was a greater victory for antislavery than for the cause of slavery. With heightened will and solidarity, blacks and their white allies made good their vow that no fugitive would ever again be returned to slavery from the city of Boston.

As the civil rights movement in the mid-twentieth century caused many Americans to clarify their positions on segregation and racial justice, so the fugitive slave cases made it difficult for many Bostonians of the mid-nineteenth century to remain neutral on the question of slavery. Even the most conservative men in the city admitted the injustice and the inhumanity of the slave system at this time. In 1844, Ralph Waldo Emerson distinguished between those Whig congressmen in the Massachusetts legislature who were motivated by "conscience" and those motivated by "cotton."[86] The latter group for the most part consisted of older, more conservative textile manufacturers who depended upon southern raw materials. They had been the gentlemen who supported the anti-abolitionist mobs of the 1830s and 1840s. Among these "Cotton Whigs" were many of Boston's wealthiest and most influential citizens. Men like Rufus Choate, Abbott Lawrence, Nathan Appleton, and Robert C. Winthrop saw militant abolitionism as a dangerous threat to the peace of Boston, to orderly trade with the southern states, and to the maintenance of the Union.

Given the conservative, anti-abolitionist bias of these Cotton Whigs it is especially significant that they were so profoundly disturbed by the capture and return of Anthony Burns. During Burns' trial his lawyer, Richard Henry Dana, was surprised by the support of many of these conservative gentlemen for efforts to free the fugitive. Rufus Choate admitted he had been wrong in his previous anti-abolitionist attitudes and expressed a willingness to help Burns in any way possible. Amos A. Lawrence, claiming to represent "active 1850 men" offered to finance Burns' defense in "any amount."[87] A measure of the impact of the Burns affair is the dramatic change in Lawrence's attitude. In 1851, during the Thomas Sims case, Lawrence had volunteered his services to U.S. Marshal Butman in the return of the fugitive. By 1854, however, Lawrence informed Boston Mayor J. V. Smith that he would rather see the total destruction of the federal courthouse than see Burns returned to bondage.[88] There can be little doubt that after the Burns case "the commercial classes of the city took a new position on the great question of the day" as Cotton Whigs and conservative businessmen gave "their influence on the antislavery side."[89]

This conversion of some Boston industrialists was relatively short-lived, however. The Panic of 1857 caused greater dependence upon southern markets, which were far less depressed than those in the West. This dependence in turn led to greater tolerance of southern ideology among these men and a growing unwillingness to directly attack slavery. Many Cotton Whigs who had supported the Free Kansas movement limited or withdrew their support. When Jefferson Davis visited Boston in the fall of 1858, he and his family received a gracious welcome. Faneuil Hall was packed to overflowing with many of Boston's prominent citizens, come to hear Davis' address. By 1859 Lawrence, too, had returned to a position sympathetic to southerners on the question of slavery.[90]

Yet reaction to Burns' arrest and trial did have considerable effect and led directly to an effort to extend the Personal Liberty Act of 1843. Petitions were circulated, but in 1855 the Massachusetts attorney general in a letter to the governor expressed the opinion that this extension should not be allowed to become law because it directly conflicted with the federal fugitive slave law. He insisted that the extension would therefore be unconstitutional. Heeding this advice, the governor vetoed the bill. Abolitionist sentiment, however, was strong in the state legislature and public pressure throughout the state, especially in Boston, was growing. As a result, a measure extending the Personal Liberty Law was passed over the governor's veto.[91] Further, the next state and local election witnessed the political power of the growing abolitionist sentiment as conservative, anti-abolitionist elements were turned out of office. In the city and in the state the antislavery cause had gained respectability. The spectacle of fugitive slave captures and the drama of antislavery reaction had brought the central question of the morality of slavery squarely before Boston's citizenry. Men of good will were forced to take a position regarding that peculiarly southern institution; often abolitionist forces gained support. This did not mean that there was a complete abatement of prejudice or discrimination toward local blacks. Racism which limited the opportunities and protections of Boston's blacks remained an ever-present reality.

9/A Decade of Militancy

The decade of the 1850s was a crucial one for black Bostonians and for all American blacks. It began with the issuance of a political compromise including a new fugitive slave law and ended with a federal attack on black citizenship and a violent attack on slavery by an abolitionist. During the middle years of the decade, there was open warfare between proslavery and antislavery forces in the Kansas territory. The need to aid and protect fugitive slaves in Boston continued.

During the 1850s, Boston blacks increasingly felt their rights under attack from a federal government that seemed more interested in protecting property rights than in defending human freedom. Blacks became less willing to follow the early admonitions of their leaders to be loyal to their country and became more conscious of a loyalty to their state. The state personal liberty law of 1843 and its extension in 1855 stood in stark contrast to federal action during this decade. The changing public stance of many black leaders reflected a general shift among blacks towards greater militancy and a greater willingness to "go it alone," if necessary, in the continuing struggle.

Although Boston blacks had never been entirely happy with Garrison's pacifism, black leaders in the city during the 1840s had been willing to restrain their public remarks. When Henry Highland Garnet, a black minister from Troy, New York, spoke before the National Colored Convention in Buffalo in 1843, boldly declaring Denmark Vesey and Nat Turner heroes and calling slaves to violent resistance, Boston's leaders were among the slim majority that voted against endorsement of Garnet's words. They hesitated to give public support to the speech, fearing that Garnet's remarks, "Rather die freemen than live to be slaves," would call forth retribution on free blacks in southern and border states.[1] Sentiment was changing, however, and four years later there proved to be less unfavorable opinion regarding Garnet's words at the convention.[2]

Some ardent Garrisonians like Charles Lenox Remond had been among those expressing concern over Garnet's daring. Yet by 1854 Remond's interpretation of the Garrisonian concept of disunion with slaveholders seemed remarkably congruent with Garnet's sentiments of a decade earlier.

In a speech before the American Antislavery Convention in that year Remond called upon the memory of such Massachusetts citizens as John Adams, Samuel Adams, and John Hancock to support a move which, he felt, would redeem Massachusetts. Remond urged the defiance of federal law, encouraging the rescue of the fugitive slave Anthony Burns and asserted that with the dissolution of the Union and the withdrawal of northern support from federal proslavery laws, slaves themselves would take care of the problem of slavery.[3]

Blacks in Boston had advocated many antislavery means throughout the antebellum period. There were always a few who advocated slave uprisings, but during the 1830s and 1840s a commitment to less drastic means was more common. The changes apparent in the sentiments of black leaders echoed the transition in community sentiment as federal actions escalated the conflict between proslavery and antislavery forces. Gradually the options available to abolitionists seemed to grow more limited.

In 1845, Frederick Douglass had spoken in opposition to Garnet's call for the violent overthrow of slavery. In that year Douglass' stance had approximated that of Boston's black community, condoning violence only in specific instances of self-defense. After 1854, Douglass' growing militancy reflected that of blacks throughout the North, fueled by the "crime" of the Compromise of 1850. After the fugitive slave law and especially after the Burns affair, Boston blacks were more willing than ever to use violence if necessary to protect fugitives. Those who had been involved in the attempt to rescue Burns became community heroes.

In the years after 1850, the militant statements and actions of black Bostonians reflected an increasingly cynical turn of mind about the possibility of justice at the hands of federal law. Many in the community, feeling abandoned by the federal government, armed themselves as a defense against slave catchers and kidnappers. Two young black men arrested on the Boston Common for carrying weapons justified their actions as necessary to their determination to remain free men.[4]

If the fugitive slave law in 1850 and the recapturing of fugitives in Boston had angered and heightened the cynicism of the city's blacks, the actions of the federal court in the latter years of the decade inflamed black sentiment even more. On March 6, 1857, the Supreme Court of the United States announced the Dred Scott decision. Dred Scott, a slave born in Virginia, claimed his freedom on the grounds that he had lived outside the slave states for some five years, from 1834 to 1838, and in so doing had become a free citizen. The Circuit Court of St. Louis found in Scott's favor, but this decision was reversed by a higher tribunal. At the urging of Henry Taylor Blow, a Free Soil supporter, and with the legal assistance of Montgomery Blair and George Tincknor Curtis, Scott became involved in an abolitionist test case which, had it succeeded, might have established grounds upon which a slave could gain liberty through federal courts.[5]

The opposition represented by Reverdy Johnson of Maryland, former

U.S. attorney general, and Senator Henry S. Geyer of Missouri argued, among other things, that slavery would exist for all time, and its expansion was essential for the preservation of constitutional freedom in the United States. Such statements angered blacks and abolitionists and focused a great deal of attention upon the case as it was argued before the Supreme Court. The decision finally handed down dealt a crushing blow to the hopes of those attempting to obtain civil and constitutional rights for blacks and to those seeking to limit or abolish the institution of slavery. Chief Justice Roger B. Taney, in delivering the ruling opinion of the court, declared that Congress had no power to exclude slavery from the nation's territories, thus nullifying the Missouri Compromise of 1820. Even more important for the black community and the history of constitutional law in America, Taney proclaimed that the rights and privileges set forth in the Declaration of Independence and the Constitution did not extend to blacks, slave or free. Blacks, said the Court, were not and could not be American citizens and thus had "no rights which the white man was bound to respect."[6]

The impact of this decision on blacks was predictably intense. On April 3, 1857, at a protest meeting in Philadelphia, Remond addressed an enraged crowd. "We owe no allegiance," he said, "to a country which grinds us under its iron heel and treats us like dogs. The time has gone by for colored people to talk of patriotism."[7] Remond's speech and the militant anger of the Philadelphia crowd reflected the sentiment which galvanized Boston's black community. Blacks felt that the federal government had abandoned them to the kidnappers and the slaveholders. They organized for self-defense throughout Massachusetts and across the nation. At a state convention of Massachusetts' blacks held in the city hall of New Bedford during the first week of August 1858, Robert Morris called for cooperative action for the defense of blacks throughout the state.[8]

In a speech which brought the convention to its feet, Morris asserted the willingness of blacks in Boston to aid sister communities in the continual process of sheltering and protecting fugitives. He acknowledged that such protection might involve violence but pledged assistance to any black man in need of aid. He proclaimed, "If any man comes here to New Bedford and they try to take him away, you telegraph us in Boston, and we'll come down 300 strong, and stay with you; and we won't go until he's safe."[9] Remond then shifted the convention to an even more aggressive posture by suggesting that a committee of five be established to prepare a call for slave insurrection. Remond probably never expected this resolution to pass but had intended his speech to symbolize the feeling of a growing number of blacks who believed that a clash of slave and free interests was imminent. This resolution was meant to clear the field of "half-way fellows" in favor of those increasingly vocal black militants calling for greater black unity, some even for separatism.[10]

A year later, on August 1 and 2 of 1859, a convention of Colored Citizens of New England gathered in Boston to petition Congress in protest of the

Dred Scott decision. The convention called for black solidarity, encouraging support of black trades, arts and professions, and attacked ministers who did not speak out against slavery as being "college made, money-called and Devil-sent."[11]

This call for black unity may not only be seen as an angry response to the Supreme Court decision of 1857 but also as a part of a growing feeling of solidarity among blacks in Boston and in other cities during the 1850s. This took the form of a renewed interest in African colonization for a minority of blacks, but centered for the majority upon a drive for black unity and collective, independent action. Some blacks expressed the desire to purge black organizations of white leadership or to establish new black groups. Douglass advocated a "Union of the Oppressed for the Sake of Freedom" which would meet more often than the National Negro Convention and function under, presumably, more effective organization.[12] This idea was abandoned however, largely because of weak response. There was a significant move toward increased black unity and self-help at the Rochester National Negro Convention in the summer of 1853. This gathering of the most distinguished and influential blacks in the country placed considerable emphasis upon concerted and independent action nationally to improve the condition of free blacks. A number of committees were established to organize a manual labor school, to initiate the formation of a consumer protection and cooperative buying union, and to improve relations with the American press. Also to be established was a general reference library on black affairs, with a museum and reading room, and a committee to defend the race against unfair and libelous attacks.[13]

The programs, without openly attacking integration as a common goal, leaned heavily toward separate, independent action. It is significant that three of Boston's most prominent black leaders, Grimes, Nell, and Remond, represented their city and supported the programs of this convention. The 1850s were for Boston's black community a period of increased pride in black heroes and leaders. Beginning in 1851, blacks made continuous attempts to have the city erect a monument in the name of Crispus Attucks, the "first martyr in the Boston Massacre."[14] These efforts did not culminate in success until 1888. In 1852, after petitions for the monument were rejected by the Massachusetts legislature, frustration was apparent in Nell's bitter declaration that "the rejection of this petition was to be expected, for blacks would never receive justice or proper consideration in America except by mistake."[15]

It was during the late 1840s and the early 1850s that Nell began work on his books, *Services of Colored Americans in the Wars of 1776 and 1812*, published in 1851, and *The Colored Patriots of the American Revolution*, published in 1855. Both these works told the story not only of black contributions during American warfare but also of the black struggle for freedom and equality. Nell's books were expressions of pride in the accomplishments of the race in spite of grave obstacles. Nell believed that the history of black contributions and achievements would serve to illustrate the worth of the race to all Americans. He also hoped that an awareness of black history would encourage black pride and continued accomplishments.

A more vocal pride and militancy throughout the decade demanded that blacks act independently if need be to properly honor black heroes. Accordingly, as a symbolic rejection of the Dred Scott decision, the first annual Crispus Attucks Day celebration was held in Boston in 1858. After a parade and a number of speeches, Nell denounced despotism in America, the suppression of free speech in the South and the "annihilation of the citizenship of Colored Americans by the Dred Scott decision." Although there were white participants on this occasion, it was clearly a black community affair.[16]

The most controversial speech made at the celebration was delivered by John Rock. Although he was only thirty-three years old in 1858, Rock's health was failing. His speech was abbreviated but still a strong illustration of the pride of race that had great appeal for his predominately black audience. Rock's initial remarks were addressed to statements by some whites that blacks had not resisted enslavement to the extent that native Americans had or white Americans would have. The enslavement of blacks, Rock explained, had nothing to do with black submission but rather with the extent of white military power. He appealed to history to illustrate the courage of African people and suggested that slaves in the American South might soon strike for their freedom. "Now, it would not be surprising if the brutal treatment which we have received for the past two centuries should have crushed our spirits," he continued, "but this is not the case." Rock then went on to praise slave resistance.[17]

Rock asserted that "Sooner or later, the clashing of arms will be heard in this country, and the black man's service will be needed: 150,000 freemen capable of bearing arms, and not all cowards and fools, and three quarters of a million slaves, wild with the enthusiasm caused by the dawn of the glorious opportunity of being able to strike a genuine blow for freedom, will be a power," Rock explained, paraphrasing the wording of the Dred Scott decision, "which white men will be 'bound to respect'." Rock spoke for many of his fellow black Bostonians when he upbraided the Supreme Court and "this wicked [federal] Government" and vowed that black people would outlast both.[18]

He then turned to the question of color prejudice, assuring the crowd that black was indeed beautiful in his eyes regardless of what certain whites believed. Rock suggested that he was not overly fond of the physical appearance of Caucasian features:

> If old mother nature had held out as well as she commenced, we should, probably, have had fewer varieties in the races. When I contrast the fine tough muscular system, the beautiful, rich color, the full broad features, and the gracefully frizzled hair of the

> Negro, with the delicate physical organization, wan
> color, sharp features and lank hair of the Caucasian,
> I am inclined to believe that when the white man was
> created, nature was pretty well exhausted—but determined
> to keep up appearances, she pinched up his features, and
> did the best she could under the circumstances.[19]

Rock's comments brought the house to its feet with laughter and applause.

Black Bostonians were proud of what they had accomplished in their city. Progress in Boston made federal rulings which were unfavorable to blacks even more intolerable and made the government in Washington, D.C., appear even more remote and hostile. Most agreed that blacks must not allow the values of whites, with reference to color, to supersede their own racial loyalty. As Rock put it, "I not only love my race, but am pleased with my color . . . I shall feel it my duty, my pleasure and my pride, to concentrate my feeble efforts in elevating to a fair position a race to which I am especially identified by feelings and by blood."[20]

Honoring Cripus Attucks was indicative not only of a pride in black heroes but also of a growing sentiment within the black community and among some white abolitionists that slavery and racial injustice would only be overcome by a "new American Revolution." The racial pride and separatism of the 1850s aided the effort to establish an independent black military company. Anticipating a violent conflict to free the slaves, blacks led by Morris and Remond petitioned the Massachusetts legislature in 1852 for the establishment of a black military company. After an initial failure the question was resubmitted to the legislature in 1853. In support of the request, Morris cited an old Massachusetts law which, during colonial days, had required blacks sixteen years and over to enroll in a militia company under pain of a twenty-shilling fine. In an eloquent plea to the legislature, Morris asserted a "hunger and thirst for propriety and advancement," and asked the aid of the legislature in securing this military organization to serve as a symbol of black pride and unity. The legislature rejected the request a second time on the grounds that establishment of a black military company would conflict with the Constitution and the decisions of the Supreme Court.[21]

The broad spectrum of blacks supporting the drive for the military company attested to the general popularity of the proposal. Among the boosters of the project were workers like waiters Thomas Brown and Henry L. W. Thacker and laborers J. J. Fatal and George Washington. Also participating were the community leaders Nell, Morris, Hayden, and Remond, as well as well-to-do men like Benjamin P. Bassett, an independent hairdresser and salon owner, and clothing-shop owners John P. Coburn and John Wright.[22] As a result of this support, the military company was organized in 1854 without state sponsorship under the name "Massasoit Guards."[23]

A year later, when the guard applied to the state for aid in the form of arms and other equipment, the request was rejected.[24] In 1859, Governor N. P. Banks vetoed a bill that would have authorized blacks to join the state militia, calling it unconstitutional. So far as equipment was made available to the black company, it was provided through private and community contributions.[25]

The drive for a black military company was an expression of solidarity and an assertion of potency in the face of federal attack. Blacks felt themselves embattled: the positive, visible, even inspirational presence of disciplined, organized, and armed community members served not only to discourage slave catchers but also to bolster the courage of the threatened community. Although the military company was seen by some as preparation for an impending conflict, others undoubtedly saw its value in encouraging blacks to remain in Boston with strengthened resolve to resist the slave catchers and kidnappers who, with the support of the federal government, threatened the security and freedom of fugitive and freeborn alike.

In some circles, debate over African colonization was revived during the 1850s. The actions of the federal government convinced some former opponents of colonization of the impossibility of racial justice within the United States. In 1858, the African Civilization Society was launched in Philadelphia with Henry Highland Garnet as its president. Garnet, who had opposed African colonization in the 1840s became disillusioned with the black man's chances for freedom and political equality in America after the developments of the 1850s. He proved effective in his new role, placing the case for colonization before black Americans in open debate with Frederick Douglass. The new society planned a vast publicity campaign to attract blacks to their cause. Robert Campbell, of the British West Indies, was sent to Central Africa to explore the area and its prospects for settlement. His report, given upon his return in 1860, recommended such settlement. "With as good prospects in America as colored men generally," Campbell wrote, "I have determined, with my wife and children, to go to Africa to live. . . . "[26]

Colonization was, however, still a minority movement, as a resolution passed at the Negro Convention of 1853 clearly showed. Liberian colonization was seen as "in violation of the physical laws of the human constitution." It was obvious that the vast majority of members of the convention had no sympathy with African colonization, "having long since determined to plant our trees on American soil, and repose beneath their shade."[27] Opposition to this latest move toward African colonization was particularly strong in Boston. Virtually every black leader in the city stood opposed to emigration, and sentiment within the black community generally was unfavorable. Remond, Rock, Nell, Grimes, and others were outspoken in their opposition. Not only did Nell disapprove of colonization; he was not entirely in favor of the National Negro Convention's program of independent racial action. Douglass accused Nell and a number of blacks from the Ohio delegation of plotting to blunt the effectiveness of independent action. Indeed, Nell was likely to vote against those measures which sought to deny the leadership of Garrison in favor of all-black leaders. In this Nell was joined in the May 8, 1855, meeting of the council by Remond, with both standing for integrated action.[28]

Although Douglass, Remond, and Nell did not agree on the question of independent versus integrated action, they were united in their anticolonization feeling even after emigration began to attract the prominent black support of Henry Highland Garnet, James M. Whitfield, and Martin R. Delany. Douglass had advocated independent black action to improve the condition of free blacks as a specific alternative to emigration. Except for advocating the settlement of a thousand black families in Kansas in 1854 to help maintain the nonslave character of the territory, Douglass was consistent in his opposition to black emigration.[29] At the end of the decade he was still convinced that regardless of what the Supreme Court had ruled, "America is our native land . . . our home . . . we are American citizens."[30] At a convention of blacks held in Boston in 1859, called to discuss the question of suffrage, anti-colonization feeling was obvious. By August of 1859 a full-scale bitter controversy was underway, with most blacks in Boston opposing Garnet and his emigrationist forces.[31]

Although anti-colonization feeling ran high in black Boston, there were a few black colonizationists who spoke out in favor of this movement. One of these was John Sella Martin. Martin saw in West Africa the opportunity for blacks to establish an independent nation that would stand as a symbol of black achievement. He also believed that American blacks could bring much to African civilization that would speed its progress toward modernity. In the spring of 1860 Martin paired with Garnet in defending colonization in a meeting held at New York City's Zion Church. The meeting quickly became the forum for a debate between proponents of colonization and opposing forces. The latter were strongly supported by the crowd gathered to listen to the debate. Friction was so great that the meeting was broken up by fist fights. In fact, the intensity of opposition to emigration caused Garnet to arrange for "controlled" meetings thereafter. These controls insured that opposition forces received virtually no representation. Even many advocating emigration objected to this "undemocratic" method of stifling critical debate. Martin withdrew his active support of Garnet as a protest of this practice.[32]

The emigration controversy was not limited to the continent of Africa as a location for a black colony. There were some who favored the establishment of a colony in the western hemisphere. During the early 1850s Martin R. Delany had favored the colonization of blacks within the American tropics. He was joined by men like J. Theodore Holly, a former shoemaker, who advocated emigration of blacks to Haiti. Holly set forth his views on black nationalism in *A Vindication of the Capacity of the Negro for Self-Government* in 1857 and in a series of articles in *The Anglo-African Magazine* in 1859.[33]

James Redpath, a white man born under the British crown, also became an important advocate of Haitian colonization. In conjunction with President

Fabre Giffard, Haiti's chief executive after the revolution of 1859, Redpath organized the "Haytian Bureau of Emigration" which was funded to the extent of twenty thousand dollars by the Haitian government. In 1860, Redpath established general offices in Boston and recruited a number of black leaders as agents and organizers. A year later he founded the emigrationist organ, *Pine and Palm*, which was published in Boston and New York.[34]

One of Redpath's agents was William Wells Brown, a figure well known in Boston's black community. Yet Boston's blacks were no more ready to adopt the concept of Haitian colonization than they were to support plans for African colonization. John Rock eloquently expressed the feelings of most Boston blacks when he explained: "This being our country we have made up our minds to remain in it, and to try to make it worth living in." Douglass warned blacks in 1860 that "the place for the free colored people is the land where their brothers and sisters are held in slavery, and where circumstances might some day enable them to contribute an important part to their liberation."[35] In 1861, Boston's blacks resolved at a large public meeting to reject Haitian emigration and to regard those who advocated emigration to Haiti with "suspicion, and deprecate both their counsel and advice."[36] A year later another community meeting was held. The city's blacks rejected any form of emigration or colonization in any location and vowed that if they left the United States it would be under duress.[37] Although President Lincoln made tenative approaches to the idea of colonization as a complement to emancipation, for Boston's black community the question was closed.

Black Bostonian opposition to emigration was rooted in the feeling of earned citizenship in the United States, in a loyalty to those enslaved, a determination to bring an end to slavery, and a general optimism that ebbed but never completely disappeared even during the trying experiences of the 1850s. The great possibilities for interracial cooperation through organized abolitionist groups and the continuing reverence for the dedication of William Lloyd Garrison and respect for other white abolitionists like Wendell Phillips helped sustain their allegiance to their native land. Blacks in this old city felt a part of New England and Massachusetts in a way that even the growing economic pressure from the immigrants could not destroy. Most of these black New Englanders would have been more willing to support the removal of their region from the federal union than to have removed their community from New England.

Rather than following the lead of emigrationists like Garnet and Delany, blacks in Boston were more inclined towards the racial solidarity of Frederick Douglass and New York's James McCune Smith and the program endorsed by the black convention of 1853 in Rochester. This plan called for the establishment of national and regional councils by which programs for improved academic education and vocational training would be instituted. It was intended that united action might improve the political and economic position of blacks and could more effectively "grapple with the various systems of injustice."[38]

By the late 1850s, it was the feeling of many blacks that sectional antagonism would lead to war between the North and South. Such a war would sound the death knell for slavery. Unwilling to wait for such an eventuality, some men moved to attempt the direct, violent, and immediate destruction of slavery. On October 16, 1859, John Brown, with thirteen whites and five blacks, attacked Harper's Ferry, Virginia, as a first step in a rather ambitious plan to free slaves by force. Although the raid failed, the enthusiasm generated within Boston's black community testified to the anger and frustration blacks everywhere experienced. Although many felt Brown acted prematurely and had been ill-advised to attack Harper's Ferry, he was hailed as a martyr to the cause of freedom. Blacks openly supported his attempt to liberate slaves. Brown and his sons had been the house guests of Lewis Hayden on several trips to Boston. It is extremely likely that Hayden, Rock, and other Boston blacks aided Brown directly or indirectly by donating money to his venture or by helping to recruit volunteers for his band. In 1860, Hayden was almost subpoenaed to appear before the Select Committee of the Senate appointed to inquire into the Brown affair, but the summons was withdrawn at the last minute. John Sella Martin, in the *Liberator*, answered assertions of Brown's insanity saying that if Brown were insane, his madness had not only "a great deal of method in it but a great deal of philosophy and religion" as well.[39]

Solemn gatherings were held in Boston on the day of Brown's execution. Black businessmen closed their doors and draped their shops in mourning. Individuals wore black armbands and a continuous two-day vigil was kept at the Twelfth Baptist Church. Virtually all black community members attended meetings held at the Twelfth Baptist Church or the integrated meeting at Tremont Temple. Speakers included Grimes, Remond, Nell, and Martin. At the Twelfth Baptist Church meetings, prayers were offered by both the eloquent and the unlettered. The emotions aroused found an outlet in the singing of antislavery and protest songs well into the night.[40]

The sentiments expressed in these meetings persisted during the pre-Civil War years. Although there were many differences of opinion on other subjects, blacks were united in their acclamation of John Brown. Both William C. Nell and John Sella Martin, on opposite sides of the emigration question, unreservedly supported Martyr's Day, the anniversary of John Brown's death.[41]

In the spring of 1860, blacks gathered to honor Crispus Attucks on the anniversary of the Boston Massacre. Addressing this gathering, John Rock characterized John Brown as the Crispus Attucks of the second American Revolution. In militant tones Rock charged that the only events worth commemoration in American history were the founding of the American Anti-Slavery Society, Nat Turner's slave rebellion, and John Brown's raid. While the leader John Brown was remembered, it was important too, some said, to remember his band of followers. Blacks were proud that five of their number had stood with John Brown at Harper's Ferry. Nell urged the collection of information about the blacks who fought at Harper's Ferry.[42]

A year after John Brown's death, the memory of his daring act was still vivid in the minds of black Bostonians. Gatherings to commemorate the anniversary of his execution were held, one of which took place on December 3, 1860, at Tremont Temple. Douglass, who had fled to Canada after being charged by the state of Virginia as a conspirator in Brown's plan, returned to address the gathering. He praised John Brown and supported all methods of abolition. He was cheered when he gave support and praise to slave uprisings in the South. Douglass called for the preservation of the Union only if federal troops were used to free slaves and unite the country under an antislavery president. He expressed a willingness if necessary to dissolve the Union and to free slaves by armed invasion of the South. In criticism of Garrison's more tentative approach, he remarked that to appeal to the moral sense of a slaveholder was not enough and explained that "the only way to make the fugitive slave law a dead letter [was] to make a few dead slave catchers." The crowd cheered and applauded his remarks.[43]

While the meeting was in progress, an anti-abolition mob, mainly Irishmen said to have been hired by commercial interests, gathered outside. They invaded the meeting and attacked Douglass, who fought back like "a trained pugilist" but was thrown down the staircase to the floor of the hall. Phillips, who had also taken part in the meeting, was assisted to his home on Essex Street by some forty volunteers who protected him from the threatening mob.[44]

Refusing to be silenced, blacks organized a second meeting to be held that evening at the black Baptist Church on Joy Street. Phillips, Douglass, John Brown, Jr., and Martin, the church's minister, joined with others in eulogizing John Brown, while anti-abolitionist forces surrounding the church were prevented from disrupting this meeting by city police. Previously, police had been used to prevent an antislavery meeting; by 1860 they were used to prevent the disruption of one.

The growing schism between the federal government's efforts to prevent sectional conflict by compromising with slaveholding interests and public sentiment in Massachusetts was apparent to abolitionists and to the black community. Although the governor's veto, in 1859, of the state legislature's bill that would have permitted blacks to serve in the state militia was discouraging, the opening of the new decade seemed promising.[45] The election of an abolitionist governor, John A. Andrew, in 1860 and the outbreak of war a year later gave new hope that military necessity would force the repeal of state militia laws and federal laws excluding blacks from the military. Andrew had served one term in the Massachusetts legislature, where he had established himself as a leader of antislavery forces.[46] His election augured well for Boston's blacks.

Blacks were not accepted into the military immediately, however, and in Boston, as in other cities in the North, they complained bitterly of this discriminatory treatment. In the spring of 1861, at a meeting held at the Twelfth Baptist Church, Boston's blacks called for the repeal of laws against black military service. Morris expressed the eagerness of his fellows to take part in the fight for freedom, asserting that, "If the Government would only take away the disability, there was not a man who would not leap for his knapsack and musket and they would make it intolerable hot for old Virginia."[47] Blacks did not wait for favorable governmental action. The antebellum experience had taught them that great pressure must be applied to achieve even the most modest advance. Accordingly, a black drill society was organized in Boston on April 29, 1861, and petitions were forwarded to the Massachusetts legislature in which the black men of the state claimed "as recognized citizens of Massachusetts, that they ought to be permitted to test the validity of that act of Congress complained of, before the proper judicial tribunals; and to this end they ask the obliteration of the word 'white' from the militia law of the State."[48] As with the struggle for a black military company in the 1850s, the state legislature did not take favorable action.

Governor Andrew did prove to be a powerful and important ally. He consulted with Secretary of War Stanton about the possibility of raising black troops first in North Carolina. When that plan fell through, he received authorization, after "many and frequent interviews with the President," to raise black troops in Massachusetts.[49] The 54th Massachusetts Infantry began as an idealistic project headed by white liberals dedicated to the task of constructing "a model for all future colored Regiments." The regiment was the first of its kind to be established in the North, and its supporters were well aware that "its success or its failure [would] go far to elevate or to depress the estimation in which the character of the Colored American will be held throughout the world." A white officer, Robert Gould Shaw, then captain with the 2nd Massachusetts Infantry, was chosen to command the new unit. He was offered the rank of colonel but, aware of the ridicule and abuse he would surely face as the white commander of black troops, Shaw accepted the assignment with reluctance. His second in command was Norwood P. Hallowell, formerly captain with the 20th Massachusetts, who was given the rank of lieutenant colonel.[50]

George L. Stearns, a wealthy white abolitionist, was given the task of raising funds for recruitment and a number of black leaders, among them Douglass and Remond, served as recruiting agents. Yet in 1863 Boston's blacks were less willing to volunteer for military service than they had been in 1861. From this largest black community in Massachusetts came scarcely one company. Abolitionist Charles Russell Lowell explained the indifference as the effect of increasing employment possibilities resulting from the booming wartime economy. "Blacks here are too comfortable," he wrote, "to do anything more than talk about freedom."[51] This would appear to be a harsh assessment of a situation that was not nearly so simple. There were a number of reasons which might have explained the reluctant black response to this belated call to arms. One undoubtedly resulted from indication that the Confederacy would not treat captured black troops as prisoners of war. According to a Confederate Congressional ruling, captured officers of black units could be executed, while black enlisted men who were captured might be sold into slavery or put to death. In addition, much resentment was caused by the fact that black troops were provided with less pay than white troops and with inferior equipment.

Another important obstacle to black enlistment, especially for Boston's blacks, was the restriction of commissioned officer ranks to whites. Morris was one of those who objected bitterly to the exclusion of blacks from the officer ranks. He joined with other blacks in a protest visit to the State House to confront Governor Andrew on the issue. The governor, in response to mounting pressure on this question, addressed a meeting of community members at the Twelfth Baptist Church to explain his position. Black leaders verbally attacked the governor. Morris told the gathering that he considered any black justified in refusing to enlist.[52]

Actually, the governor was powerless to correct this discriminatory situation. Andrew had wanted to grant commissions and provide promotion opportunities to qualified blacks but this plan had been overruled by Secretary of War Stanton and President Lincoln.[53] They reasoned that the commissioning of black officers would be ill-received by northern public opinion. Blacks in Boston and throughout the North resented this decision. Robert Purvis from Philadelphia, wrote that, "it argues a sad misapprehension of the character, aspirations and self-respect of colored men, to suppose that they would submit to the degrading limitations which the government imposes in regard to the officering of said regiments."[54] Given this resentment, the choice of officers for the black unit became crucial. Shaw, from a prominent abolitionist family, proved to be an excellent choice. Black leaders finally consented to aid in recruitment only because they were satisfied that Colonel Shaw would act fairly towards blacks under his command. Even so, recruitment was so slow at first that it became necessary to induct blacks from outside Massachusetts to fill out the unit.

By the spring of 1863, the efforts of black recruiters were bearing fruit, as the number of black volunteers grew rapidly. By the end of March, five companies of the 54th Regiment were filled, a training camp had been established in Readville, outside of Boston, and recruits were coming in at a rate of one hundred a week. During April, the number of recruits reached over eight hundred, and on May 15 Governor Andrew reported that the 54th would be ready for duty in five days and that a second unit, the 55th Infantry, was in the making.[55] Immediately orders were received assigning the regiment to Major General Hunter in South Carolina.

Although the initial response of many of Boston's blacks had been negative, by the spring of 1863 the 54th had the community's full support. It gave its encouragement and its prayers. It also gave food and clothing as tokens of support. Most of all, it gave its young men. At least 137 young black men, about 40 percent of all black males of military age in Boston, enlisted in the 54th and 55th Massachusetts Infantry Regiments.[56] It was a spring-like day at the end of May when the 54th Massachusetts Infantry in full-dress uniform marched through the streets of Boston to the Common, where ceremonies were held in honor of their departure. The streets of the city were hung with flags. The regiment displayed a number of flags, one of which had been presented by several young black women, and another given by the Colored Ladies Relief Society. The Reverend Grimes offered a prayer, after which Governor Andrew addressed the regiment and the thousands gathered on the Common. After a brief response by Colonel Shaw, the regiment passed in review to the cheers of the crowd of onlookers.[57] For abolitionists the event marked the beginning of a most important experiment, one which they believed might prove the fitness of black men to fight for the preservation of the nation and for the freedom of their fellows. For blacks, their fitness to fight had already been established in the American Revolution and the War of 1812. Whereas before they had fought for the freedom of the American nation, they would now fight for their own freedom within that nation. The formation of the black regiment marked the culmination of almost one hundred years of community action.

The departure of the black regiment and the black role in the Civil War brought no new racial equality. Nor was the basic question of the status of blacks in American society settled. For the black community in Boston, there remained the pressing concerns of prejudice and discrimination which made life difficult and frustrating. Yet the formation of the 54th and 55th regiments symbolized the coalescence of community and activism, as Boston blacks joined in offering their young men in a united drive toward freedom for all black Americans.

Appendix A
*Occupational Classifications**

I. Professional

- doctor
- minister
- music teacher
- schoolteacher
- lawyer

II. Skilled and Entrepreneurial

- barber
- seamstress
- clothing dealer
- blacksmith
- hairdresser
- carpenter
- tailor
- printer
- clerk
- shoemaker
- barkeeper
- boarding-house operator
- mason
- trader
- artist
- gilder
- merchant tailor
- sailmaker
- baker
- tanner
- eating house
- boxing master
- painter
- grocer
- dry-goods-store operator
- matron in old-age home
- butcher
- cigar maker
- mantua maker
- messenger
- engraver
- brush peddler
- variety-store operator
- hostler
- machinist
- engineer
- keeper
- jeweler
- upholsterer
- straw dealer
- carrier
- law student
- fruit dealer
- "puni" maker
- caterer
- wheelwright
- shirtmaker
- billiard saloon operator
- musician
- restaurant operator
- gymnast
- tobacconist
- restorer
- clothes cleaner
- paperhanger

*The occupational classifications in this study were derived from city directory or census data. They were chosen to roughly approximate traditional class distinctions. Such distinctions have not been used because of the confusion that results from having to explain why a black barber might be considered middle class. In black Boston, there was no doubt that a barber was a person of respectability and influence far greater than his white counterpart. Although a teacher might have been considered middle class among white Bostonians, he/she was clearly of the professional group, a step above the middle class for blacks.

III. Unskilled and Semi-skilled

domestic	cook	bootblack
seaman	steward	stevedor
laborer	whitewasher	chimney sweep
waiter	teamster	apprentice blacksmith
jobber	tender	apprentice tailor
porter	bartender	coachman
washer	gardener	soapstone worker

An effort was made to use the occupational classifications employed by Stephen Thernstrom in his studies of nineteenth- and twentieth-century communities. Because his white workers held a wide range of jobs, he found it helpful to divide his occupations into a number of categories including high and low white-collar levels. Since Boston's black working community was small and the range of jobs was limited, it was impractical to use these categories. Subdividing black workers into high white collar, low white collar, skilled manual, and so forth, would have resulted in categories too small for meaningful analysis. The present classification was devised as a compromise that would have meaning for the social and economic organization of nineteenth-century black society.

Skill-level requirements of the work were particularly important. There are, however, difficulties with this system. A messenger's skill level may be less important than the fact that he is employed by the state government, a relatively reliable employer. In an economically insecure society, stability in employment was uncommon.

A mantua maker, a skilled producer of fancy lacework, was included in the middle level because of the skill required for the work. The authors of this study do not know what a "puni" was, but since the female worker involved was listed with a number of seamstresses, it seemed reasonably certain that "puni" making was some specialized cloth work. At any rate, there was only one such occupation filled by a black in Boston.

Appendix B
Black Households

BLACK HOUSEHOLD SIZE

	Number of Households	
Number in Household	*1850*	*1860*
1	62	51
2	123	149
3	89	119
4	73	93
5	64	50
6	31	40
7	25	21
8	13	13
9	6	7
10	5	5
11	2	4
12	3	2
13	2	1
14	0	2
17	0	1
19	0	1
23	1	0
26	1	0
Total	500	559
Mean =	3.8	3.7
Standard Deviation =	2.6	2.4

BOARDERS BY NATIVITY[a]

	1850			1860		
	Children	*Adults*	*Total*	*Children*	*Adults*	*Total*
Massachusetts	57	185	242	42	209	251
Other New England	6	52	58	11	80	91
Other North	2	21	23	5	41	46
Total North	65	258	323	58	330	388
South	3	80	83	6	157	163
Foreign	4	48	52	6	101	107
Total	72	386	458	70	588	658

[a]Includes only those boarders with birthplace listed in the census.

SEX AND NATIVITY IN SINGLE-PERSON HOUSEHOLDS

	1850		1860	
	Male	*Female*	*Male*	*Female*
Massachsuetts	2	22	6	11
Other New England	1	5	2	6
Other North	0	3	3	2
Total North	3	30	11	19
South	7	7	5	8
Foreign	0	3	5	3
Unknown	5	7	0	0
Total	15	47	21	30

Appendix C
Marriage Patterns

MARRIAGES BY BIRTHPLACE OF HUSBAND AND WIFE, 1850[a]

Birthplace of Wife	Birthplace of Husband: *Massa-chusetts*	*Other North*	*Total North*	*South*	*Foreign Coun-tries*	*Unknown*	*Total*
Massachusetts	53	19	72	24	6	2	104
Other North	20	50	70	16	11	4	101
Total North	73	69	142	40	17	6	205
South	7	5	12	42	4	1	59
Foreign Countries	6	7	13	12	22	1	48
Unknown	2	0	2	1	0	35	38
Total	88	81	169	95	43	43	350

[a]For northern born, southern born, and foreign born only, $\chi^2 = 184.12$ and $T = .55$.

MARRIAGES BY BIRTHPLACE OF HUSBAND AND WIFE, 1860 [a]

Birthplace of Wife	*Birthplace of Husband:* *Massachusetts*	*Other North*	*Total North*	*South*	*Foreign Countries*	*Unknown*	*Total*
Massachusetts	41	18	59	23	9	0	91
Other North	18	50	68	30	11	3	112
Total North	59	68	127	53	20	3	203
South	5	7	12	77	9	1	99
Foreign Countries	14	17	31	16	43	1	91
Unknown	1	0	1	0	0	2	3
Total	79	92	171	146	72	7	396

[a]For northern born, southern born, and foreign born only, $\chi^2 = 225.31$ and T = .54.

Appendix D
School Attendance

SCHOOL ATTENDANCE BY OCCUPATION OF HEAD OF HOUSEHOLD, 1850[a]

Occupation	*Attending School*	*Attending School*	*Total*	*% Attending School*
Professional	2	0	2	100.0
Skilled and Entrepreneurial	42	26	68	61.8
Semi-skilled and Unskilled	90	51	141	63.9
None listed	104	37	141	73.8
Total	238	114	352	66.3

[a]Includes only children between the ages of 5 and 15.

SCHOOL ATTENDANCE BY OCCUPATION OF HEAD OF HOUSEHOLD, 1860[a]

Occupation	*Number Attending School*	*Number Not Attending School*	*Total*	*% Attending School*
Professional	3	6	9	33.3
Skilled and Entrepreneurial	44	26	70	62.9
Semi-skilled and Unskilled	125	49	174	71.9
None listed	55	28	83	66.3
Total	227	109	336	67.6

[a]Includes only children between the ages of 5 and 15.

Notes

Preface

1. Lorenzo Johnston Green, *The Negro in Colonial New England, 1620–1776* (New York, 1942; reissued 1966), pp. 167–190.

2. Ibid., p. 84.

3. Ibid., p. 17.

4. Often the descendants of these slaves returned to Boston. They thus accounted, in large part, for the significant proportion of Canadian-born Boston blacks around 1850 and 1860.

5. Oliver Warner, *Abstract of the Census of Massachusetts, 1865* (Boston, 1867).

Notes to Introduction

1. Theodore Hershberg, "Free Blacks in Antebellum Philadelphia: A Study of Ex-Slaves, Freeborn, and Socioeconomic Decline," *Journal of Social History* 2 (winter 1971–72): 183–209; Stephan Thernstrom, *Poverty and Progress* (New York, 1969); Stephan Thernstrom, *The Other Bostonians* (Cambridge, Mass., 1973); Peter R. Knights, *The Plain People of Boston, 1830–1860* (New York, 1971); Elizabeth Hafkin Pleck, *Black Poverty* (New York), forthcoming.

2. For a discussion of underenumeration, see John B. Sharpless and Ray M. Shortridge, "Biased Underenumeration in Census Manuscripts: Methodological Implications," *Journal of Urban History* 4 (1975): 409–439.

3. Peter R. Knights, "City Directories as Aids to Ante-Bellum Urban Studies: A Research Note," *Historical Methods Newsletter* 4 (1969): 1–10.

4. Leonard Curry, "Economic Opportunities for Urban Blacks: North and South, 1800–1860," unpublished paper delivered at the Organization of American Historians convention, April 1975.

5. Civil War Pension Records, Record Group 15, Records of the Veterans Administration (National Archives, Washington, D.C.).

Chapter 1

1. William C. Nell, "Farewell to the *Liberator*," Boston, October 21, 1865, MHS.

2. Thomas H. O'Connor, *Lord of the Loom* (New York, 1968), pp. 26–29, 31–33.

3. Ibid., pp. 95, 42–57.

4. Oscar Handlin, *Boston's Immigrants* (Cambridge, 1959), p. 97; *Fifth United States Census* (1830). The Boston black community was the largest black community in Massachusetts throughout the antebellum period.

5. Age distribution from United States census (1830–1860).

6. *Report by City Registrar of Births, Marriages and Deaths in City of Boston, 1854* (Boston, 1855); *Bill of Mortality 1810–1840, City of Boston* (Boston, 1893).

7. Information on black residential patterns from *Seventh United States Census* (1850); *Eighth United States Census* (1860); Peter Knights, *The Plain People of Boston* (New York, 1971), p. 31.

8. Ibid.; Handlin, *Boston's Immigrants*, pp. 90, 242.

9. Edward H. Savage, *A Chronological History of the Boston Watch and Police From 1631 to 1865* (Boston, 1865), p. 311.

10. Kenneth L. Kusmer, *A Ghetto Takes Shape: Black Cleveland, 1870–1930* (Urbana, Illinois, 1976), p. 31; Ira Berlin, *Slaves without Masters* (New York, 1974), pp. 257–258; Nathan Kantrowitz, "The Index of Dissimilarity; A Measure of Residential Segregation for Historical Analysis," *Historical Methods Newsletter* 7 (1974): 285–289. Only Chicago came close to duplicating the segregated residential patterns of Boston. When ten black households scattered on the fringes of the sixth ward are eliminated, the average black household in that ward was within 1.5 dwellings of another black household in 1860.

11. Boston city directories for the years 1830 through 1860; United States census (1850 and 1860).

12. Ibid.

13. Ibid.; Edward S. Abdy, *Journal of a Residence and Tour in the United States of North America from April 1833 to October 1834* (London, 1835), I, p. 136.

14. Mulattoes were 21 percent and 37 percent of the black population in 1850 and 1860 respectively, while they accounted for only 31 percent of the total black population in the North. In the South, 41 percent of free blacks were recorded as mulatto in 1860. Berlin, *Slaves without Masters*, p. 178.

15. Although it is difficult to trace black employment before 1850 because the census, the most useful source of such information, does not note employment before that year, it is possible to estimate relative percentages using the *Boston City Directory* and the "Records of the Boston Tax Assessor." Both these sources are skewed toward the most stable, skilled, entrepreneurial, and professional workers in black society, since these groups were most likely to find their way into such records. The figures provided here are, no doubt, low estimates of the number and percentage of unskilled, unemployed, and underemployed in black Boston. These figures can only provide an indication of the limited employment situation which blacks faced.

While the city directory listed slightly over 61 percent of black household heads as employed in unskilled and semi-skilled jobs, the tax records listed 78 percent of its black household heads in such positions. It is probably realistic to place the percentage of blacks employed in unskilled and semi-skilled positions in the 1830s and 1840s as somewhere between 70 and 80 percent.

16. The disproportionate representation of southern-born blacks in skilled occupations is compatible with Leonard Curry's findings that black workers in the South were more likely to be skilled workers than their northern counterparts.

17. Boston city directories for the years 1830 through 1860; United States census (1850 and 1860).

18. Handlin, *Boston's Immigrants,* pp. 60–70. Handlin paints a far rosier picture of the black occupational structure than seems warranted by our analysis of census occupational data.

19. Boston city directories for years 1830 through 1860; United States census (1850 and 1860).

20. Selected Boston city directories, 1830 to 1850; "Records of the Boston Tax Assessor," 1850; "Records of the Overseers of the Poor," 1839. Since the social structure of nineteenth-century black society was not parallel to that of nineteenth-century white society, the use of traditional class distinctions may be confusing. Black society, excluded from full participation in the economic and social life of the nation, developed socioeconomic distinctions which have meaning only within the context of that group. For example, teachers who might be considered middle class by white society would be upper class by black standards.

21. Information concerning occupational mobility compiled from city directories. Precise figures for mobility are not given because of the shortcomings of the city directory already noted.

22. George W. Forbes, "Typescript Biographical Sketch of E. M. Bannister," unpublished manuscript (undated), B.P.L.; "Robert Morris, Sr., In Memoriam" (1882), M.H.S.

23. *Boston City Directory* (1837, 1839); "Records of the Overseers of the Poor," (1839), M.H.S.

24. *Boston City Directory* (1837, 1841, 1845, 1848–49).

25. "Records of the Overseers of the Poor" (1839). Theodore Hershberg notes a decline in black occupational status in Philadelphia by 1860 in "Free Blacks in Antebellum Philadelphia: A Study of Ex-Slaves, Freeborn and Socioeconomic Decline," *Journal of Social History* 5, no. 2 (winter, 1971–72): 183–209.

26. *Boston City Directory,* passim (1830–1860); United States census (1850 and 1860).

27. Herbert G. Gutman, "Persistent Myths About the Afro-American Family," *Journal of Interdisciplinary History* 6 (autumn, 1975): 195.

28. Information on property holding in this chapter was compiled from the "Records of the Boston Tax Assessor" (B.P.L.) and United States census information. Since the census of 1850 lists only real property, information on personal property for that year comes only from tax assessor's records.

29. "Records of the Tax Assessor" (1840). The economic distribution described above is congruent with the findings of Paul J. Lammermeier in his study of the urban black family in the Ohio Valley. Lammemeier reports finding little relationship between occupation and property holding. "Steamboat and hotel stewards," he says, "were as apt to own real estate as a teacher, barber or whitewasher." Paul J. Lammermeier, "The Urban Black Family of the Nineteenth Century: A Study of Black Family Structure in the Ohio Valley, 1850–1880." *Journal of Marriage and the Family* 35 (1973): 445.

30. *Boston Evening Transcript,* March 3, 1854.

31. William C. Nell, *The Colored Patriots of the American Revolution* (Boston, 1855); Nell, *Services of Colored Americans in the Wars of 1776 and 1812* (Boston, 1851).

32. United States census (1850 and 1860). Boston black illiteracy was high, however, when compared to white illiteracy in New England. In 1860 white illiteracy in New England was only .26 percent. Illiteracy among Boston's blacks in that year was roughly equal to illiteracy among whites in the state of Virginia, where 8.7 percent of the white population was illiterate. *Compendium of the Ninth United States Census* (Washington, D.C., 1870), pp. 458, 459.

Chapter 2

1. *Seventh United States Census* (1850); *Eighth United States Census* (1860). Seventy-four percent of black children in 1850 and 65 percent in 1860 lived in two-parent families.

2. See Lawrence A. Glasco, "Computerizing the Manuscript Census," *Historical Methods Newsletter* 1 (1969): 1–4.

3. A test of the reliability of the relationships assumed in this study was conducted using the 1880 United States census as a control. For 100 blacks listed consecutively in the 1880 census for Boston, the method employed in this study for determining these relationships proved 100 percent accurate in determining immediate familial relationships. All statistical data in this chapter, unless otherwise indicated, is derived from the United States census (1850 and 1860).

4. U.S. census (1850); *Boston City Directory* (1848–49).

5. Ibid. Since the censuses of 1850 and 1860 do not designate the relationship of household members to the head of the household, those adults with different family names from the household head have been considered boarders. In some cases, these boarders may have actually been relatives of the household head or of the spouse of the household head. Speculation on relationships to the household head, beyond the immediate family, has not generally been

attempted because of the lower reliability already noted. Boarders, then, include both unrelated individuals and families and adult members of the extended family. Adults with the same family name, other than the spouse of the household head, were also considered boarders.

6. In 1850, almost one-quarter of the female-headed households had boarders; by 1860 over 45 percent of these households had boarders.

7. In 1850, 53 percent of all boarders were between the ages of 18 and 30; by 1860, 54 percent were. Those between the ages of 31 and 50 were almost 23 percent of all boarders in 1850 and 28 percent in 1860. Those over 50 were about 9 percent in 1850 and 7 percent in 1860.

8. A rise of six percentage points.

9. It may be possible to argue that the increase in blacks living with family members is indicative of improvement in the economic conditions which in 1850 might have driven blacks out of the city, thus enabling them to remain in the city in 1860. However, other economic information available concerning the depression of 1857, and the growing competition from immigrant, particularly Irish, labor, suggests that the increase in single adults living with family members was rather a response to worsened economic opportunities.

10. Herbert G. Gutman, *The Black Family in Slavery and Freedom, 1750–1925* (New York, 1976). The household of clothing dealer Lewis Hayden, as listed in the census of 1850, is interesting in this regard, considering the fact that Hayden was a well-known activist in the underground railroad and often harbored fugitive slaves. In addition to his wife and two children, Hayden's household included three tenders and a tailor from South Carolina, a tailor from Pennsylvania, William and Ellen Craft, fugitives from Georgia, a cook from Virginia, and a white English woman who was a domestic. By the 1860 census, the Hayden household had dwindled to Hayden, his wife and son, artist William Simpson from New York, and a porter from North Carolina.

11. Ibid., pp. 222, 226–228.

12. Only one-third of the homeless children lived in households that already had children in 1860. Fifty-eight percent were taken in by two-parent families. While only 16 percent of natural-born children lived in one-parent families, 42 percent of homeless children lived in one-parent families. For information on this practice in contemporary society, see Robert B. Hill, *Informal Adoption among Black Families* (Washington, D.C., 1977).

13. Gutman describes this practice among slaves in *Black Family,* p. 222.

14. Carol B. Stack, *All Our Kin* (New York, 1974), p. 60.

15. Civil War Pension Records of Elias Hall, Record Group 15, Records of the Veterans Administration (National Archives, Washington, D.C.); hereafter referred to as Pension Records (with name of applicant).

16. The information on shopping was compiled from various sources: Abdy, *Journal of a Residence,* I, pp. 142–143, 152; Pension Records of Burrill Smith, Jr.; the *Boston Evening Transcript* (May 30, 1854).

17. Pension Records of Elias Hall.

18. Pension Records of William H. Lee and George Henry Albert.

19. The importance of black women to the support of their families is a persistent theme in black history. See Elizabeth H. Pleck, "A Mother's Wages: Income Earning among Married Italian and Black Women, 1896–1911," in *The American Family in Socio-Historical Perspective,* ed. Michael Gordon. (New York, 1978), pp. 490–511, and John W. Blassingame, *Black New Orleans, 1860–1880* (Chicago, 1973), pp. 92–94.

20. A comparison of census and city directory listings with tax records, statements found in pension records, and newspapers confirms this observation.

21. *The Journal of Charlotte L. Forten,* ed. Ray Allen Billington (New York, 1967), pp. 8–10.

22. *Report of the City Registrar of the Births, Marriages and Deaths in the City of Boston . . .* (Boston, 1854, 1855, 1859).

23. Regarding the mulatto designation: officially, the children of interracial couples but probably listed at the determination of the census taker or the person reporting. The percentage of mulatto men marrying mulatto women fell from 90 percent in 1850 to 78 percent by 1860, when

there were fewer than one-third as many mulatto men married to black women as married to white women. There is a body of literature dealing with the roles and relationships of mulattoes in the black community. Some of the most important early work in this area was done by Frazier. See E. Franklin Frazier, *The Negro Family in Chicago* (Chicago, 1932), *The Negro in the United States* (New York, 1957), and *Black Bourgeoisie* (New York, 1957). More recently, historians have discussed the function of color in black society. See Berlin, *Slaves without Masters*, pp. 195–198; Blassingame, *Black New Orleans*, pp. 21–22; and Carl N. Degler, *Neither Black Nor White* (New York, 1971), pp. 205–265.

24. For a discussion of North End boardinghouses and their importance for immigrant and transient blacks, see James O. Horton, "Black Migrants' Adaptive Mechanisms in Antebellum Boston," unpublished paper presented at the Ninth Annual Conference on Social-Political History, State University College at Brockport, Brockport, New York (October, 1976).

25. Pension Records of Washington Perkins.

26. Pension Records of Henry Tillman.

27. Pension Records of William H. Lee. Lee joined the 54th black infantry regiment to fight in the Civil War.

28. Horton, "Black Migrants," p. 12.

29. Pension Records of Joseph Henry Green.

30. Pension Records of Elias Hall.

31. One hundred sixty-seven in 1850 and 234 in 1860.

32. Their median age was 28 years, with an age range from 10 to 78 years. The average age was 31 years. Females accounted for 84 percent of the group.

33. Their median age was 26 years and their average age was 25.4 years.

34. Robert Roberts, *House Servants' Directory* (Boston, 1827), p. 10.

35. Stack, *All Our Kin*, pp. 32–44.

Chapter 3

1. Alexis de Tocqueville, *Democracy in America* (London, 1835, 1840; rpt. New York: Mentor-NAL, 1956), p. 198.

2. Greene, *The Negro in Colonial New England*, p. 196; *Journal of the House of Representatives of Massachusetts* 15 (1735): 172–175.

3. Ibid.

4. *Laws of the Sons of the African Society, Instituted at Boston, Anno Domini, 1798* (Boston, 1808); William C. Nell, *The Colored Patriots of the American Revolution* (Boston, 1855), p. 97; Jedidiah Morse, "Discourse Delivered at the African Meeting House in Boston, July 14, 1808."

5. *Laws of the African Society*, p. 16.

6. Ibid.

7. Temperance was certainly a divisive issue within the community, one that tended to further separate unskilled laborers and sailors, who were less likely to find the cause of temperance attractive, from some middle-class people who did.

8. *Laws of the African Society*, p. 16.

9. Ibid.

10. *Laws of the African Society*, p. 16.

11. Nell, *Colored Patriots*, p. 29.

12. Donn A. Cass, *Negro Freemasonry and Segregation* (Chicago, 1957).

13. Ibid.

14. Prince Hall, "A Charge Delivered to the African Lodge, June 24, 1797, at Menotomy" in *Afro-American History: Primary Sources*, edited by Thomas R. Frazier (New York, 1970), pp. 46–52.

15. Nell, *Colored Patriots*, pp. 61–64.

16. John Daniels, *In Freedom's Birthplace* (Cambridge, Mass., 1914), p. 452.

17. *Laws of the African Society.* By 1825 the average wage for mill workers was fifty-six cents a day, the daily wage for black unskilled workers was probably comparable. See Robert G. Layer, *Earnings of Cotton Mill Operatives, 1825–1914* (Cambridge, Mass., 1955), p. 22.

18. For information on Charleston's Brown Fellows Society, see Berlin, *Slaves without Masters.* There is no evidence of shade of color distinction in any of these Boston groups, such as that found among the Brown Fellows.

19. Edmond Quincy, *Introductory Lecture Delivered before the Adelphic Union, November 19, 1838* (Boston, 1838). The price of tickets reveals much about the potential audience for these lectures.

20. William Wells Brown, *The Black Man, His Antecedents, His Genius, and His Achievements* (New York, 1863), p. 240.

21. *Genius of Universal Emancipation,* March 1832.

22. Ibid.

23. Daniels, *In Freedom's Birthplace,* p. 452.

24. *Liberator,* April 3, 1833.

25. *New England Telegraph,* October 1834; see also Nell. Of course, the community also sponsored schools, which will be discussed in the sixth chapter.

26. Arthur La Brew, "Studies in Nineteenth-Century Afro-American Music" (unpublished manuscript, 1975).

27. Ibid.

28. Ibid.

29. Ibid.

30. Ibid.

31. *Boston Evening Transcript,* April 14, 1855.

32. Savage, *A Chronological History,* p. 131.

33. Ibid.

34. Pension Records of Joseph Henry Green.

35. Pension Records of Henry Tillman.

36. *Boston Evening Transcript,* April 4, 1855.

37. Ibid., August 29, 1854; February 16, 1854.

38. Ibid., September 5, 1854; August 5, 1854; and July 5, 1854.

39. Unless otherwise noted, statistics on black incarcerations are taken from *United States Census* (1850 and 1860).

40. *Report on Goals and Houses of Correction in the Commonwealth of Massachusetts . . .* 1833, Mass. House Doc. No. 36 (Boston, 1834), 30; *Abstract of Returns of Inspectors and Keepers of Jails and Houses of Correction,* Mass. House Doc., No. 32 (Boston, 1838); *Abstract of Returns of Keepers of Jails and Overseers of the Houses of Correction . . . 1843,* Mass. House Doc. [unnumbered] (Boston, 1844); Lemuel Shattuck, *Report to the Committee of the City Council . . . Census for Boston . . . 1845* (Boston, 1846), 12–15, 17; Josiah Curtis, *Report of the Joint Special Committee on the Census of Boston, May 1855* (Boston, 1856), 23.

41. Savage, *Chronological History,* p. 311.

42. *Boston Evening Transcript,* October 9, 1854.

43. *Colored American and Advocate,* September 15, 1838.

44. Ibid.; and *Colored American,* June 27, 1840.

45. Walker, *Walker's Appeal in Four Articles* (Boston, 1830), p. 33.

46. Helen T. Catterall, ed., *Judicial Cases Concerning American Slavery and the Negro* (Washington, D.C., 1936), IV, pp. 160–161; *Boston Evening Transcript,* May 27, 1854, May 29, 1854, and May 30, 1854. Seamen and laborers arrested in connection with attempts to rescue fugitive slaves include James Scott, Wesley Bishop, John C. Cluer, Nelson Hopewell, James Bellows, Lewis Osgood, and John J. Roberts.

47. Daniels, *In Freedom's Birthplace,* p. 57.

48. Ibid. John J. Smith later became a politician himself. He was elected to the State House of Representatives in 1868 and again in 1872.

49. Pension Records of William H. Lee.

50. Ibid.

51. At the almshouse on Deer Island in 1850, for example, there were 3 black inmates out of a total inmate population of 328. There were 204 Irish inmates.

Chapter 4

1. For a discussion of the role of the black church, see, for example, C. Eric Lincoln. ed., *The Black Experience in Religion* (New York, 1974); Charles V. Hamilton, *The Black Preacher in America* (New York, 1972); and E. Franklin Frazier, *The Negro Church in America* (New York, 1963).

2. George W. Williams, *History of the Negro Race in America, 1619–1880* (New York, 1883) vol. 1, p. 198. For a biographical sketch of Phillis Wheatley, see Edward D. Seeber, "Phillis Wheatley," *Journal of Negro History* 24 (1939); 259–262.

3. Abdy, *Journal of a Residence*, I, p. 134.

4. Nell, *Colored Patriots*, pp. 33–35.

5. *The American Baptist Magazine*, (July, 1831), pp. 221–225; Charles L. Coleman, "A History of the Negro Baptist in Boston" (unpublished masters thesis, 1956).

6. *The American Baptist Magazine*, pp. 221–225.

7. *First Baptist Church of Boston, Church Records*, Books 2 and 3; *Second Baptist Church of Boston, Church Records*, Books 1 and 2; *Minutes of the Boston Baptist Association* (Boston, 1812–1867) [hereafter cited as *Minutes*], p. 26. In presenting a brief history of the church, only the males (7 among the 22 original members) were noted by name in the latter. They were Scipio Dalton, Abraham Fairfield, James Bromfield, Charles Bailey, Richard Winslow, John Bassett, and Obediah Robbins.

8. *Minutes* (1812).

9. *First Baptist Church of Boston, Church Records,* Books 2 and 3; *Second Baptist Church of Boston, Church Records,* Books 1 and 2; *Minutes* (1812–1867).

10. *Minutes* (1813–1819).

11. Ibid.

12. *Minutes* (1829–1839).

13. George W. Williams, *History of the Twelfth Baptist Church* (Boston, 1874), pp. 21–22; Williams, *History of the Negro Race,* pp. 505–506.

14. Nell, *Colored Patriots,* pp. 364–365.

15. *Minutes* (1841).

16. George A. Levesque, "Inherent Reformers—Inherited Orthodoxy: Black Baptists in Boston, 1800–1873," *Journal of Negro History* 4 (1975): 491–525. Levesque drew evidence from statements by evangelists Charles Grandison Finney and Francis Wayland, but did not explain why it is reasonable to believe that they were spokesmen for black Baptists. The most convincing evidence he used was a statement from an 1842 "people's convention" of Boston blacks that, Levesque claimed, condemned black ministers for their lack of involvement in abolition. In fact, the resolution from this group called for greater intellectual leadership from black ministers. Levesque edited the resolution so that it appeared to support his thesis, leaving out the important phase "in reference to the promulgation of the arts and sciences among us as a people." For a complete text of the resolution, see Nell, *Colored Patriots,* p. 363. For Levesque's edited version, see page 511 of his article.

17. Nell, *Colored Patriots; Liberator,* April 13, 1831; *Minutes* (1829–1843).

18. Nell, *Colored Patriots,* p. 364.

19. Daniels, *In Freedom's Birthplace,* p. 61; William H. Hester, *One Hundred and Five Years by Faith* (Boston, 1946), p. 17; for a list of delegates to the Boston Baptist Association, see Levesque, "Inherent Reformers," pp. 520–522.

20. Thomas R. Watson, *A Sketch of the Past and Present Conditions of the Twelfth Baptist Church* (Boston, 1880), pp. 13–14.

21. Edgar C. Lane, *A Brief History of Tremont Temple* (Boston, 1949).

22. Walker, *Walker's Appeal.*
23. Lincoln, ed., *The Black Experience in Religion*, p. 1.
24. *Minutes* (1845).
25. *United States Census,* 1860.
26. Daniels, *In Freedom's Birthplace,* p. 452.
27. For more information on church services and the role of the black minister, see Charles V. Hamilton, *The Black Preacher in America* (New York, 1972).
28. *Boston Sunday Herald,* July 14, 1889, as quoted in Pleck, *Black Poverty.*
29. Melville Herskovitz, *The Myth of the Negro Past* (New York, 1941); see, for example, Gutman, *The Black Family,* pp. 329–343; 351–353.
30. Eugene D. Genovese, *Roll, Jordan, Roll* (New York, 1974), p. 266.
31. Carter G. Woodson, ed., *The Mind of the Negro as Reflected in Letters Written during the Crisis, 1800–1860* (Washington D.C., 1926), pp. 164–165.
32. Nell, *Colored Patriots,* p. 364.
33. William Wells Brown, *The Rising Sun: or the Antecedents and Advancement of the Colored Race* (Boston, 1874), p. 534.
34. Williams, *History of the Negro Race,* p. 506.
35. S. S. Jocelyn to Amos Phelps, March 20, 1843.
36. Daniels, *In Freedom's Birthplace*, p. 452.
37. Brown, *The Rising Sun*, pp. 535–536.
38. Ibid.
39. Peter Randolph, *From Slave Cabin to Pulpit* (Boston, 1893), pp. 28–32.
40. James Pike, ed., *History of the Churches of Boston* (Boston, 1833).
41. *Liberator,* January 3, 1857; Oliver Johnson, *William Lloyd Garrison and His Times* (Boston, 1880), pp. 71–72.
42. Ibid.
43. Francis Jackson, "Vigilance Committee Account Book" (unpublished).
44. *Liberator,* April 11, 1851.
45. "Papers Relating to Negroes at Harvard" (unpublished); Harvard University "Medical Faculty Minutes," November 4, 1850, December 26, 1850, and November 16, 1853.
46. Nell, *Colored Patriots,* p. 344.
47. Genovese, *Roll, Jordan, Roll.*
48. See, for example, Martin Luther King, *Stride toward Freedom: The Montgomery Story* (New York, 1958) or Louis Lomax, *The Negro Revolt* (New York, 1962).
49. Original program announcements reproduced in La Brew, "Studies in Nineteenth Century Afro-American Music."
50. Beth Bower and Duncan Ritchie, "Preliminary Archeological Investigations at the African Meeting House, Boston, Mass." [unpublished report], 1975. James Oliver Horton, "Black Migrant Adaptive Mechanisms in Ante-bellum Boston" (unpublished manuscript presented at the Ninth Annual Conference on Social-Political History, State University College, Brockport, New York, 1976).
51. Civil War Pension Records of Washington Perkins.
52. Lincoln, ed., *The Black Experience in Religion*, p. 3.

Chapter 5

1. Names were gathered from such sources as the *Liberator*, the *Boston Evening Transcript*, the *Colored american*, membership lists of the New England Anti-Slavery Society, the Massachusetts General Colored Association, and the Boston Vigilance Committee.
2. Southern-born blacks represented 17 percent of the black population of Boston in 1850 and 24 percent in 1860. Mulattoes accounted for 21 percent of the black population of Boston in 1850 and 37 percent in 1860. These percentages were compiled from U.S. Census figures.
3. Southern-born blacks accounted for 40 percent of all black skilled workers by 1860.

4. Brown, *The Rising Sun*. Hayden was assisted in his escape by both Fairbanks and Miss Delia A. Webster. Miss Webster served several months in prison, and Fairbanks served over ten years before Hayden could secure $650 to pay for his release.

5. N. P. H., "The Lewis and Harriet Hayden Scholarship," December 28, 1893, p. 2.

6. Francis Jackson, "The Account-Book of the Boston Vigilance Committee."

7. Austin Bearse, *Reminiscenses of Fugitive Slave Days in Boston* (Boston, 1880).

8. N.P.H., "Hayden Scholarship."

9. "Robert Morris, Sr., In Memoriam," 1882, p. 31.

10. Ibid., p. 33.

11. Robert F. Lucid, ed., *The Journal of Richard Henry Dana, Jr.* (Cambridge, 1968), II, p. 478; Benjamin R. Curtis, *A Memoir of Benjamin Robbins Curtis, LL.D.* (Boston, 1870), pp. 60–62.

12. "In Memoriam," p. 35.

13. Ibid., p. 36.

14. "Members of the Committee of Vigilance."

15. "In Memoriam," p. 36.

16. Ibid., pp. 34–38.

17. Ibid.

18. For autobiographical information on Nell, see Nell, *Colored Patriots*. For additional biographical information on Nell, see George W. Forbes, "Typescript Biographical Sketch of William Cooper Nell" (undated) and Robert P. Smith, "William Cooper Nell: Crusading Black Abolitionist," *Journal of Negro History* 55 (July, 1970): 182–199.

19. Ibid.

20. Ibid., quoted by Forbes.

21. Martin R. Delany, *The Condition, Elevation, Emigration, and Destiny of the Colored People of the United States* (Philadelphia, 1852), p. 123.

22. *Liberator*, December 12, 1845.

23. George W. Forbes, "Typescript Biographical Sketch of John S. Rock" (undated).

24. *Liberator*, March 12, 1858.

25. Ibid.

26. Forbes, "Sketch of John S. Rock."

27. John Daniels, *In Freedom's Birthplace*, p. 57.

28. *Liberator*, December 12, 1845, and July 20, 1838.

29. Garrison to his wife, New York, May 15, 1840; Remond to Rev. C. B. Ray, London, June 30, 1840.

30. Garrison to his wife, London, July 3, 1840.

31. *Emancipator and Free American*, May 12, 1842.

32. Ibid., p. 115.

33. Charles Lenox Remond, "Before the Legislative Committee in the House of Representatives of Massachusetts respecting the rights of colored citizens in traveling, etc." *Liberator*, February 25, 1842.

34. Frederick Douglass, *The Life and Times of Frederick Douglass* [rpt. of the rev. ed. of 1892] (New York, 1962), p. 213.

35. Ibid., pp. 215–219.

36. Anne Weston to Maria W. Chapman, June 5, 1849; Samuel May to J. S. Estlin, September 30, 1847; Samuel May to Estlin, October 31, 1847.

37. Anne Weston to Maria W. Chapman, June 5, 1849.

38. Samuel May to Richard Webb, Boston, March 9, 1858.

39. Samuel May to J. S. Estlin, October 31, 1848.

40. Anne Weston to Maria W. Chapman, June 5, 1849.

41. Garrison to Samuel May, September 23, 1853.

42. "Liberatas to the Editor of the *Liberator*," *Liberator*, June 26, 1847.

43. Forbes, "William Cooper Nell."

44. Ibid.

45. "Boston Negro Proceedings" (1855), original records. For a slightly different view of the importance of local leaders, see Nell Painter, *The Exodusters* (New York, 1976).

46. Ibid.; *Boston City Directory*, passim (1830–1860).

47. "Annual Report of the Boston Female Anti-Slavery Society" (1836); "Proceedings of the Anti-Slavery Convention of American Women, held in Philadelphia" (1838).

48. *Liberator*, May 17, 1834, February 15, 1834, April 13, 1833, and December 26, 1835.

49. Susan Paul to Garrison, April 1, 1834.

50. Forbes, "William Cooper Nell."

51. Nina Morre Tiffany, *Samuel E. Sewall: A Memoir* (Boston, 1898), p. 63; Leonard W. Levy, "The Abolition Riot: Boston's First Slave Rescue," *New England Quarterly* 25 (1952): 85–92.

52. Jackson, "Account Book."

53. Garrison to his wife, New York, May 15, 1840; Remond to Rev. C. B. Ray, London, June 30, 1840; Garrison to his wife, London, June 29, 1840.

54. *North Star*, July 28, 1848.

55. James Oliver Horton, "Generations of Protest: Black Families and Social Reform in Ante-Bellum Boston," *New England Quarterly* 49 (1976): 242–256.

Chapter 6

1. Frederick Douglass, *Life and Times of Frederick Douglass* [rpt. of rev. ed. of 1892]; (New York, 1962), pp. 223–225.

2. S. Davenport to Anne Warren Weston, Boston, June 3, 1840.

3. Charles Lenox Remond to Rev. Charles B. Ray, London, June 30, 1840.

4. *Liberator*, June 18, 1847; *McCrey* v. *Marsh, Judicial Cases Concerning American Slavery and the Negro*, edited by Helen Tunnicliff Catterall, vol. 4 (Washington, D.C., 1936).

5. George W. Forbes, "Typescript Biographical Sketch of William Cooper Nell" (undated).

6. *Boston Evening Transcript*, March 3, 1854.

7. Ibid., August 12, 1854.

8. "Babolition of Slavery Grand Selebrashum by de Africum Shocietee and Reply Babolition of Slavery" (undated).

9. Forbes, "William Cooper Nell."

10. Thomas Cole to Brother Johnson, Newport, Rhode Island, August 7, 1840.

11. *Liberator*, February 25, 1842.

12. Louis Ruchames, "Race, Marriage and Abolition in Massachusetts," *Journal of Negro History* 11 (1955): 250–273.

13. *Liberator*, February 10, 1843.

14. Williams, *History of the Negro Race*, p. 162; Stanley K. Schultz, *The Culture Factory: Boston Public Schools, 1789–1860* (New York, 1973), pp. 157–60. The thrust of Schultz's argument is that before 1800 blacks voluntarily separated themselves in all black schools. An adequate explanation of the hostile atmosphere that existed in Boston public schools and forced blacks to see separation as desirable is not provided.

15. Williams, *History of the Negro Race*, p. 162.

16. Walker, *Walker's Appeal*, p. 33.

17. Charles Sumner, *Works of Charles Sumner*, Vol. 2 (Boston, 1874), pp. 342–343.

18. *Liberator*, August 21, 1846; Sumner, *Works*, vol. 2, p. 349; "Report to the Primary School Committee, June 15, 1846, on the petition of sundry colored people for the abolition of the schools for colored children" (1855), p. 7.

19. *Report of a Special Committee of Grammar School Board Presented August 29, 1849, on the Petition of Sundry Colored Persons Praying for the Abolition of the Smith School* (Boston, 1849).

20. *City of Boston Census* (Boston, 1845); Carleton Mabee, *Black Freedom* (New York, 1970). p. 170. Mabee states that there were fifty-three blacks in the school by 1849.

21. For a full account of the Roberts case, see Leonard W. Levy, with Douglass Jones, "Jim Crow Education: Origins of the 'Separate but Equal' Doctrine," in Leonard W. Levy, *Judgments* (Chicago, 1972), pp. 316–341; *Roberts* v. *City of Boston, Judicial Cases*, p. 512.

22. *Liberator*, June 14, 1850; *Roberts* v. *City of Boston, Judicial Cases*, p. 205; "Arguments of Charles Sumner, Esq., Against the Constitutionality of Separate Schools in the Case of Sarah C. Roberts v. the City of Boston. Before the Supreme Court of Massachusetts," December 4, 1849, pp. 24–25.

23. "Argument of Charles Sumner, Esq.," pp. 24–25.

24. *Roberts* v. *City of Boston, Judicial Cases*, pp. 198, 206; *Liberator*, June 14, 1850.

25. Forbes "William Cooper Nell"; *Liberator*, February 15, 1850, February 8, 1850, and May 23, 1854.

26. *Liberator*, June 28, 1844 and August 2, 1844.

27. David Lee Child, "Committee Report on the Memorial for Joseph Woodson."

28. Thomas Paul Smith to James McCune Smith, August 2, 1849; *Liberator*, January 4, 1850.

29. Mabee, *Black Freedom*, pp. 171–172.

30. Ibid.

31. Eric Foner, *Free Soil, Free Labor, Free Men* (New York, 1970), pp. 240–241.

32. Forbes, "William Cooper Nell."

33. A second suit was brought against the City of Boston in 1853 on behalf of Edward Pindall, a child of Caucasian, Native American, and Negro ancestry, who was excluded from the public school nearest his home by order of the school board. Robert Morris was engaged as counsel for the child. The court ruled against Pindall in 1854. See Mabee, *Black Freedom*, p. 176.

34. "Boston Negro Proceedings," 1855.

35. Mabee, *Black Freedom*, p. 173.

36. Ibid.; Brown, *The Black Man*, p. 239; *Liberator*, December 17, 1855.

37. Hosea Easton, *A Treatise on the Intellectual Character and Condition of the Colored People of the United States* (Boston, 1837), p. 34.

38. Amos A. Phelps on behalf of B. F. Roberts, Boston, May 16, 1838.

39. Daniels, *In Freedom's Birthplace*, p. 452.

40. Figures cited in Handlin, *Boston's Immigrants*, pp. 238–264.

41. *Frederick Douglass' Paper*, March 4, 1853.

42. Information used in occupational comparisons gathered from the *United States Census*, 1850 and 1860.

43. A long discussion of industrial schools may be found in the minutes of the Colored Conventions, Oct. 16–18, 1855, in *Minutes of the Proceedings of the National Negro Convention, 1830–1864*, edited by Howard Holman Bell (New York, 1969); quoted in "Learn Trades or Starve," *Frederick Douglass' Paper*, March 4, 1853.

44. *Frederick Douglass' Paper*, March 4, 1853, and March 11, 1853.

45. Philip S. Foner, *The Life and Writings of Frederick Douglass*, vol. 2 (New York, 1950), pp. 34–37.

46. Ibid., p. 35.

47. Jane H. Pease and William H. Pease, *They Who Would Be Free* (New York, 1974), p. 141.

48. Handlin, *Boston's Immigrants*, p. 242.

49. Cambridge grew from 77 to 141 blacks, Charlestown from 129 to 206, and Roxbury from 26 to 107. Figures compiled from Oliver Warner, *Abstract of the Census of Massachusetts, 1865* (Boston, 1867), p. 228; Lemuel Shattuck, *Report to the Committee of the City Council on the Census of Boston for 1845* (Boston, 1846), p. 43; Josiah Curtis, *Report of the Joint Special Committee on the Census of Boston, May 1855* (Boston, 1856), p. 7.

50. *Douglass' Monthly*, November, 1859.

51. Benjamin Quarles, *The Negro in the Civil War* (Boston, 1953), p. 101.

Chapter 7

1. Wendell Phillips Garrison and Francis Jackson Garrison, eds. *William Lloyd Garrison*, vol. 1 (New York, 1885), p. 148.
2. Amos A. Phelps on behalf of B. F. Roberts, Boston, May 16, 1838; "For the *Liberator*," F. W. Barker (undated letter), *Liberator*, May 4, 1838 and October 12, 1838.
3. B. F. Roberts to Amos A. Phelps, Boston, June 19, 1838.
4. *Liberator*, April 1, 1853.
5. *Liberator*, September 28, 1849 and October 5, 1849.
6. George W. Forbes, typescript biographical sketch of William Cooper Nell (undated).
7. Garrison, eds., *William Lloyd Garrison*, vol. I, pp. 277–278.
8. Ibid., pp. 279–282.
9. Paul Dean, "A Discourse delivered before the African Society . . . 1819."
10. Garrison, *William Lloyd Garrison*, vol. I, pp. 284, 330.
11. Walter M. Merrill, ed., *The Letters of William Lloyd Garrison*; idem, vol. I (Cambridge, Mass., 1971), pp. 216–217.
12. Garrison, *William Lloyd Garrison*, vol. II, p. 29; Theodore Lymann III, *Papers Relating to the Garrison Mob* (Cambridge, Mass., 1870).
13. Billington, ed., *Journal of Charlotte L. Forten*, p. 45.
14. Garrison to Oliver Johnson, August 7, 1862. Years later, Mitchell was elected to the Massachusetts state legislature after serving in the Union army and losing a leg during the Civil War.
15. Garrison to Francis Jackson Garrison, November 23, 1866.
16. Garrison to George W. Benson, June 25, 1844.
17. Garrison, *William Lloyd Garrison*, vol. I. pp. 329–330.
18. Frederick Douglass, *Life and Times of Frederick Douglass* [rpt. of rev. ed. of 1892]; New York, 1962), p. 214.
19. Nell, *Colored Patriots*, p. 369.
20. Merrill, *Letters*, I, p. 222.
21. Garrison, *William Lloyd Garrison*, vol. I, pp. 502–503.
22. "Records of the Boston Tax Assessor," 1850, 1855, 1860.
23. Leon F. Litwack, *North of Slavery* (Chicago, 1961), pp. 84–87.
24. Merrill, *Letters*, I, p. 425.
25. Foner, ed., *Life and Writings of Frederick Douglass*, vol. II, p. 67.
26. Benjamin Quarles, *Black Abolitionists* (New York, 1969), pp. 168–169.
27. Martin Robinson Delaney, *The Condition, Elevation, Emigration, and Destiny of the Colored People of the United States* (Philadelphia, 1852), p. 123; "Robert Morris, Sr., In Memoriam," 1882, p. 45.
28. Merrill, *Letters*, III, p. 604.
29. William C. Nell, "Circular," December 10, 1856.
30. *Liberator*, December 10, 1852.
31. *Liberator*, September 5, 1856.
32. For a full discussion of Garrison's political beliefs, see John L. Thomas, *The Liberator: William L. Garrison* (Boston, 1963), and Aileen S. Kraditor, *Means and Ends in American Abolitionism* (New York, 1967).
33. For an interesting acccount of non-violence among abolitionists, see Mabee, *Black Freedom*.
34. *First Annual Report of the Board of Managers of the New England Anti-Slavery Society* (Boston, 1833), p. 7.
35. Ibid., p. 8.
36. *A Few Facts Respecting the American Colonization Society* (Washington, D.C., 1830), p. 3.
37. Nell, *Colored Patriots*, p. 74; Floyd J. Miller, *The Search for a Black Nationality: Black Emigration and Colonization, 1787–1863* (Urbana, Ill., 1975), p. 22.

38. John H. Bracey, Jr., August Meier, and elliott Rudwick, eds., "Paul Cuffe to R. Finley, January 8, 1817," in *Black Nationalism in America* (New York, 1970); Miller, in *The Search for a Black Nationality*, argues that Cuffe advocated African colonization as a measure for establishing legitimate trade alternatives to slaves between the United States and West Africa, as well as a measure for bringing the gospel to Africans.

39. "To Paul Cuffe from Prince Saunders, Secretary, Thomas Jarvin, Chairman, and Perry Locks, President of the African Insititution of Boston," in Bracey, *Black Nationalism*, p. 22.

40. "Paul Cuffe to the President, Senate and House of Representatives of the United States of America," in Bracey, *Black Nationalism*, pp. 41–43.

41. "To Paul Cuffe From Prince Saunders . . ."

42. Nell, *Colored Patriots*, p. 74; *A Few Facts*, pp. 5, 8.

43. *The Emancipator*, June 30, 1835.

44. Garrison, *William Lloyd Garrison*, vol. I, p. 148.

45. Garrison, *Thoughts on African Colonization*, part I (Boston, 1832), pp. 5–15.

46. *Liberator*, January 1, 1831; Garrison, *Thoughts*, part II, p. 21.

47. Garrison, *Thoughts*, part II, pp. 21, 29, 31, 44.

48. *Minutes of the Boston Baptist Association, 1838* (Boston, 1839), p. 14.

49. Williams, *History of the Negro Race*; Austin Steward to William C. Nell, Wilberforce, December 1835, in Woodson, ed., *The Mind of the Negro*, p. 637.

50. Howard Holman Bell, *A Survey of the Negro Convention Movement, 1830–1861* (New York, 1969).

51. Garrison, *Thoughts*, part II, p. 26.

53. Ibid., p. 33.

53. *Liberator*, January 13, 1843, April 28, 1843, and June 8, 1849.

54. Litwack, *North of Slavery*, pp. 111–112, 264.

55. *Liberator*, March 16, 1860.

56. Ibid.

57. "Constitution of the New England Anti-Slavery Society," Article I, 1832, pp. 3, 4.

58. Nell, *Colored Patriots*, p. 345.

59. *James Russell Lowell Anti-Slavery Papers*, vol. I (Boston, 1902), pp. 21–22.

60. James Freeman Clark, *Slavery in the United States* (Boston, 1843), p. 24.

61. Charles Sumner, *The Works of Charles Sumner*, vol. VII (Boston, 1874), p. 226.

62. For a discussion of "romantic racism" among white abolitionists, see George M. Frederickson, *The Black Image in the White Mind* (New York, 1971).

63. Anne W. Weston to Deborah Weston, February 4, 1842 and November 8–9, 1842.

64. James Mott to Anne W. Weston, June 7, 1838.

65. For a detailed discussion of the Free Soil philosophy, see Foner, *Free Soil, Free Labor, Free Men*.

66. Caroline Weston to Deborah Weston, March 3, 1837.

67. Deborah Weston to Mary Weston, February 23, 1835.

68. Martin B. Duberman, *James Russell Lowell* (Boston, 1966), p. 185.

Chapter 8

1. Catteral, ed., *Commonwealth* v. *John Robinson and Sophia Robinson*, in *Judicial Cases*, p. 501.

2. Ibid., *Commonwealth* v. *Aves*, p. 506.

3. William H. Freeling, *Prelude to Civil War* (New York, 1965), pp. 111–116.

4. *Boston City Directory*, 1830 and 1840; "Records of the Boston Tax Assessors," 1830 and 1840.

5. John Tidd to Arthur Jones, April 6, 1834; see chapter 4.

6. George F. Hoar, *Autobiography of Seventy Years*, vol. I, (New York, 1903), pp. 24–28.

7. Catteral, *The Cynosure*, p. 511. This practice continued throughout the antebellum period.

8. *Liberator*, December 10, 1852; Tiffany, *Samuel E. Sewall*, p. 630.

9. Easton, *Treatise*, as quoted in Herbert Aptheker, ed., *Documentary History of Negro People in the United States* (New York, 1951), p. 166.

10. Remond to Garrison, Newcastle-on-Tyne, March 7, 1841.

11. Catteral, *Commonwealth* v. *Tracy*, 5 Metcalf 536ff.

12. Austin G. Elbridge, *Statement of the Facts Connected with the Arrest and Emancipation of George Latimer* (Boston, 1842), p. 70.

13. Massachusetts Legislature, Original papers of Chapter 69 of "An act to Protect the rights and Liberties of the people of the Commonwealth of Massachusetts," March 24, 1843.

14. *Liberator*, December 12, 1845 and August 28, 1846.

15. Adams, who by 1846 was seventy-nine years old, had defended slaves who captured a Spanish ship, the *Amistad*, in 1839. Through his efforts, the slaves were freed and returned to Africa in 1844.

16. *Address of the Committee Appointed by a Public Meeting, Held at Faneuil Hall, September 24, 1846, for the Purpose of Considering the Recent Case of Kidnapping from our Soil, and of Taking Measures to Prevent the Recurrence of Similar Outrages* (Boston, 1846).

17. Ibid.

18. "Members of the Committee of Vigilance."

19. Francis Jackson, "Vigilance Committee Account Book."

20. Wilbur H. Siebert, "The Underground Railroad in Massachusetts," *Proceedings of the American Antiquarian Society*, 1936, series XLV, p. 43.

21. Jackson, "Vigilance Committee Account Book."

22. *Liberator*, October 20, 1848.

23. Nell, *Colored Patriots*, pp. 356, 365; *Liberator*, June 8, 1849.

24. Philip Foner, *Life and Writings of Frederick Douglass*, vol. 2. (New York, 1950), pp. 19–38.

25. As quoted in *The Fugitive Slave Law and its Victims*, The American Anti-Slavery Society (New York, 1861), pp. 1–2.

26. Ibid.

27. Wilbur H. Siebert, *The Underground Railroad* (New York, 1898), p. 246.

28. Ibid.

29. Quarles, *Black Abolitionists*, p. 200; Daniels, *In Freedom's Birthplace*, p. 61; *Minutes of the Boston Baptist Association, 1852* (Boston, 1853).

30. Siebert, "The Underground Railroad in Massachusetts," *The Underground Railroad*, p. 43.

31. *Liberator*, November 1, 1850.

32. Nell, *Colored Patriots*, pp. 392–393.

33. *Liberator*, October 18, 1850.

34. William Wells Brown to Garrison, as quoted in Aptheker, *Documentary History*, p. 277; *Liberator*, May 9, 1851.

35. William Craft, *Running a Thousand Miles for Freedom* (London, 1860), pp. 319–320.

36. Archibald H. Grimke, "Anti-Slavery in Boston," *New England Magazine* (December 1890): 458.

37. Siebert, "The Underground Railroad," pp. 67–68.

38. Lucid, *Journal of Richard Henry Dana, Jr.*, II, p. 478; Curtis, *A Memoir of Benjamin Robbins* Curtis, LL.D., pp. 60–62.

39. Stanley J. Robboy and Anita W. Robboy, "Lewis Hayden: From Fugitive Slave to Statesman," *New England Quarterly*, 46, no. 4: 597–613; Thomas Wentworth Higginson, *Cheerful Yesterdays* (Boston, 1898), p. 137; John P. Hale was nominated for the presidency by the Free Soil Party in 1852.

40. John A. Andrew to James Freeman Clark, March 5, 1857.

41. *Liberator*, March 19, 1852.

42. Robert Morris to Richard H. Dana, January 1, 1852; Robert Morris to John P. Hale, January 1, 1852.
43. Thomas W. Higginson to *Newport Union* (undated).
44. Savage, *Chronological History*, pp. 375–378.
45. Theodore Parker, "The Boston Kidnapping—A Discourse to Commemorate the Rendition of Thomas Sims," Boston Vigilance Committee, April 12, 1852.
46. Lawrence Lader, *The Bold Brahmins* (New York, 1961), pp. 174–177.
47. "Slave Catchers and Kidnappers," Broadside (1851).
48. Account of illegal search case in Massachusetts Senate Document #89, 1851, "Report on the Freedom of the Inhabitants Passim."
49. *Fugitive Slave Law and Its Victims; Twelfth Annual Report of the Massachusetts Anti-Slavery Society,* Boston, January 28, 1852.
50. Savage, *Chronological History*, p. 380.
51. *Fugitive Slave Law and Its Victims,* pp. 17–18; *Twelfth Annual Report of the Massachusetts Anti-Slavery Society*, p. 23.
52. *Douglass' Monthly*, June, 1863.
53. Theodore Parker, "The Boston Kidnapping"; Siebert, "Underground Railroad in Massachusetts," pp. 75–76.
54. *Boston Evening Transcript*, January 30, 1854.
55. *Boston Slave Riot and Trial of Anthony Burns* (Boston, 1854), pp. 5–7.
56. Lucid, *Journal of Richard Henry Dana*, vol. II, p. 628; R. H. Dana, Jr., to J. P. Hale, Boston, November 28, 1853.
57. *Liberator*, July 7, 1854.
58. *American Freeman*, Vigilance Committee of Boston (Boston, 1854).
59. Nell, *Colored Patriots*, pp. 372–374.
60. *Boston Slave Riot*, p. 8; *Boston Evening Transcript*, May 27, 1854.
61. There is some question as to whether Batchelder was stabbed or shot.
62. T. W. Higginson to wife, May 27, 1854; *Boston Evening Transcript*, May 27, 1854.
63. Higginson, *Cheerful Yesterdays*, pp. 154–162; Higginson to wife, May 27, 1854.
64. *Fugitive Slave Law and its Victims*, p. 35.
65. *Boston Evening Transcript*, May 30, 1854.
66. *Boston Slave Riot*, pp. 5–7.
67. "To the Yeomenry of New England," Boston Vigilance Committee, May 27, 1854.
68. *Boston Evening Transcript*, May 29, 1854.
69. Ibid.
70. Ibid.
71. Ibid., May 27, 1854.
72. Higginson, *Cheerful Yesterdays*, p. 162.
73. *Boston Evening Transcript*, May 29, 1854.
74. Ibid., May 30, 1854, and May 31, 1854.
75. *Liberator*, August 13, 1858.
76. *Boston Slave Riot*, p. 85.
77. *Liberator*, August 15, 1858.
78. *Boston Evening Transcript*, April 12, 1855.
79. *Frederick Douglass' Paper*, June 2, 1854.
80. *Liberator*, July 7, 1854.
81. Nell, *Colored Patriots*, pp. 372–373.
82. Information concerning Wesley Bishop compiled from Boston city directories, the United States census, and *Judicial Cases*.
83. Jackson, "Vigilance Committee Account Book"; Catteral, *The Cynosure*.
84. *Boston Evening Transcript*, May 30, 1854.
85. Lucid, *Journal of Richard Henry Dana*, vol. II, p. 638.
86. E. W. Emerson and W. E. Forbes, *Journal of Ralph Waldo Emerson*, vol. III. (Boston, 1903–1914) p. 13.

87. Charles Francis Adams, *Richard Henry Dana*, vol. I (Boston, 1891), pp. 269–270.
88. Amos A. Lawrence to Mr. Andrews, May 26, 1854; "Amos A. Lawrence Letterbook," vol. II, p. 335.
89. *Boston Times*, May 30, 1854.
90. O'Connor, *Lords of the Loom*, p. 133.
91. Massachusetts Legislature, Original papers of Chapter 487, "An Act to protect the rights and liberties of the people of the Commonwealth of Massachusetts, Extension." May 21, 1855.

Chapter 9

1. Henry Highland Garnet, "An Address to the Slaves of the United States of America" (Buffalo, New York, 1843); reprinted in Frazier, ed., *Afro-American History*, pp. 113–120.
2. "National Colored Convention, 1847" in *Minutes of the Proceedings of the National Negro Conventions, 1830–1834*, ed. Howard H. Bell (New York, 1969.)
3. *Annual Report of the American Anti-Slavery Society* (New York, 1854).
4. *Liberator*, April 11, 1851. These young men were the sons of Samuel Snowdon.
5. *Dred Scott* v. *Sanford* (1857), 19 Howard, 393.
6. Ibid.
7. "Address by Charles L. Remond," April 3, 1857, in Aptheker, *Documentary History*, p. 394.
8. *Liberator*, August 13, 1858.
9. Ibid.
10. Ibid.
11. Ibid.
12. See *The North Star*, August 10 and 24, September 7, October 12 and 26, 1849.
13. *Minutes of the Proceedings of the National Negro Convention* (Rochester, 1853) in Bell, *National Negro Conventions*.
14. *Liberator*, February 22, 1851.
15. William C. Nell, *Services of Colored Americans*, p. 9.
16. *Liberator*, March 12, 1858.
17. Ibid.
18. Ibid.
19. Ibid.
20. Ibid.
21. Nell, *Colored Patriots*, pp. 101–102.
22. "List of those taxes on $6,000 and upwards in 1853," Boston, 1854. Coburn reportedly had $5,000 in real property and $1,000 in personal property; Wright had $5,000 in personal property.
23. *Liberator*, September 14, 1855; Nell, *Colored Patriots*, pp. 110–111. Massasoit was an Indian chief who in 1621 signed the original treaty of friendship with the settlers of the Plymouth Colony. See Benjamin Quarles, *Allies for Freedom* (New York, 1974), p. 69.
24. *Douglass' Paper*, September 7, 1855.
25. Quarles, *Black Abolitionists*, p. 230.
26. Martin R. Delany and Robert Campbell, *Search for a Place*, with an introduction by Howard H. Bell (Ann Arbor, Mich. 1969), p. 151.
27. *Minutes of the Proceedings of the National Negro Convention* (Rochester, 1853) in Bell, *National Negro Conventions.*
28. See *Frederick Douglass' Paper*, May 5 and 9, July 28, 1854; *Liberator*, July 27, 1855.
29. *Frederick, Douglass' Paper*, September 15, 1854.
30. *Douglass' Monthly*, January 1859.
31. *Liberator*, June 3, 1859, and July 11, 1859.

32. *Weekly Anglo-African*, April 5, 1860.
33. Delany and Campbell, *Search for a Place*, pp. 12–14.
34. James Redpath, *A Guide to Haiti* (Boston, 1861), pp. 9–11.
35. *Liberator*, February 3, 1860.
36. *Anglo-African*, November 16, 1861.
37. *Liberator*, May 2, 1862.
38. *North Star*, August 10, 1849.
39. Quarles, *Allies for Freedom*, pp. 157–158; *Liberator*, December 9, 1859.
40. Quarles, *Allies for Freedom*, p. 126.
41. Ibid., pp. 125–126, 152.
42. Ibid., p. 85.
43. *Boston Evening Transcript*, December 3 and 6, 1860.
44. Ibid.
45. Francis W. Bird, *Review of Governor Banks' Veto of the Revised Code, on Account of its Authorizing the Enrollment of Colored Citizens in the Militia* (Boston, 1860).
46. Henry G. Pearson, *The Life of John A. Andrew, Governor of Massachusetts, 1861–1865*, vol. I (Boston, 1904), pp. 68–95.
47. *Liberator*, April 26, 1861.
48. Ibid., May 17, 1861.
49. *The National Republican*, January 28, 1863.
50. John A. Andrew to Francis G. Shaw, January 30, 1863, in Pearson, II, pp. 74, 75.
51. Edward W. Emerson, ed., *Life and Letters of Charles Russell Lowell*, (Boston, 1907), pp. 233–234.
52. "Robert Morris, Sr., In Memoriam," 1882, p. 38.
53. Pearson, *Life of John A. Andrew*, II, pp. 71–74.
54. "Robert Purvis to J. M. McKim" in James M. McPherson, *The Negro's Civil War* (New York, 1965), p. 175.
55. "John A. Andrew to Edwin M. Stanton," May 15, 1863, in *The War of the Rebellion: Official Records*, series 2, vol. V (Washington, D.C., 1899), p. 207.
56. *Massachusetts Soldiers, Sailors and Marines in the Civil War*, vol. IV (The Massachusetts' Adjutant General's Office, 1932).
57. William Wells Brown, *The Negro in the American Rebellion* (Boston, 1867), pp. 147–159.

Bibliography

Manuscripts

Abbreviations and Locations:

(A.N.T.S.) = Andover Newton Theological School, Newton, Massachusetts.
(B.P.L.) = Boston Public Library, Boston, Massachusetts.
(M.H.S.) = Massachusetts Historical Society, Boston, Massachusetts.
(M.S.A.) = Massachusetts State Archives, Boston, Massachusetts.

"Amos A. Lawrence Letterbook," Vol. II (M.H.S.)
"Annual Report of the Boston Female Anti-Slavery Society," 1836 (B.P.L.)
Anti-Slavery Papers (B.P.L.)
Amos A. Phelps on behalf of B. F. Roberts, Boston, May 16, 1838.
B. F. Roberts to Amos A. Phelps, Boston, June 19, 1838.
Charles Lenox Remond to Rev. C. B. Ray, London, June 30, 1840.
John Tidd to Arthur Jones, April 6, 1834.
"*Liberator* Extra," Boston Female Anti-Slavery Society, 1840.
Nell, William C. "Circular, December 10, 1856."
Robert Morris to John P. Hale, January 1, 1852.
Robert Morris to Richard H. Dana, January 1, 1852.
Samuel May to Estlin, October 31, 1841; September 30, 1847, and October 31, 1848.
Thomas Cole to Bro. Johnson, Newport, R. I., August 7, 1840.
Thomas W. Higginson to *Newport Union*, n.d.
Thomas W. Higginson to wife, May 27, 1854.
William C. Nell to George Downing, September 12, 1854.
"Babolition of Slavery Grand Selebrashum by de Africum Shocietee and Reply Babolition of Slavery," n.d. (B.P.L.)
"Boston Negro Proceedings," 1855 (M.H.S.)
Bower, Beth, and Duncan Ritchie. "Preliminary Archeological Investigations at the African Meeting House, Boston, Mass." Unpublished report, 1975.

Child, David Lee. "Committee report on the memorial for Joseph Woodson" (M.H.S.)
Coleman, Charles L. "A History of the Negro Baptist in Boston." Master's thesis, 1956 (A.N.T.S.)
"Constitution of the New England Anti-Slavery Society," 1832.
Curry, Leonard. "Economic Opportunities for Urban Blacks: North and South, 1800–1860." Paper delivered at the Organization of American Historians convention, April 1975.
Dean, Paul. "A Discourse before the African Society . . . 1819." (B.P.L.)
Forbes, George W. "Typescript Biographical Sketch of E. M. Bannister," n.d. (B.P.L.)
——. "Typescript Biographical Sketch of John S. Rock," n.d. (B.P.L.)
——. "Typescript Biographical Sketch of William Cooper Nell," n.d. (B.P.L.)
Garrison Papers (B.P.L.)
Douglass to Garrison, November 11, 1859.
"For the *Liberator*" from F. W. Barker, n.d.
Garrison to George W. Benson, June 25, 1844.
Garrison to Francis Jackson Garrison, November 23, 1866.
Garrison to Oliver Johnson, August 7, 1862.
Garrison to Samuel May, September 23, 1853.
Garrison to wife, New York, May 15, 1840.
Garrison to wife, London, July 3, 1840.
Remond to Garrison, Newcastle-on-Tyne, March 7, 1841.
Susan Paul to Garrison, April 1, 1834.
Gutman, Herbert G., and Laurence A. Glasco. "The Buffalo, New York Negro, 1855–1875: A Study of the Family Structure of Free Negroes and Some of Its Implications." Paper prepared for the Wisconsin Conference on the History of American Political and Social Behavior, May 1968.
Hershberg, Theodore. "*Time on the Cross* and Black Family History." Paper presented at the University of Rochester Conference, "*Time on the Cross*: A First Appraisal," October 24–26, 1974.
Hill, Adelaide. "The Negro Upper Class in Boston: Its Development and Present Social Structure." Ph.D. Thesis, Radcliffe College, 1952.
Horton, James O. "Black Migrants' Adaptive Mechanisms in Ante-bellum Boston." Unpublished paper presented at the Ninth Annual Conference on Social-Political History, State University College at Brockport, Brockport, New York, October 1976.
Jackson, Francis. "Vigilance Committee Account Book." (M.H.S.)
Jacobs, Donald M. "A History of the Boston Negro from Revolution to Civil War." Ph.D. Dissertation, Boston University, 1968.
La Brew, Arthur. "Studies in Nineteenth Century Afro-American Music." Unpublished manuscript, 1975.

"Medical Faculty Minutes," November 4, 1850, December 26, 1850, and November 16, 1853 (Harvard University).
"Members of the Committee of Vigilance."
"Membership List," Boston Female Anti-Slavery Society (B.P.L.)
Morse, Jedidia. "A Discourse Delivered at the African Meeting House in Boston, July 14, 1808." (Boston Atheneum)
N. P. H., "The Lewis and Harriet Hayden Scholarship," December 23, 1893 (Harvard University, Widner Archives)
"Papers Relating to Negroes at Harvard" (Harvard Manuscript Archives)
Parker, Theodore. "The Boston Kidnapping—A Discourse to Commemorate the Rendition of Thomas Sims." Talk held before Boston Vigilance Committee, April 12, 1852.
"Proceedings of the Anti-Slavery Convention of American Women, Held in Philadelphia." Philadelphia, Pa., 1838.
Richard H. Dana to Edmund T. Dana, March 2, 1851 (M.H.S.)
R. H. Dana, Jr., to J. P. Hale, Boston, November 28, 1853 (M.H.S.)
"Robert Morris, Sr., in Memoriam," 1882 (M.H.S.)
"Slave Catchers and Kidnappers," Broadsides, 1851 (M.H.S.)
Smith, Marilyn. "Paul Cuffe and the Colonization of American Negroes." Paper read at Brandeis University, 1967.
"To the Yeomenry of New England," May 27, 1854, Vigilance Committee of Boston (B.P.L.)
Vinovskis, Maris A. "The Field of Early American Family History: A Methodological Critique." Paper delivered at the American Studies Association meeting, San Francisco, October 1973.
Weston Papers (B.P.L.)
  Anne W. Weston to Deborah Weston, February 4, 1842, and November 8–9, 1842.
  Anne W. Weston to Maria W. Chapman, June 5, 1849.
  Caroline Weston to Debra Weston, March 3, 1837.
  Debra Weston to Mary Weston, February 23, 1835.
  James Mott to Anne W. Weston, June 7, 1838.
  S. Davenport to Anne W. Weston, Boston, June 3, 1838.

Government Documents

Abstract of Returns of Inspectors and Keepers of Jails and Houses of Correction, Mass. House Doc., No. 32. Boston, 1838.
Abstract of Returns of Keepers of Jails and Overseers of the Houses of Correction . . . 1843, Mass. House Doc. (unn.). Boston, 1844.
"Argument of Charles Sumner, Esq., against the Constitutionality of Separate Schools in the Case of Sarah C. Roberts v. the City of Boston. Before the Supreme Court of Massachusetts," December 4, 1849.

Bills of Mortality, 1810–1849, City of Boston. Boston, 1893.

Boston City Directory, 1830–1860.

Chickering, Jesse. *Report of the Committee Appointed by the City Clerk*, City Document No. 60. Boston, 1851.

City of Boston Census, 1845.

Civil War Pension Records, Record Group 15, Records of the Veterans Administration (National Archives, Washington, D.C.)

Compendium of the Ninth Census, 1870.

Curtis Josiah, *Report of the Joint Special Committee on the Census of Boston, May 1855*. Boston, 1856.

Dred Scott v. *Sanford* (1857), 19 Howard 393.

Journal of the House of Representatives of Massachusetts, 1735, vol. XV.

"List of Qualified Voters in the City of Boston," 1838, 1839, 1844, 1845 (M.H.S.)

"List of those taxed on $6,000 and upwards in 1853." Boston, 1854.

Massachusetts Legislature, Original Papers of (M.S.A.)

- Chapter 53 of "Resolve Memorial to Crispus Attucks, Samuel Gary, Jonas Caldwell, Samuel Maverick, and Patrick Carr," May 17, 1887.
- Chapter 69 of "An Act to protect the rights and liberties of the people of the commonwealth of Massachusetts," March 24, 1843.
- Chapter 74 of "Resolve relating to slavery and the slave trade in the District of Columbia and territory of the United States," April 23, 1838.
- Chapter 75 of "Resolve condemning tabling in Congress of all Anti-Slavery Petitions," April 12, 1837.
- Chapter 97 of "Resolve for the abolition of slavery in the District of Columbia and nonsupport of federal government for slavery," May 1, 1850.
- Chapter 256 in "Amendment of an Act concerning public schools passed March 24, 1845," February 21, 1855.
- "Report to the Primary School Committee, June 15, 1846, on the Petitions of Sundry Colored People for the abolition of the Schools for Colored Children," 1855.
- Chapter 487 of "An Act to protect the rights and liberties of the people of the commonwealth of Massachusetts, Extension," May 21, 1855.

Massachusetts Soldiers, Sailors and Marines in the Civil War. Vol. 4. The Massachusetts' Adjutant General's Office, 1932.

Moynihan, Daniel Patrick. *The Negro Family: The Case for National Action*. Office of Policy Planning and Research, United States Department of Labor, March 1965.

Negro Population of the United States, 1790–1915. U.S. Bureau of the Census. Washington, D.C., 1918.

"Records of the Boston Overseers of the Poor," miscellaneous records, 1809–1860 (M.H.S.)

"Records of the Boston Tax Assessor," 1850, 1855, and 1860 (B.P.L.)

"Records of the Overseers of the Poor," 1837, 1839 and 1845 (M.H.S.)

Report by the City Registrar of the Births, Marriages and Deaths in the City of Boston, 1854. Boston, 1855.

Report by the City Registrar of the Births, Marriages and Deaths in the City of Boston, 1855. Boston, 1856.

Report by the City Registrar of the Births, Marriages and Deaths in the City of Boston, 1859. Boston, 1860.

Report of a Special Committee of Grammar School Board Presented August 29, 1849, on the Petition of Sundry Colored Persons Praying for the Abolition of the Smith School: With an Appendix, Documents of the City of Boston for the year 1849. Boston, 1849.

Report of the Committee Appointed by the City Clerk: Population of Boston in 1850, City Document No. 60. Boston, 1851.

Report of the Minority of the Committee upon the Petition of John T. Hilton and others, Colored Citizens of Boston, Praying for the Abolition of the Smith School and that colored children may be permitted to attend the other schools of the City; Documents of the City of Boston for the year 1849. Boston, 1849 (M.S.A.)

Report on Goals and Houses of Correction in the Commonwealth of Massachusetts . . . 1833, Mass. House Doc. No. 36. Boston, 1834.

"Report on the Freedom of the Inhabitants Passim," Massachusetts Senate Document No. 89, 1851.

"Report to the Primary School Committee, June 15, 1846, on the Petition of Sundry Colored People for the Abolition of the Schools for colored children," in the original papers of Chapter 256 "in Amendment of an Act concerning public schools passed March 24, 1845," February 21, 1855 (M.S.A.)

Roberts v. *City of Boston* (1849), 5 Cush 198.

Secretary of the Commonwealth. *Abstract of the Census of Massachusetts*, 1860, 1865.

Shattuck, Lemuel. *Report to the Committee of the City Council; Report of the Joint Special Committee on the Census of Boston for 1845*. Boston, 1846.

United States Census, 1830–1860.

Warner, Oliver. *Abstract of the Census of Massachusetts, 1865*. Boston, 1867.

The War of the Rebellion: Official Records, series 2, vol. V. Washington, D.C., 1899.

Newspapers

The Abolitionist (Concord, N.H., 1835–1846)

Anglo-African Magazine (New York, 1859–1860)

Boston Evening Transcript (Boston, 1830–1860)

Boston Times (Boston, 1836–1857)
Colored American (New York, 1837–1841)
Colored American and Advocate (Boston, 1837–1841)
The Emancipator (New York, 1833–1841)
Emancipator and Free American (New York, 1841–1842; Boston, 1842–1844)
Freedom's Journal (New York, 1827–1829)
Genius of Universal Emancipation (Baltimore, 1821–1839)
Liberator (Boston, 1831–1865)
The National Republican (Rochester, N.Y., 1831–1834)
New England Telegraph (North Wrentham, Mass., 1831–1834)
New York Times (New York, 1826–1860)
The North Star (subsequently *Frederick Douglass' Paper*, then *Douglass' Monthly*) (Rochester, N.Y., 1847–1863)
Pine and Palm (New York, 1861)
Weekly Anglo-African (New York, 1859–1862)

Books and Journals

Abdy, Edward S. *Journal of a Residence and Tour in the United States of North America, from April 1833 to October 1834*. Vol. I. London: J. Murray, 1835.
Adams, Charles Francis. *Richard Henry Dana*. Vols. I and II. Boston: Houghton Mifflin, 1891.
Address of the Committee Appointed by a Public Meeting, Held at Faneuil Hall, September 24, 1846, for the Purpose of Considering the Recent Case of Kidnapping from Our Soil, and of Taking Measures to Prevent the Recurrence of Similar Outrages. Boston, 1846.
The American Baptist Magazine, July 1831.
American Freeman. Vigilance Committee. Boston, 1854.
Annual Report of the American Anti-Slavery Society. New York, 1834–1860.
Annual Report of the Board of Managers of the New England Anti-Slavery Society. Boston, 1834.
Annual Report of the Massachusetts Anti-Slavery Society. Boston, 1836, 1844, 1845, 1851.
Aptheker, Herbert. *The Negro in the Abolitionist Movement*. New York: International Publishers, 1941.
——, ed. *Documentary History of Negro People in the United States*. New York: Citadel Press, 1951.
Bacon, Edwin M. *Boston: A Guide Book*. Boston: Ginn, 1908.
Bardolph, Richard. *The Negro Vanguard*. New York: Negro Univ. Press, 1959.
Barnes, Gilbert H., and Dwight L. Dumond, eds. *Letters of Theodore*

Dwight Weld, Angelina Grimke Weld, and Sarah Grimke, 1822–1844. 2 vols. New York: DaCapo Press, 1934.
Bates, Frederick L., and Lloyd Bacon. "The Community as a Social System." *Social Forces* 50 (1972): 371–379.
Bearse, Austin. *Reminiscences of Fugitive Slave Days in Boston*. Boston: W. Richardson, 1880.
Bell, Howard Holman. *A Survey of the Negro Convention Movement, 1830–1861*. New York: Arno, 1969.
———, ed. *Minutes of the Proceedings of the National Negro Conventions, 1830–1864*. New York: Arno, 1969.
Berlin, Ira. *Slaves without Masters: The Free Negro in the Antebellum South.* New York: Pantheon Books, 1974.
Bernard, Jessie. *Marriage and Family among Negroes*. Englewood Cliffs, N.J.: Prentice-Hall, 1966.
Billingsley, Andrew. "Black Families and White Social Science." In *The Death of White Society*, edited by Joyce Ladner. New York: Friendship Press, 1973, pp. 431–450.
Billington, Ray Allen, ed. *Journal of Charlotte Forten.* New York: Collier, 1967.
Bird, Francis W. *Review of Governor Banks' Veto of the Revised code; an Account of its Authorizing the Enrollment of Colored Citizens in the Militia*. Boston: J. P. Jewett, 1860.
Blassingame, John W. "Before the Ghetto: The Making of the Black Community in Savannah, Georgia, 1865–1880." *Journal of Social History* 6 (1972): 463–488.
———. *Black New Orleans, 1860–1880.* Chicago: Univ. of Chicago Press, 1973.
———. *The Slave Community*. New York: Oxford Univ. Press, 1972.
Bloomberg, Susan E., et al. "A Census Probe into Nineteenth-Century Family History: Southern Michigan, 1850–1880." *Journal of Social History* 1 (1971): 26–45.
"The Boston Mutual Lyceum." *The Abolitionist*. Vol. I. September 9, 1833.
Boston Slave Riot and Trial of Anthony Burns. Boston: Fetridge, 1854.
Bracey, John H., Jr., August Meier, and Elliott Rudwick, eds. *Black Matriarchy: Myth or Reality?* Belmont, Calif.: Wadsworth, 1971.
———. *Black Nationalism in America*. Indianapolis, Ind.: Bobbs-Merrill, 1970.
Brown, William Wells. *The Black Man, His Antecedents, His Genius and His Achievements*. New York: T. Hamilton, 1863.
———. *The Negro in the American Rebellion.* Boston: Lee and Shepard, 1867.
——— *The Rising Sun: or the Antecedents and Advancement of the Colored Race*. Boston: A. G. Brown, 1874.
Cass, Donn A. *Negro Freemasonry and Segregation*. Chicago: E. A. Cook Publications, 1957.

Catterall, Helen Tunnicliff, ed. *Judicial Cases Concerning American Slavery and the Negro*. Vol. IV, 1936; rpt. New York: Negro Univ. Press, 1968.

Clark, David B. "The Concept of Community: A Re-examination." *Sociological Review* 3 (1975): 397–416.

Clarke, James Freeman. *The Rendition of Anthony Burns*. Boston: Crosby, Nichols, 1854.

———. *Slavery in the United States.* Boston: B. F. Greene, 1843.

Craft, William. *Running a Thousand Miles for Freedom*. London, 1860; rpt. New York: Arno, 1969.

Crawford, Mary C. *Romantic Days in Boston*. Boston: Little, Brown, 1910.

Cross, Whitney R. *The Burned-Over District*. Ithaca: Cornell Univ. Press, 1950.

Curtis, Benjamin R. *A Memoir of Benjamin Robbins Curtis, LL.D.* Boston: Little, Brown, 1879.

Daniels, John. *In Freedom's Birthplace*. Cambridge, Mass.: Houghton Mifflin, 1914.

Davis, David Brian, ed. *The Fear of Conspiracy*. Ithaca: Cornell Univ. Press, 1971.

Davis, William T. *Professional and Industrial History of Suffolk County, Massachusetts*. Vol. I. Boston: Boston History Co., 1894.

Degler, Carl N. *Neither Black nor White*. New York: Macmillan, 1971.

Delany, Martin R., and Robert Campbell. *Search for a Place*, with an introduction by Howard H. Bell. Ann Arbor: Univ. of Michigan Press, 1969.

———. *The Condition, Elevation, Emigration, and Destiny of the Colored People of the United States*. Philadelphia: privately printed, 1852.

Douglass, Frederick. *Life and Times of Frederick Douglass*. Rpt. of rev. ed. of 1892. New York: Collier, 1962.

Duberman, Martin B., ed. *The Antislavery Vanguard*. Princeton: Princeton Univ. Press, 1965.

———. *James Russell Lowell*. Boston: Houghton Mifflin, 1966.

Dumond, Dwight Lowell. *Antislavery*. Ann Arbor: Univ. of Michigan Press, 1961.

———. *Antislavery Origins of the Civil War in the United States*. Ann Arbor: Univ. of Michigan Press, 1939.

Draper, Theodore. *The Rediscovery of Black Nationalism*. New York: Viking, 1970.

Drake, St. Claire, and Horace R. Clayton. *Black Metropolis: A Study in Negro Life in a Northern City*. Vol. II. New York: Harcourt Brace, 1945.

Du Bois, W. E. B. *The Philadelphia Negro: A Social Study*. New York: B. Blom, 1899.

Easton, Hosea. *A Treatise on the Intellectual Character and Condition of the Colored People of the United States*. Boston: I. Knapp, 1837.

Elbridge, Austin G. *Statement of the Facts Connected with the Arrest and Emancipation of George Latimer*. Boston, 1842.

Elkins, Stanley M. *Slavery: A Problem in American Institutional and Intellectual Life*. Chicago: Univ. of Chicago Press, 1959.

Emerson, E. W., and W. E. Forbes, eds. *Journals of Ralph Waldo Emerson*. Vols. I-X. Boston: Houghton Mifflin, 1909–1914.

——. *Life and Letters of Charles Russell Lowell*. Vol. I. Boston: Houghton Mifflin, 1907.

Feldstein, Stanley. *Once a Slave*. New York: Morrow, 1971.

First Anniversary of the Boston South Baptist Association. Boston, 1849.

First Annual Report of the American Anti-Slavery Society. New York, 1834.

First Annual Report of the Board of Managers of the New England Anti-Slavery Society. Boston, 1833.

First Baptist Church of Boston, Church Records. Books 1, 2, and 3. Boston, 1665–1855.

Fogel, Robert William, and Stanley L. Engerman. *Time on the Cross: The Economics of American Negro Slavery*. Boston: Little, Brown, 1974.

Foner, Eric. *Free Soil, Free Labor, Free Men*. New York: Oxford Univ. Press, 1970.

Foner, Philip, ed. *Life and Writings of Frederick Douglass*. Vols. I and V. New York: International Publishers, 1950.

Formisano, Ronald P. "Analyzing American Voting, 1830–1860: Methods." *Historical Methods Newsletter* 2 (1969): 1–11.

Franklin, John Hope. *From Slavery to Freedom*. 3rd rev. ed. New York: Knopf, 1967.

Frazier, E. Franklin. *Black Bourgeoisie*. Glencoe, Ill.: Free Press, 1957.

——. *The Free Negro Family*. Nashville: Fisk Univ. Press, 1932.

——. *The Negro Church in America*. New York: Schocken Books, 1963.

——. *The Negro Family: A Study of Family Origins before the Civil War*. Nashville: Fisk Univ. Press, 1932.

——. *The Negro Family in Chicago*. Chicago: Univ. of Chicago Press, 1932.

——. *The Negro Family in the United States*. Chicago: Univ. of Chicago Press, 1966.

——. *The Negro in the United States*. Rev. ed. New York: Macmillan, 1957.

Frederickson, George M. *The Black Image in the White Mind*. New York: Harper & Row, 1971.

Freehling, William W. *Prelude to Civil War*. New York: Harper & Row, 1965.

The Fugitive Slave Law and Its Victims. The American Anti-Slavery Society. New York, 1861.

Furstenberg, Frank F., Jr., Theodore Hershberg, and John Modell. "The

Origins of the Female-Headed Black Family: The Destructive Impact of the Urban Experience." *Journal of Interdisciplinary History* 6 (June 1975): 211–233.

Garrison, Wendell Phillips, and Francis Jackson Garrison, eds. *William Lloyd Garrison*. Vols. I and II. New York: Century, 1885.

Garrison, William Lloyd. *Thoughts on African Colonization*. Boston: Garrison and Knapp, 1832.

Gatell, Frank Otto. *John Gorham Palfrey and the New England Conscience*. Cambridge: Harvard Univ. Press, 1963.

Genovese, Eugene D. *Roll, Jordan, Roll*. New York: Pantheon Books, 1974.

Glasco, Laurence A. "Computerizing the Manuscript Census." *Historical Methods Newsletter* 1 (1969): 1–4.

Glazer, Nathan, and Daniel Patrick Moynihan. *Beyond the Melting Pot*. Cambridge: M.I.T. Press, 1963.

Graff, Harvey J. "Notes on Methods for Studying Literacy from the Manuscript Census." *Historical Methods Newsletter* 1 (1971): 11–16.

Grandy, Moses. *Narrative of the Life of Moses Grandy*. Boston: O. Johnson, 1844.

Green, James W., and Selz C. Mayo. "A Framework for Research in the Actions of Community Groups." *Social Forces* 4 (1953): 320–327.

Greene, Lorenzo. *The Negro in Colonial New England, 1620–1776*. New York: Atheneum, 1942.

Griffin, Clifford S. *Their Brothers' Keepers: Moral Stewardship in the United States, 1800–1865*. New Brunswick: Rutgers Univ. Press, 1960.

Grimke, Archibald H. "Anti-Slavery in Boston." *New England Magazine* (Dec. 1890): 441–459.

Gutman, Herbert G. *The Black Family in Slavery and Freedom, 1750–1925*. New York: Pantheon Books, 1976.

———. "Persistent Myths about the Afro-American Family." *Journal of Interdisciplinary History* 6 (Autumn 1975): 181–210.

Hall, Prince. "A Charge Delivered to the African Lodge, June 24, 1797, at Menotomy." In *Afro-American History: Primary Sources*, edited by Thomas R. Frazier. New York: Harcourt Brace Jovanovich, 1970, pp. 46–52.

Hamilton, Charles V. *The Black Preacher in America*. New York: Morrow, 1972.

Handlin, Oscar. *Boston's Immigrants*. Cambridge: Belknap Press of Harvard Univ. Press, 1959.

Hareven, Tamara K., ed. *Anonymous Americans* New York: Prentice-Hall, 1971.

Hershberg, Theodore. "Free Blacks in Antebellum Philadelphia: A Study of Ex-Slaves, Freeborn, and Socioeconomic Decline." *Journal of Social History* 2 (Winter 1971–72): 183–209.

Herskovitz, Melville. *The Myth of the Negro Past*. Boston: Beacon Press, 1958.

Hester, Rev. William H. *One Hundred and Five Years by Faith: A History of the Twelfth Baptist Church*. Boston: privately printed, 1946.

Higginson, Thomas W. *Cheerful Yesterdays*. Boston: Houghton Mifflin, 1898.

Hill, Robert B. *Informal Adoption among Black Families*. Washington, D.C.: National Urban League, 1977.

Hoar, George F. *Autobiography of Seventy Years*. Vol. I. New York: Scribner, 1903.

Horton, James O. "Generations of Protest: Black Families and Social Reform in Ante-Bellum Boston." *New England Quarterly* 49 (1976): 242–256.

Howe, Julia Ward. "First Years in Boston." In *The Many Voices of Boston*, edited by Howard Mumford Jones and Bessie Zoban Jones. Boston: Little, Brown, 1975, pp. 196–202.

Howe, M. A. DeWolfe. *Boston, The Place and the People*. New York: Macmillan, 1903.

Jaher, Frederic Cople. "Nineteenth-Century Elites in Boston and New York." *Journal of Social History* 1 (Fall 1972): 32–77.

James Russell Lowell Anti-Slavery Papers. Vol. I. Boston: Houghton Mifflin, 1902.

Jay, William. *American Colonization and American Anti-Slavery Societies*. London: F. Westley and A. H. Davis, 1835.

Johnson, Oliver, ed. *William Lloyd Garrison and His Times*. Boston: B. B. Russell, 1880.

Kantrowitz, Nathan. "The Index of Dissimilarity: A Measure of Residential Segregation for Historical Analysis." *Historical Methods Newsletter* 7 (1974): 285–289.

Katzman, David M. *Before the Ghetto: Black Detroit in the Nineteenth Century*. Urbana: Univ. of Illinois Press, 1973.

Kaufman, Harold F. "Toward an Interactional Conception of Community." *Social Forces* 1 (1959): 8–17.

King, Martin Luther. *Stride Toward Freedom: The Montgomery Story*. New York: Harper & Row, 1958.

Knights, Peter R. "Accuracy of Age Reporting in the Federal Censuses of 1850 and 1860." *Historical Methods Newsletter* 3 (1971): 79–83.

———. "City Directories as Aids to Ante-Bellum Urban Studies: A Research Note." *Historical Methods Newsletter* 4 (1969): 1–10.

———. *The Plain People of Boston, 1830–1860*. New York: Oxford Univ. Press, 1971.

Kraditor, Aileen S. *Means and Ends in American Abolitionism*. New York: Vintage-Random House, 1967.

Kusmer, Kenneth L. *A Ghetto Takes Shape: Black Cleveland, 1870–1930*. Urbana: Univ. of Illinois Press, 1976.

Lader, Lawrence. *The Bold Brahmins*. New York: Dutton, 1961.

Lammermeier, Paul J. "The Urban Black Family of the Nineteenth Century:

A Study of Black Family Structure in the Ohio Valley, 1850–1880." *Journal of Marriage and the Family* 35 (1973): 440–457.
Lane, Edgar C. *A Brief History of Tremont Temple*. Boston, 1949.
Lane, Roger. *Policing the City: Boston, 1822–1885*. Boston: Harvard Univ. Press, 1967.
Laws of the Sons of the African Society, Instituted at Boston, Anno Domini, 1798. Boston, 1802.
Layer, Robert G. *Earnings of Cotton Mill Operatives, 1825–1914.* Cambridge: Harvard Univ. Press, 1955.
Levesque, George A. "Inherent Reformers—Inherent Orthodoxy: Black Baptists in Boston, 1800–1873." *Journal of Negro History* 4 (1975): 491–525.
Levy, Leonard W. "The Abolition Riot: Boston's First Slave Rescue." *New England Quarterly* 25 (1952): 85–92.
———, and Douglas Jones. "Jim Crow Education: Origins of the 'Separate But Equal' Doctrine." In *Judgments: Essays on American Constitutional History*, by Leonard W. Levy. Chicago, 1972, pp. 316–341.
Lincoln, C. Eric, ed. *The Black Experience in Religion*. Garden City, N.Y.: Anchor-Doubleday, 1974.
Litwack, Leon F. *North of Slavery*. Chicago: Univ. of Chicago Press, 1961.
Lomax, Louis E. *The Negro Revolt*. New York: Harper & Row, 1962.
Lucid, Robert F., ed. *The Journal of Richard Henry Dana, Jr.* Vol. II. Cambridge: Belknap Press of Harvard Univ. Press, 1968.
Lyman, Theodore, III. *Papers Relating to the Garrison Mob.* Cambridge, Mass: Welch, Bigelow, 1870.
Mabee, Carleton. *Black Freedom.* New York: Macmillan, 1970.
Maginnes, David R. "The Case of the Court House Rioters in the Rendition of the Fugitive Slave Anthony Burns, 1854." *Journal of Negro History* 1 (1971): 31–43.
May, Samuel J. *Discourse on Slavery in the United States*. Boston: Garrison and Knapp, 1832.
———. *Some Recollections of our Antislavery Conflict*. Boston: Fields, Osgood, 1869.
McPherson, James M. *The Negro's Civil War*. New York: Pantheon Books, 1965.
———. *The Struggle for Equality*. Princeton: Princeton Univ. Press, 1964.
Mehlinger, Louis R. "The Attitudes of the Free Negro Toward African Colonization." *Journal of Negro History* (July 1916): 284–285.
Merrill, Walter M., ed. *The Letters of William Lloyd Garrison*. Vols. I and III. Cambridge: Belknap Press of Harvard Univ. Press, 1971.
Miller, Floyd J. *The Search for a Black Nationality: Black Emigration and Colonization, 1787–1863*. Urbana: Univ. of Illinois Press, 1975.
Minutes of the Boston Baptist Association. Boston, 1812–1867.
Minutes of the South Boston Baptist Association, 1849–1860 (A.N.T.S.)

Nell, William C. *Services of Colored Americans in the Wars of 1776 and 1812*. Boston: Prentiss and Sawyer, 1851.

——. *The Colored Patriots of the American Revolution*. Boston: R. F. Wallcut, 1855.

Nevins, Allan. *The Emergence of Lincoln*. Vols. I and II. New York: Scribner, 1950.

O'Connor, Thomas H. *Lords of the Loom*. New York: Scribner, 1968.

Painter, Nell. *The Exodusters*. New York: Knopf, 1976.

Pearson, Henry G. *The Life of John A. Andrew, Governor of Massachusetts, 1861–1865*. Vols. I and II. Boston: Houghton Mifflin, 1904.

Pease, Jane H., and William H. Pease. *They Who Would Be Free*. New York: Atheneum, 1974.

Perry, Lewis. *Radical Abolitionism: Anarchy and the Government of God in Antislavery Thought*. Ithaca: Cornell Univ. Press, 1973.

Pike, James, ed. *History of the Churches of Boston*. Boston: Ecclesia, 1883.

Pleck, Elizabeth Hafkin. "A Mother's Wages: Income Earning among Married Italian and Black Women, 1896–1911." In *The American Family in Socio-Historical Perspective*, 2nd ed., edited by Michael Gordon. New York: St. Martin's Press, 1978, pp. 490–510.

——. *Black Poverty: Migration, Work, and Family among Blacks in Boston, 1870–1900*. New York: Academic Press, forthcoming.

——. "The Two-Parent Household: Black Family Structure in Late Nineteenth-Century Boston." *Journal of Social History* 6 (1972): 3–31.

Proceedings of the Colored National Convention at Philadelphia, 1855.

Pulszky, Francis, and Theresa Pulszky. *White, Red, Black: Sketches of Society in the United States*. London: Trübner, 1853.

Quarles, Benjamin. *Allies for Freedom*. New York: Oxford Univ. Press, 1974.

——. *Black Abolitionists*. New York: Oxford Univ. Press, 1969.

——. *The Negro in the Civil War*. Boston: Little, Brown, 1953.

Quincy, Edmund. *Introductory Lecture Delivered before the Adelphic Union, November 19, 1838*. Boston: I. Knapp, 1839.

Quincy, Josiah. *A Municipal History of the Town and City of Boston During Two Centuries*. Boston: Little, Brown, 1852.

Randolph, Peter. *From Slave Cabin to Pulpit*. Boston: J. H. Earle, 1893.

Rawick, George P. *From Sundown to Sunup*. Westport, Conn.: Greenwood Press, 1972.

Redpath, James. *A Guide to Hayti*. Boston: Haytian Bureau of Emigration, 1861.

Robboy, Stanley J., and Anita W. Robboy. "Lewis Hayden: From Fugitive Slave to Statesman." *New England Quarterly* 46 (Dec. 1973): 591–613.

Roberts, Robert. *House Servants' Directory*. Boston: Monroe and Francis, 1827.

Ross, Majorie Drake. *The Book of Boston: The Federal Period.* New York: Hastings House, 1961.

———. *The Book of Boston: The Victorian Period.* New York: Hastings House, 1964.

Ruchames, Louis. "Jim Crow Railroads in Massachusetts." *American Quarterly* 8 (1956): 61–75.

———. "Race, Marriage and Abolition in Massachusetts." *Journal of Negro History* 40 (1955): 250–273.

———. *The Abolitionists.* New York: Putnam, 1963.

Savage, Edward H. *A Chronological History of the Boston Watch and Police from 1631 to 1865.* Boston: privately printed, 1865.

Schultz, Stanley K. *The Culture Factory: Boston Public Schools, 1789–1860.* New York: Oxford Univ. Press, 1973.

Second Baptist Church of Boston, Church Records. Books 1 and 2, 1788–1847.

Seeber, Edward D. "Phillis Wheatley." *Journal of Negro History* 24 (July 1939): 259–262.

Sharpless, John B., and Ray M. Shortridge. "Biased Underenumeration in Census Manuscripts: Methodological Implications." *Journal of Urban History* 4 (1975): 409–439.

Siebert, Wilbur H. *The Underground Railroad.* New York: Macmillan, 1898.

———. "The Underground Railroad in Massachusetts." *Proceedings of the American Antiquarian Society* 45 (1936): 25–100.

Smith, Robert P. "William Cooper Nell: Crusading Black Abolitionist." *Journal of Negro History* 55 (1970): 182–199.

Sons of Africa: An Essay on Freedom. Boston: African Society, 1808.

Sorin, Gerald. *Abolitionism: A New Perspective.* New York: Praeger, 1972.

Spear, Allan H. *Black Chicago.* Chicago: Univ. of Chicago Press, 1967.

Stacey, Margaret. "The Myth of Community Studies." *British Journal of Sociology* 2 (1969): 134–147.

Stack, Carol B. *All Our Kin.* New York: Harper & Row, 1974.

Stevens, Charles Emery, *Anthony Burns.* Boston: J. P. Jewett, 1856.

Sumner, Charles. *Works of Charles Sumner.* Vol. II. Boston: Lee and Shepard, 1874.

Thernstrom, Stephan. *Poverty and Progress.* Cambridge: Harvard Univ. Press, 1964.

———. *The Other Bostonians.* Cambridge: Harvard Univ. Press, 1973.

———, and Richard Sennett, eds. *Nineteenth-Century Cities.* New Haven: Yale Univ. Press, 1969.

Thomas, John L. *The Liberator: William L. Garrison.* Boston: Little, Brown, 1963.

Tiffany, Nina Moore. *Samuel E. Sewall: A Memoir.* Boston: Houghton Mifflin, 1898.

Tocqueville, Alexis de. *Democracy in America.* London, 1835, 1840; rpt. New York: Mentor-New American Library, 1956.

"To P. Cuffe from Prince Saunders, Secretary; Thomas Jarvis, Chairman; and Perry Locks, President of the African Institution of Boston. Boston, August 3, 1812." In *Black Nationalism*, edited by John H. Bracey, Jr., August Meier, and Elliott Rudwick. Indianapolis, Ind.: Bobbs-Merrill, 1970, pp. 41–43.

Twelfth Annual Report of the Massachusetts Anti-Slavery Society. Boston, January 28, 1852.

Van Deusen, Glyndon G. *The Jacksonian Era, 1828–1848*. New York: Harper & Row, 1959.

Vinovskis, Maris A. "American Historical Demography: A Review Essay." *Historical Methods Newsletter* 4 (1971): 141–148.

———. "Mortality Rates and Trends in Massachusetts before 1860." *Journal of Economic History* 32 (1972): 184–213.

Walker, David. *Walker's Appeal in Four Articles*. Boston, privately printed, 1830.

Watson, Thomas R. *A Sketch of the Past and Present Conditions of the Twelfth Baptist Church*. Boston, 1880.

White, Arthur O. "Prince Saunders: An Instance of Social Mobility among Antebellum New England Blacks." *Journal of Negro History* 4 (1975): 526–535.

Wilkinson, Kenneth P. "Phases and Roles in Community Action." *Rural Sociology* 1 (1970): 54–68.

Williams, George W. *History of the Negro Race in America, 1619–1880.* Vols. I and II. New York: Putnam, 1883.

———. *History of the Twelfth Baptist Church*. Boston, 1874.

———. *The Negro as a Political Problem*. Boston: A. Mudge, 1884.

Willson, E. B. *The Bad Friday: A Sermon*. Boston, 1854.

Woodson, Carter G. *Negro Orators and Their Orations*. New York, 1925; rpt. New York: Russell and Russell, 1969.

———. *The History of the Negro Church*. Washington, D.C.: Associated Pub., 1921.

———. "The Negro in Cincinnati prior to the Civil War." *Journal of Negro History* 1 (Jan. 1916): 1–22.

———. "The Relation of Negroes and Indians in Massachusetts." *Journal of Negro History* 5 (Jan. 1920): 45–57.

———, ed. *The Mind of the Negro as Reflected in Letters Written during the Crisis, 1800–1860.* Washington, D.C.: Associated Pub., 1926.

Woodward, C. Vann. *American Counterpoint*. Boston: Little, Brown, 1970.

Wright, John S. *Lincoln and the Politics of Slavery*. Reno: Univ. of Nevada Press, 1970.

Young, Joshua. *God Greater than Man: A Sermon*. Burlington, Vt.: S. B. Nichols, 1854.

Zilversmit, Arthur. *The First Emancipation: The Abolition of Slavery in the North*. Chicago: Univ. of Chicago Press, 1967.

Index